James Merrick

The Psalms

Translated or paraphrased in English verse

James Merrick
The Psalms
Translated or paraphrased in English verse

ISBN/EAN: 9783337043155

Printed in Europe, USA, Canada, Australia, Japan

Cover: Foto ©ninafisch / pixelio.de

More available books at **www.hansebooks.com**

PSALMS,

TRANSLATED OR PARAPHRASED

In ENGLISH VERSE,

By JAMES MERRICK, M. A.
LATE FELLOW OF TRINITY COLLEGE, OXFORD.

THE SECOND EDITION.

READING,
Printed and sold by J. CARNAN and Co.
Sold also by Mr. NEWBERY in St. Paul's Church-Yard,
and Mr. DODSLEY in Pall-Mall, London; and by
Mr. FLETCHER and Mr. PRINCE in Oxford.
M DCC LXVI.

PREFACE.

THE following attempt on the Psalms, though a mixture of Translation and Paraphrase, will, I hope, be found to contain little more of the latter kind than what may be useful either in opening the sense, or in pointing out the connexion, of the Original. The defects of it, great as they must be, would probably have been much greater, had it not been favoured with a revisal by a gentleman, whose various and well-known abilities, together with his singular acquaintance with the Hebrew Poetry, rendered him peculiarly qualified for the office. The Reverend Doctor LOWTH, Prebendary of Durham, having read a part of the work, was pleased to express a desire of seeing the whole: The Author of it was too sensible of the advantage which was likely to result from his inspection of it, to decline such an offer; and takes this opportunity of publicly acknowledging the very great service which he has received from this gentleman's assistance; who, after having in a most friendly and candid manner proposed his objections where he judged them necessary, was pleased to encourage and advise the publication of the work. My thanks are also particularly due to my very worthy and learned neighbour JOHN LOVEDAY, Esq; to whose perusal the several parts of the work were submitted, almost as soon as composed, and whose accurate criticisms have rendered it less unworthy of the public light; to which, without consulting such judicious friends as himself and the gentleman above-mentioned, it had been presumption to expose it: As the latter of these gentlemen (whose son Mr. JOHN LOVEDAY,

PREFACE.

LOVEDAY, of Magdalen College, Oxford, a young gentleman of distinguished abilities and learning, has seconded him in every office of friendship and humanity towards me) has most readily assisted me in considering the sense of the Original whenever I have applied to him, so the former has favoured me with a great number of observations on the Hebrew Text; which I may hereafter (if God give me health) commit to the press, together with many others communicated to me by persons of very great learning and eminence, and with such remarks as have occurred to myself in comparing my Version or Paraphrase with the Original. Though the annotations which I have received from Dr. LOWTH were written in a very expeditious manner, without consulting many commentators, yet the singular attention which that learned gentleman appears (in his admirable lectures on the Hebrew Poetry) to have paid to the Psalms, as well

PREFACE.

as to the other poetical parts of Holy Scripture, had so prepared him for the work which he has thus obligingly taken upon him, that they will, I am persuaded, be found worthy of their author. As those annotations which have been put into my hands are (many of them at least) such as will not be understood by any persons who have not applied themselves to the study of the learned languages, I have rather chosen to reserve them for a separate volume than to subjoin them to the Version or Paraphrase which is here presented to the reader. The inconveniences arising from my situation, remote from any of the most public libraries, have been in a great measure remedied by my access to the large and well-chosen libraries of a gentleman before mentioned, and of my late pious, learned, and ingenious friend, the Reverend Doctor BOLTON Dean of Carlisle, as also by the favour of the most Reverend the Lord Archbishop of CANTERBURY;

TERBURY; who has (in addition to the many other instances, which I have experienced, of his Grace's goodness and condescension) been pleased to honour me, on this occasion, with the voluntary offer, and the use, of some of the most considerable expositions of the Psalms; such as those of Geierus, Michaelis, and Houbigant; together with Celsius's Hierobotanicon, Hillerus's Hierophyticon, and several new Versions of the Psalter in different languages. As the communication of these valuable helps demands my humblest gratitude, so it likewise encourages me to hope (though my own incapacity and a long course of ill health will scarce allow me to think of attempting a regular Comment on the Psalms) that it may be in my power, in some instances, to confirm by sufficient authorities such interpretations of several difficult texts as I have followed, and, in others, to discover the errors which I have committed.

PREFACE.

It may be proper to advertise the reader, that The Version or Paraphrase of the Psalms now put into his hands has not been calculated for the uses of public Worship. The translator knew not how, without neglecting the Poetry, to write in such language as the common sort of people would be likely to understand: For the same reason he could not confine himself in general to stanzas, nor, consequently, adopt the measures to which the tunes used in our Churches correspond. However, as his measures are all of the Lyric kind, his work may, he hopes, answer the purposes of private devotion. Two of the Psalms, the hundred and eleventh and the hundred and twelfth, have indeed been purposely translated or paraphrased in the measure which answers to the tune of the hundredth Psalm, as it is sung in the Church, on account of its known excellence.

PREFACE.

The judicious reader will not, it is hoped, be offended, if he finds the same phrases, and even the same lines, sometimes occur in different Psalms, when he considers what liberty of repetition the Hebrew Poetry admits in one and the same Poem, and, consequently, how often the same expressions are likely to be found in a collection of many Hebrew Poems composed on similar subjects. The candid Critic may the better judge what degree of indulgence the translator of such a work may stand in need of, if he knows to how great difficulties no less able a writer than CORNEILLE was reduced on a like occasion: whose words, in the Preface to his poetical Version and Paraphrase of Thomas a Kempis, are as follows.——
Sur tout les redites y sont si fréquentes, que quand nostre Langue seroit dix fois plus abondante qu' elle n' est, je l' aurois épuisée fort aisément, et j' avoüe que je n' ay pû trouver le secret de diversifier mes expressions,

toutes

PREFACE.

toutes les fois que j' ay eu la mesme chose à exprimer.

Whatever imperfections may be discovered in the following performance, when examined with a critical view, I shall by no means think my labour either useless or unrecompenced, if any pious persons shall find their devotion assisted and improved by it, or their love more strongly excited towards the great Author of our Salvation, so evidently pointed out in the course of these divine Compositions.

June 5, 1765.

A VERSION or PARAPHRASE OF THE PSALMS.

PSALM I.

O How blest the Man, whose ear
Impious counsel shuns to hear,
Who nor loves to tread the way
Where the Sons of Folly stray,
Nor their frantic mirth to share, 5
Seated in Derision's chair,
But, possess'd with sacred awe,
Meditates, great God, thy Law,
This by day his fix'd employ,
This by night his constant joy. 10
Like the Tree that, taught to grow
Where the streams irriguous flow,
Oft as the revolving Sun
Through the destin'd Months has run,

Regular,

Regular, its season knows, 15
Bending low its loaded boughs,
He his verdant branch shall spread,
Nor his sick'ning leaves shall shed;
He, whate'er his thoughts devise,
Joyful to the work applies, 20
Sure to find the wish'd success
Crown his hope, his labour bless.
See, ah! see a diff'rent fate
God's obdurate foes await;
See them, to his wrath consign'd, 25
Fly like chaff before the wind.
When thy Judge, O Earth, shall come,
And to Each assign their doom,
Say, shall then the impious Band
With the Just assembled stand? 30
These th' Almighty, These alone,
Objects of his Love shall own,
While his vengeance who defy
Whelm'd in endless ruin lie.

PSALM II.

WHY thus enrag'd, ye Tribes profane?
   Why strive the Nations thus in vain?
Earth's scepter'd Lords rebellious rise
Against the Ruler of the Skies,
And Him on whose distinguish'd head 5
His hand the sacred oil has shed.
" Quick let us each renounce their Sway,
" And cast their hated bands away."

PSALM II.

God from on high their threats shall hear,
Laugh, as the tumult meets his ear, 10
And, arm'd with vengeance, thus aloud
Superior quell the frantic Croud:
" Yet, Mortals, yet your Monarch see,
" And bow to Him the humble knee;
" His throne on *Sion*'s hill my hand 15
" Has built, and what I build shall stand."
Thy Will, great Father, I obey;
Pleas'd I accept the offer'd Sway,
And through the Earth's extended frame
The Counsels of thy Love proclaim. 20
" Thou art my Son, on this blest Day
" Begotten; (thus I hear thee say;)
" Prefer thy wish, and to thy hand
" Lo! I consign each heathen Land,
" And bid thee rule the Nations round, 25
" Far as to Earth's remotest bound.
" Though join'd in firmest league, thy foes
" With vain attempt thy pow'r oppose:
" Thy arm the iron rod extends;
" Behold them, as the stroke descends, 30
" Crush'd like the potter's brittle store,
" And scatter'd, to unite no more."
Ye Kings, from Error's sleep arise,
Ye Judges of the Earth, be wise.
While Ye in duteous zeal conspire, 35
And serve with joy th' eternal Sire,
O, lest Ye perish from the way
That leads to realms of endless day,

With awful love, with holy fear,
His Son, the World's great Hope, revere: 40
If yet but kindling in his hand
The vengeful bolt uplifted stand,
Thrice happy, who on Him depend,
And thankful own th' almighty Friend.

PSALM III.

BEHOLD, my God, what num'rous foes
  With dire intent my steps inclose,
While, flush'd with hope, the impious Band
In haughty triumph round me stand:
" Lo! there, they cry, our obvious prey, 5
" The wretch, whom God has cast away."
But see Omnipotence my shield!
My head aloft by Thee upheld,
Thy fav'ring beams around me shine;
Thou, Lord, from *Sion*'s hallow'd shrine 10
With kind regard shalt hear my cry,
And instant grant the wish'd reply.
Oppress'd with toil, I sought repose,
I laid me down, I slept, I rose;
For Thou, my God, wert waking still, 15
To guard my slumbring head from ill.
Though Myriads, leagu'd, against me rise,
My heart secure their rage defies.
Thy aid, blest Lord, indulgent yield:
Oft, as I trod the doubtful field, 20
Each hostile cheek has felt thy stroke;
Thy rod their teeth vindictive broke;
                                  O yield

PSALM III.

O yield (nor shall I ask in vain,)
That oft experienc'd aid again.
'Tis thine, great God, 'tis thine to save
Thy Servants from th' expecting grave,
'Tis thine to bless them from above,
And crown them with eternal Love.

PSALM IV.

DEFENDER of my rightful cause,
While anguish from my bosom draws
The deep-felt sigh, the ceaseless pray'r,
O make thy servant still thy care.
That aid, which oft my griefs has heal'd,
That aid again, intreated, yield.
How long, ye sons of pride, how long
Shall falshood arm your impious tongue,
And erring rage your breast inflame,
My pow'r to thwart, my acts defame?
To God my heart shall vent its woe,
Who, prompt his blessings to bestow
On each whose breast has learn'd his fear,
Bows to my plaint the willing ear.
Him wouldst thou please? With rev'rent awe
Observe the dictates of his Law:
In secret on thy couch reclin'd
Search to its depth thy restless mind,
Till hush'd to peace the tumult lie,
And wrath and strife within thee die.
With purest gifts approach his shrine,
And safe to Him thy care resign.

I hear a hopeless train demand,
"Where's now the wish'd Deliv'rer's hand?"
Do Thou, my God, do Thou reply,　　25
And let thy presence from on high
In full effusion o'er our head
Its all-enliv'ning influence shed.
What joy my conscious heart o'erflows!
Not such th' exulting lab'rer knows,　　30
When to his long expecting eyes
The vintage and the harvests rise,
And, shadowing wide the cultur'd soil,
With full requital crown his toil.
My weary eyes in sleep I close,　　35
My limbs, secure, to rest compose;
For Thou, great God, shalt screen my head,
And plant a guard around my bed.

PSALM V.

THE words that from my lips proceed,
　　My thoughts (for Thou those thoughts canst read,)
My God, my King, attentive weigh,
And hear, O hear me, when I pray.
With earliest zeal, with wakeful care,　　5
To Thee my soul shall pour its pray'r,
And, e'er the dawn has streak'd the sky,
To Thee direct its longing eye:
To Thee, whom nought obscur'd by stain
Can please; whose doors to feet profane　　10

Inexorable

PSALM V.

Inexorable stand; whose Law
Offenders from thy sight shall awe.
Let each whose tongue to lies is turn'd,
Who lessons of deceit has learn'd,
Or thirsts a brother's blood to shed, 15
Thy hate and heaviest vengeance dread.
But I, whose hope thy Love supports,
(How great that Love!) will tread thy Courts,
My knees in lowliest rev'rence bend,
And tow'rd thy shrine my hands extend. 20
Do Thou, just God, my path prepare,
And guard me from each hostile snare;
O lend me thy conducting ray,
And level to my steps thy way.
Behold me by a troop inclos'd, 25
Of falshood and of guilt compos'd:
Their throat a sepulchre displays,
Deep, wide, insatiate; in their praise
Lurks flatt'ry, and with specious art
Belies the purpose of their heart. 30
O let the mischiefs they intend
Retorted on themselves descend,
And let thy wrath correct their sin,
Whose hearts thy mercy fails to win.
May All whose trust on Thee is plac'd 35
Peace and delight perpetual taste,
Sav'd by thy care, in songs of joy
Their ever grateful voice employ,
And share the gifts on those bestow'd,
Who love the name of *Jacob*'s God. 40

To each, who bears a guiltless heart,
Thy grace its blessing shall impart;
Strong as the brazen shield, thy aid
Around him casts its cov'ring shade.

PSALM VI.

O Spare me, Lord, nor o'er my head
   The fulness of thy vengeance shed.
With pitying eye my weakness view,
Heal my vex'd Soul, my strength renew,
And O, if yet my sins demand   5
The wise corrections of thy hand,
Yet give my pains their bounds to know,
And fix a period to my woe.
Return, great God, return, and save
Thy servant from the greedy grave.   10
Shall Death's long-silent tongue, O say,
The records of thy pow'r display,
Or pale Corruption's startled ear
Thy praise within its prison hear?
By languor, grief, and care, oppress'd,   15
With groans perpetual heaves my breast,
And tears, in large profusion shed,
Incessant lave my sleepless bed.
My life, though yet in mid career,
Beholds the winter of its year   20
(While clouds of grief around me roll,
And hostile storms invade my soul,)
Relentless from my cheek each trace
Of youth and blooming health erase,

PSALM VI.

And spread before my wasting sight 25
The shades of all-obscuring night.
   Hence, ye profane: My Saviour hears;
While yet I speak, he wipes my tears,
Accepts my pray'r, and bids each foe
With shame their vain attempts forgo, 30
And, struck with horror from on high,
In wild disorder backward fly.

PSALM VII.

O Save me, Lord, and to my foes
   Do Thou (in Thee I trust) oppose
Thy pow'r, and let the arm divine,
Stretch'd in my cause, bespeak me thine:
Lest, while I mourn thy absent aid, 5
The Lion fierce my soul invade,
Pleas'd, with my blood his thirst allay,
And rend the unresisting prey.
My God, if truth their censure guide,
If guilt be in my facts descried, 10
If e'er from my dissembling heart
My Friend has found the hostile part,
If, urg'd by wrongs, I taught my Foe
The terrors of my hand to know,
That Foe's worst vengeance let me meet, 15
Till trampled underneath his feet
Low in the dust my life be laid,
And Earth's dark womb my glory shade.
   Rise, mightiest Lord, triumphant rise
O'er each whose hand thy pow'r defies; 20

Nor

PSALM VII.

Nor let thy foes thy wrath decline,
But hear (for judgement, Lord, is thine,)
Thy servant's pray'r: In awful state,
While circling crouds the doom await,
Ascend thy throne, great God, again,   25
And vindicate thy ways to Men.
O Thou, on whom our fates depend,
My cause, my guiltless cause, defend;
Sin's baneful growth do Thou controul,
And guard from ill the upright soul;   30
For Thou, just Lord, with searching eye
The heart and inmost reins canst try.

   To God, my Soul, for help repair,
Who makes the faithful heart his care,
Th' impartial Judge, whose eyes each day   35
Cast o'er the Earth their strict survey,
Indignant, and, where'er they turn,
New scenes of daring guilt discern.
If Man his Law refuse to know,
He whets his sword, he bends his bow,   40
His hands, in fiercest wrath applied,
The instruments of death provide,
And tip with fire the winged dart
Ordain'd to pierce th' Oppressor's heart.
With mischief teem their breasts, but woe   45
And frustrate hope attend the throe:
They dig, and with exactest care
A pit, but for themselves, prepare;
They toil, and each, condemn'd to gain
The luckless harvest of his pain,   50

Ills

Ills for a brother's head design'd
Retorted on his own shall find.
Thy justice, Lord, shall on my breast
In sure remembrance stand impress'd,
With grateful joy my heart inspire, 55
And wake to ceaseless praise my lyre.

PSALM VIII.

IMMORTAL King! Through Earth's wide frame
How great thy honour, praise, and name!
Whose reign o'er distant worlds extends,
Whose glory heav'n's vast height transcends.
From infants Thou canst strength upraise, 5
And form their lisping tongues to praise:
By these the vengeance-breathing Foe
Thy mightier terrors taught to know
In mute astonishment shall stand,
And bow beneath thy conqu'ring hand. 10
When, rapt in thought, with wakeful eye
I view the wonders of the sky,
Whose frame thy fingers o'er our head
In rich magnificence have spread,
The silent Moon, with waxing horn 15
Along th' ethereal region borne,
The Stars with vivid lustre crown'd,
That nightly walk their destin'd round,
Lord! What is Man, that in thy care
His humble lot should find a share, 20
Or what the Son of Man, that THOU
Thus to his wants thy ear shouldst bow?

His rank awhile, by thy decree,
Th' Angelic Tribes beneath them see,
Till round him thy imparted rays　　　　25
With unextinguish'd glory blaze.
Subjected to his feet by Thee
To Him all Nature bows the knee;
The beasts in Him their Lord behold,
The grazing herd, the bleating fold,　　　30
The savage race, a countless train,
That range at large th' extended plain,
The fowls, of various wing, that fly
O'er the vast desert of the sky,
And all the watry tribes, that glide　　　35
Through paths to human sight denied.

　　Immortal King! Through Earth's wide frame
How great thy honour, praise, and name!

PSALM IX.

WARM'D to its inmost depth, my breast
　　Thanks not by words to be express'd
Conceives, nor shall my grateful tongue
E'er leave thy wondrous acts unsung.
Thee, Lord, I boast my bliss supreme,　　　5
Thy praise my song's exhaustless theme:
O higher than the highest, hail!
Thou, Thou hast bid my cause prevail,
And from the terror of thine eye
My foes with stumbling step shall fly,　　　10
Or, struck by thy resistless hand,
In heaps promiscuous strew the Land.

PSALM IX.

For Justice, Lord, supports thy throne,
And Her decrees and Thine are one.
Thy stern rebuke the Heathen feel;
Their name Oblivion's shades conceal;
And o'er their guilt-polluted plain
Destruction, Death, and Horror reign;
While, where the rural waste extends,
No more the village smoke ascends,
No more their cities brave the sky,
But (ras'd by Thee,) forgotten lie,
Scarce ev'n in shapeless ruins view'd,
That mark where once the Wonder stood.
But Thou, when Time shall reach its end,
Unchang'd the scepter shalt extend,
Then fill, as now, thy awful seat,
While at thy word assembled meet
Earth's various Tribes, and hear thee thence
The true, th' impartial Doom dispense.
   Come Ye, who in the dang'rous hour
Wish for your guard the strong-built tow'r;
Each terror to the winds resign'd,
In God a surer refuge find.
The Souls, that erst oppress'd with woe
Have learn'd thy name, great God, to know,
Their hope on Thee shall still sustain,
Whom none has sought, and sought in vain.
In *Sion* God has fix'd his rest;
O be his praise aloud confest;
His Acts through ev'ry clime resound,
Far as to Earth's extremest bound.

                                           He

He from the proud Oppreſſor's hands
The poor man's guiltleſs blood demands,
And (nor with unregarding ear,) 45
His juſt complaint from heav'n ſhall hear.
Thy ſervant's woes attentive view,
While impious men my ſteps purſue,
O Thou, whoſe care prolongs my breath,
And lifts me from the gates of death: 50
So ſhall thy praiſe employ my tongue,
And *Sion*'s portals hear my ſong,
While with experienc'd heart I ſhow
What joys from thy Salvation flow.

   Low in the pit for others made 55
Th' artificers of death are laid,
And, ſtruck with dire amazement, find
Their nets around themſelves intwin'd.
His juſtice thus our God diſplays,
And miſchief with itſelf repays. 60
Behold the grave its jaws extend,
While to its depths the crouds deſcend,
Who dare in lawleſs counſels join,
Forgetful of the will divine.
For think not, O ye Good diſtreſt, 65
That in the all-remembring breaſt
Your woes and wrongs unnotic'd riſe,
That Virtue's hope for ever dies.

   Up, Lord, nor let the impious ſoul
Build ſin on ſin without controul; 70
Thy balance, mightieſt Judge, aſſume,
Paſs on the heathen race their doom,

                            And

PSALM IX.

And let thy terrors, scatter'd wide,
Correct them, till each son of pride,
By Thee convinc'd, his weakness scan,   75
And humbled own himself but Man.

PSALM X.

SAY, Lord, why thus thy aiding pow'r
   Deserts us in the needful hour,
Why clouds impervious, round thee roll'd,
Thy presence from our sight withhold.
Shall impious men escape thy view,   5
While thus the guiltless they pursue?
O let them, by themselves chastis'd,
The ills sustain for Him devis'd,
Nor longer boast their mad desires,
And acts which headlong rage inspires,   10
Or joyous grasp their lawless gain,
And Thee, the soul's best wealth, disdain.
Proud Wretch! who shuns o'er Nature's face
The footsteps of thy care to trace,
And Thee, th' all-potent Monarch, Thee   15
Denies, who gav'st himself to be.
Behold, while, high above all height,
Thy Judgements, Lord, his distant sight
Elude, this Minister of woe
Blast with his breath each obvious foe.   20
" See, proof to each assault I stand:
" What pow'r shall e'er my fear demand?
" What ill, to life's remotest day,
" Obstruct the tenour of my way?"

Thus, swoln with insolence and pride, 25
His self-deluding heart has cried:
His venom'd lips, with curses fraught,
Words ill according to his thought
Have utter'd, and beneath his tongue
Lurk fraud, and violence, and wrong. 30
Beside the solitary way,
Intent the helpless poor to slay,
He waits, and with malignant eye
Insidious marks each passer by.
As, couch'd within his bushy lair, 35
The lion fierce with hideous glare
Around him casts his wide survey,
And meditates the future prey,
So longs the man of blood to seize
The Souls that own thy just Decrees: 40
If, planted with successful care,
His nets their captive feet insnare,
Ah! what his fury shall withstand,
Or save them from the murth'rous Band,
That, leagu'd in sin, assist his toil, 45
And share with him the guilty spoil?
" Shall Heav'n's high Lord, he cries, descend
" The human actions to attend?
" The paths by Me at will pursu'd
" His mem'ry and his thought elude." 50
Rise, mightiest Lord, and lift thy hand,
Nor let the poor thy help demand
With fruitless pray'r: for why, (ah, why?)
Should impious tongues reproachful cry,

" 'Tis

PSALM X.

"'Tis not within th' Almighty's plan 55
"To scrutinize the acts of Man?"
 What eyes, like thine, eternal Sire,
Through sin's obscurest depths inquire?
What Judge, like Thee, on Virtue's foes
The needful vengeance can impose? 60
The meek observer of thy Laws
To Thee commits his injur'd cause;
In Thee, each anxious fear resign'd,
The fatherless a Father find.
O, break the arm of impious might; 65
So shall their threats no more excite
Our dread, nor thy offended eye
The triumphs of their guilt descry.
 Thine is the throne: Beneath thy reign,
Immortal King! the tribes profane 70
Behold their dreams of conquest o'er,
And vanish to be seen no more.
Thou, Lord, thy People's wish canst read,
E'er from their lips the pray'r proceed;
'Tis thine their drooping hearts to rear, 75
Bow to their wants th' attentive ear,
The weeping Orphan's cheek to dry,
The guiltless Suff'rer's cause to try,
To rein each earthborn Tyrant's will,
And bid the Sons of pride be still. 80

PSALM XI.

ON God my stedfast hopes rely:
  Why urge ye then my soul to fly,
And swift on trembling wings convey'd
To seek the mountain's cov'ring shade?
See, prompt to ill, th' insidious foe   5
Now couch'd in secret bend the bow,
Now to the string adjust the dart,
That thirsts to wound the guiltless heart.
While Justice mourns her Base o'erthrown,
Say who the injur'd cause shall own?   10
Thou, Lord, that cause wilt still sustain;
Thou, thron'd amid thy heav'nly fane,
Shalt cast, regardful, from on high
On suff'ring innocence thine eye,
Each human heart intent to prove,   15
And bid the souls that seek thy Love,
Blest objects of thy constant care,
The fulness of thy bounty share;
While lawless hands and hearts impure
Thy wrath and stedfast hate endure.   20
Behold the lightnings wing their way,
Behold the fires vindictive stray,
While from thy hand the baleful draught,
With storm and mingled sulphur fraught,
In wild amaze the impious Train   25
Low to its utmost dregs shall drain.
For (just himself,) where'er it shines
To Justice God his Love inclines,
                    Delighted

Delighted in the upright mind
His own reflected beams to find. 30

PSALM XII.

O Help me, Lord: For none I see,
   Whose acts conform to thy Decree;
Nor truth nor faith my search can trace
Amid the sons of human race:
New arts of fraud each heart has known, 5
And speaks a language not its own.
But God with vengeance arm'd shall rise,
The tongue of Flatt'ry to chastise,
And Justice to the lip of Pride
Its stroke with aim unerring guide. 10
What force, exclaims the impious Band,
Shall eloquence like ours withstand?
And say, to whom the task belongs
To fix the bridle on our tongues.
" Enough (th' eternal Sire has cried,) 15
" Enough my suff'ring Saints have sigh'd,
" To Me disclos'd their ceaseless fear,
" And pour'd their sorrows in mine ear:
" My hand shall see their wrongs redrest,
" And sooth to peace their troubled breast." 20
   Pure are thy words, almighty Lord,
As Silver, that, by art explor'd,
Has seen the sev'nth tormenting fire
Around th' inclosing vase aspire.
Thy Love thy Servants, Lord, shall share, 25
And, safe in thy protecting care,

Behold, unmov'd, an impious Age
Aim at their life its fruitless rage,
While wrong and fraud the Earth o'erspread,
And Vice triumphant lifts the head. 30

PSALM XIII.

HOW long shall I, my God, in vain,
    Prest by a weight of griefs, complain?
Say, shall I sink in deep despair,
For ever banish'd from thy care?
Condemn'd thy absent beams to mourn 5
Still to divided counsels turn
My lab'ring thought, and hear the foe
Exulting triumph in my woe?
Thy Suppliant's voice attentive weigh,
And bid, O bid, thy heav'nly ray 10
With healing influence o'er me rise,
E'er death's dark slumber close my eyes.
What transport would my fall impart
To each incens'd opposer's heart!
" Behold, the hostile tongue would cry, 15
" Beneath my feet behold him lie,
" The wretch that, hasting to his end,
" With pow'r superior durst contend."
But, while their ceaseless threats I hear,
Thy mercy, Lord, dispels my fear; 20
My hopes on thy Salvation rest,
And fill with conscious joy my breast.
Well pleas'd that mercy to proclaim,
To Thee, instinct with holy flame,

To

PSALM XIII.

To Thee my tongue from day to day 25
Shall meditate the grateful lay.

PSALM XIV.

BEHOLD the Fool, whose heart denies
   The God who form'd the Earth and Skies:
While, fearless, sin's worst paths he treads,
Mark how the dire example spreads
Through human race. Not one we find 5
To Virtue's Heav'n-taught rules inclin'd,
Who 'midst infectious times has stood
Unstain'd, and obstinately good.
Th' eternal Monarch from on high
Cast on the sons of Earth his eye, 10
If haply some he yet might see
From error's baleful influence free,
Whose lives an impious Age might shame,
Who sought his love, and own'd his name.
He look'd: but ah! not one could find 15
To Virtue's Heav'n-taught rules inclin'd:
Each, led from Wisdom's path astray,
Pursues the tenour of his way.
O say, what frenzy thus could blind
Their souls, that with remorseless mind 20
As bread my People they devour,
Nor suppliant own their Maker's pow'r.
Yet see their thoughts tumultuous roll,
See various terrors shake their soul:
For God amidst the Righteous dwells, 25
And each invading foe repells.

And

PSALM XIV.

And what are Ye, who thus deride
The souls that in their God confide,
With wise simplicity of mind
To his all-just Decrees resign'd?   30
   Who, mightiest Lord, to *Israel*'s eyes
Shall bid the wish'd Salvation rise,
From *Sion*'s hill its healing ray
Extend, and round us pour the day?
When Thou (Thy Pow'r the work demands,) 35
Shalt back recall our captive Bands,
The blest event to *Judah*'s shore
Her Songs of triumph shall restore,
And ceaseless shouts, through heav'n's wide frame
Loud-echoing, *Jacob*'s joy proclaim.   40

PSALM XV.

WHO shall tow'rd thy chosen seat
   Turn in glad approach his feet?
Who, great God, a welcome Guest,
On thy hallow'd Mountain rest?
He whose heart thy Love has warm'd,   5
He whose Will, to thine conform'd,
Bids his Life unsullied run;
He whose word and thought are one.
He who ne'er with cruel aim
Seeks to wound an honest fame,   10
Nor with gloomy joy possess'd
Can a Brother's peace molest,
Or to Slander's tongue severe
Stoops with easy faith his ear:

                               Who

PSALM XV.

Who from servile terror free
Spurns at those who spurn at Thee,
And to each who Thee obeys
Love and lowliest rev'rence pays.
What he swears, with stedfast will
To his loss he shall fulfill,
Nor by avaritious loan
Make the poor man's bread his own;
Nor can bribes his sentence guide
'Gainst the guiltless to decide.

He who thus, with heart unstain'd,
Treads the path by Thee ordain'd,
He, great God, shall own thy care,
And thy constant blessing share.

PSALM XVI.

FATHER of All! my soul defend;
On Thee my stedfast hopes depend.
" Thou, mightiest Lord, and none beside,
" Thou art my God," my heart has cried:
In vain, with grateful zeal, I burn
Thy boundless goodness to return;
In vain would gifts by Me bestow'd
Augment the treasures of my God.
Yet shall my love on All descend,
Whose Souls to thy Decrees attend,
My heart's desire to each incline,
Whose saintlike Virtue marks him Thine.
Woe to the wretch estrang'd from Thee,
Who bows to Gods miscall'd the knee;

Be witness to my guilt, if e'er 15
Their draughts of offer'd blood I share,
If, while thy breath my life sustains,
Their name my hallow'd lip profanes.
Thee, Lord, my patrimony, Thee
The portion of my cup I see: 20
Each blessing by thy care secur'd,
Life's choicest gifts around me pour'd
I view; nor finds my searching eye
A Lot, whose worth with mine shall vie.
Thee let me bless, the faithful Guide, 25
Whose counsels o'er my life preside,
And wisdom to my wakeful breast
At midnight's silent hour suggest.
In all my acts, in each intent,
Thee to my soul my thoughts present, 30
Whose sure defence my gate has barr'd,
And planted on my right a guard.
For this my heart, for this my tongue,
Shall meditate the joyful song;
And though (Thy Will has thus ordain'd,) 35
My flesh to death's dark shades descend,
Yet Hope ev'n there, its constant Guest,
Shall smooth the pillow of my rest.
Thou from the grave my soul shalt claim,
Nor leave thy Servant, in whose frame 40
Thy hallowing Spirit dwells inshrin'd,
To pale Corruption's pow'r resign'd,
But to my eyes, in full survey,
The op'ning paths of Life display;

Those

PSALM XVI.

Those paths that to thy presence bear; 45
For plenitude of Bliss is there,
And pleasures, Lord, unmix'd with woe,
At thy right hand for ever flow.

PSALM XVII.

TO Thee, the Judge inthron'd on high,
 Shall injur'd Innocence apply:
O let my pray'r by Thee be heard,
From undissembling lips prefer'd;
O let my Doom from Thee proceed, 5
And gracious mark the upright deed.
When night's dark shades were round me pour'd,
Thy thoughts my spirit have explor'd;
Say, to thy all-discerning eyes
If aught of guilt within me rise, 10
If offer'd violence and wrong
Have urg'd to Sin my thoughtless tongue.
Taught by thy Word my stedfast mind
Has each nefarious path declin'd;
O still my Guardian, still my Guide, 15
Forbid my wav'ring feet to slide.
To Thee (for Thou the pray'r canst hear,)
To Thee my suppliant voice I rear;
O treat me not with cold disdain,
Nor let my vows return in vain. 20
O Thou, whose hand th' oppressor quells,
And each invading pow'r repels
From Him whose hopes on Thee repose,
To Me thy wondrous grace disclose.

What

What care the pupil of the eye 25
Demands, that care to Me apply,
" And keep, O keep me, King of Kings,
" Beneath thy own almighty wings."
Rich in my spoils, with murth'rous hate
A pamper'd Croud around me wait, 30
Whose heart, with impious fury stung,
To mad presumption prompts their tongue.
With watchful look they mark my way,
As lurks, expectant of the prey,
The Lion, or his tawny Brood 35
To rapine born, and nurs'd in blood.
Rise, Lord, and let me, by thy aid
Preserv'd, their threatning jaws evade;
With sword unsheath'd, and lifted hand,
Preventive crush the lawless Band, 40
Whose Days, with Life's full blessings fraught,
To Earth's low scene confine their thought;
Whose eyes a num'rous race behold,
To heir their heaps of treasur'd gold.
Far other bliss my soul shall own, 45
A bliss to guilty minds unknown.
O! when, awaken'd by thy care,
Thy face I view, thy image bear,
How shall my breast with transport glow,
What full delight my heart o'erflow! 50

PSALM XVIII.

BLEST Object of my soul's desire,
To Thee my grateful thoughts aspire;
On Thee my stedfast hope I build;
My God, my Rest, my Rock, my Shield,
The Strength of my Salvation Thee,   5
And Tow'r of sure defence, I see.
What foe shall e'er my terror raise,
While thus I pay my debt of praise,
And, as the doubtful field I tread,
To God my suppliant hands outspread?   10
Woes heap'd on woes my heart deplor'd,
While Sin's proud torrents round me roar'd;
The Sepulchre's extended hands
Had wrapt me in its strongest bands,
And Death, insulting, o'er my head   15
Th' inextricable toils had spread.
My Words, as griev'd to God I pray,
Wing to his heav'nly fane their way,
Through adverse clouds their passage clear,
Nor unaccepted reach his ear: 20
With strong convulsions groan'd the ground,
The hills, with waving forests crown'd,
Loos'd from their base, their summits nod,
And own the presence of their God:
Collected clouds of wreathing smoke   25
Forth from his angry nostrils broke,
And orbs of fire, with dreadful glare,
Rush'd onward through the glowing air.

Incumbent on the bending sky
The Lord descended from on high,   30
And bade the darkness of the pole
Beneath his feet tremendous roll.
The Cherub to his car he join'd,
And on the wings of mightiest wind,
As down to Earth his journey lay,   35
Resistless urg'd his rapid way.
Thick-woven clouds, around him clos'd,
His secret residence compos'd,
And waters high-suspended spread
Their dark pavilion o'er his head.   40
In vain reluctant to the Blaze
That previous pour'd its streaming rays,
As on he moves, the clouds retire,
Dissolv'd in hail and rushing fire:
His voice th' almighty Monarch rear'd,   45
Through heav'n's high vault in thunders heard,
And down in fiercer conflict came
The hailstones dire and mingled flame.
With aim direct his shafts were sped,
In vain his foes before them fled;   50
Now here, now there, his lightnings stray,
And sure destruction marks their way:
Earth's basis open to the eye,
And Ocean's springs, were seen to lie,
As, chiding loud, his fury past,   55
And o'er them breath'd the dreadful blast.
God in my rescue from the skies
His arm extends, and bids me rise

       Emergent

PSALM XVIII.

Emergent from the flood profound,
Whose waves my struggling soul surround. 60
His hand my strongest foes repell'd,
Their force by force superior quell'd,
And I, unequal to the fight,
Ev'n I have triumph'd in his might.
Opprefs'd with languor, grief, and pain, 65
E'er yet my nerves their strength regain,
His fierce assault th' Invader gave;
But Thou wert present, Lord, to save:
My spacious path by Thee outspread,
With course secure behold me tread, 70
Blest in the favour of my God,
And speak the grace on all bestow'd,
Who guiltless hands to Him can raise,
And offer unpolluted praise.
His precepts, fix'd before my view, 75
My thoughts with stedfast aim pursue,
Nor error's cloud nor arts of sin
My soul from his obedience win.
Thou seest, eternal Judge, my breast
Each taint of inward guilt detest: 80
My will subdu'd to thy Commands,
And wash'd in innocence my hands,
Thine eyes delighted have survey'd,
Thy pow'r with fullest bliss repaid.
    Thy ways to ours conform: in Thee 85
The Holy shall the Holy see,
The Pure the Pure; the Perfect Mind
In Thee Perfection's self shall find;

Their arts the men of froward turn
By deeper art eluded mourn: 90
While These their pow'rs with effort vain
Unite, the meek and pious Train
Thou, ever watchful, ever nigh,
Defendeſt; and the haughty eye,
Chaſtis'd by thy afflicting ſtroke, 95
Bends to the earth its humbled look.
While night's thick ſhades around me ſtand,
My lamp, illumin'd by thy hand,
Pours through the gloom its ſteady ray,
And turns my darkneſs into day. 100
My arm, if Thou thine aid ſupply,
Shall bid whole hoſts before me fly,
My feet, if Thou my ſinews ſtring,
High o'er the wall exulting ſpring.
Nor ſtains of ſin thy path defile, 105
Author of Good! nor fraud nor guile
To Thee belong: On Thy bleſt Word
(By Truth's ſevereſt flames explor'd,)
On Thy bleſt Word who build their truſt,
Shall find their confidence was juſt. 110
What God but Thee ſhall *Iſrael* know,
Or Who, O Who can ſave but Thou?
'Tis God that arms me for the fight,
'Tis God that girds my ſoul with might;
From Him my feet their path have known, 115
And, wing'd with vigour not their own,
Support me, while in air ſublime,
Swift as the hind, the rock I climb,

And

PSALM XVIII.

And, safe from each invader's hand,
Fix on its craggy height my stand.   120
By Him inform'd, with surest art
My hands direct the pointed dart,
And forceful break the steely bow,
New wrested from the struggling foe.
Thou, mightiest Lord, hast o'er my head   125
The shield of thy Salvation spread;
By Thy right hand I walk'd upheld,
Great in thy mercy trod the field
With step enlarg'd, and, Thou my Guide,
Nor fear'd to fall, nor knew to slide.   130
With fierce pursuit my foes I press'd,
Beheld my spear their flight arrest,
Nor bade my sword its fury stay,
Till prostrate on the earth they lay.
They bow'd, they fell, distain'd with gore; 135
They bow'd, they fell, and rose no more.
Blest Lord! 'Twas Thy resistless pow'r
That arm'd me for the dreadful hour,
My foes beneath my feet o'erthrown,
To certain conquest led me on,   140
Their backs expos'd to many a wound,
And stretch'd them breathless on the ground.
Aloud, oppress'd with horror, cried
The rebel Throng; but None replied:
To God they call; but God their pray'r   145
Abhorrent scatters to the air.
Behold their troops before me chas'd,
As dust before the driving blast,

D 3   And

And trampled, as the yielding clay
Extended o'er the beaten way.   150
When factious Crouds againſt me roſe,
How prompt thy hand to interpoſe!
O'er realms, that but have heard my name,
Through Thee the juſt command I claim;
The Tribes, that from their God eſtrang'd   155
Through climes to Me unknown had rang'd,
With flatt'ring lip their homage pay,
And trembling own a foreign ſway.
Each dreads my vengeance to ſuſtain,
Nor walls nor forts their fears reſtrain.   160
 Bleſt be the living God, whoſe aid,
When impious foes my peace invade,
Their rage inſtructs me to decline,
And makes his wiſh'd Salvation mine;
Deals, in my right, th' avenging ſtroke,   165
And bends the Nations to my yoke,
Each force, that durſt my reign conteſt,
By His reſiſtleſs ſtrength ſuppreſs'd.
For this, thy pow'r my ſong ſhall claim,
And diſtant regions hear thy fame.   170
Behold thy *David*, to the throne
By Thee upraiſ'd: His temples own
Thy ſacred unction; fair ſucceſs
His counſels and his arms ſhall bleſs,
Thy Love on him and on his Line   175
With unextinguiſh'd luſtre ſhine.

PSALM

PSALM XIX.

GOD the Heav'ns aloud proclaim
   Through their wide-extended frame,
And the Firmament each hour
Speaks the wonders of his pow'r:
Day to the succeeding day   5
Joys the notice to convey,
And the Nights, in ceaseless round,
Each to each repeat the sound,
Prompt, without or speech or tongue,
In his praise to form the song.   10
Pleas'd to hear their voice extend
Far as to her utmost end,
Earth the Heav'n-taught knowledge boasts
Through her many-languag'd coasts,
While the Sun above her head   15
Sees his tabernacle spread,
And from out his chamber bright
Like a Bridegroom springs to sight:
See him with gigantic pace
Joyous run his destin'd race,   20
Now to farthest regions borne
Onward speed, and now return,
And to All, with welcome ray,
Life and genial warmth convey.
Warmth and life each thankful heart   25
Feels thy Law, great God, impart;
Clear from ev'ry spot it shines,
And the guilt-stain'd Thought refines;

                      Truth's

'Truth's firm base its frame upholds,
While it Mysteries unfolds, 30
Which the childlike mind explores,
And to heav'nly science soars.
Prest with sorrows, doubts, and fears,
What like this the spirit chears?
What so perfect, what so pure? 35
What to Reason's eye obscure
Can such wondrous light afford
As the dictates of thy Word?
Where thy Fear its fruit matures,
(Fruit, that endless years endures,) 40
There the mind, to Vice a foe,
Pants thy blest Decrees to know,
And (its will to thine subdu'd,)
Owns them wise, and just, and good;
Nor can Gold such worth acquire 45
From the sev'nth exploring fire,
Nor the labour of the bees
E'er in sweetness vie with These:
Taught by Them, thy Servant's breast
Joys the Blessings to attest 50
Heap'd on those whose hearts sincere
Learn thy Precepts to revere.
Best Instructor, from thy ways
Who can tell how oft he strays?
Purge me from the guilt that lies 55
Wrapt within my heart's disguise;
Let me thence, by Thee renew'd,
Each presumptuous sin exclude:

So

PSALM XIX.

So my lot shall ne'er be join'd
With the Men whose impious mind, 60
Fearless of thy just command,
Braves the vengeance of thy hand.
Let my tongue, from error free,
Speak the words approv'd by Thee;
To thy all-observing eyes 65
Let my thoughts accepted rise:
While I thus thy name adore,
And thy healing grace implore,
Blest Redeemer, bow thine ear,
God my Strength, propitious hear. 70

PSALM XX.

MAY He whom Heav'n and Earth obey
Regard thee in the dreadful day,
May *Jacob*'s Lord above thy head
His own victorious banner spread.
May He from out his hallow'd shrine 5
Reach to thy aid the hand divine,
And strength into thy soul instill
From beauteous *Sion*'s favour'd hill.
There may thy incense to the skies
In sweet memorial ever rise; 10
Thy victims there in smoke aspire,
Touch'd by his own celestial fire.
May He thy ev'ry wish approve,
May He indulgent from above
In all thy dangers intervene, 15
While We, his great Salvation seen,

Assist

PSALM XX.

Assist thy joy, thy triumphs share,
And bless the God who hears thy pray'r.
I see, I see th' Almighty shed
His blessings on th' anointed head,   20
Attentive from his holy Heav'n
Protect the crown Himself has giv'n,
And, cloth'd with terror, to thy foes
His all-subduing strength oppose.

   These urge to Fight the rattling Car,   25
And Those the fiery Steed prepare,
Unenvied Both by Us, who see
Our sure defence, great God, in Thee.
Driv'n by superior force they fly,
Or, faln, in heaps promiscuous lie,   30
While We our heads exulting raise,
And sing our great Deliv'rer's praise.
O, when we praise, and when we pray,
Do Thou, whom Heav'n and Earth obey,
Accept the praise, confirm the pray'r,   35
And make our safety still thy care.

PSALM XXI.

BY Thy unwearied strength upheld
   To Thee the King his thanks shall yield,
And, taught by blest experience, know
What joys from Thy salvation flow.
Thy cares his heart's desire complete;   5
His pray'r from Thy eternal seat,
As low to Thee his knees he bends,
In full acceptance back descends.

                                     Thou,

PSALM XXI.

Thou, Lord, preventive of his want,
The blessings of thy Love wilt grant,   10
And bid the golden circlet spread
Its purest splendors round his head.
He ask'd thee Life, and finds it giv'n,
Life, lasting as the days of Heav'n.
The conquests, which thy hands bestow,   15
With grace and glory bind his brow;
He, crown'd with bliss perpetual, He
Thy face in full display shall see,
And (for on Thee his hopes rely,)
Unmov'd each adverse shock defy.   20
Thy hand shall find each latent foe,
And vengeful strike th' unerring blow.
Fierce as the kindled furnace glows,
Whose sides the crackling thorns inclose,
Thy wrath its flames shall round them pour,   25
And quick their boasted strength devour.
Their fruit, a luckless progeny,
Uprooted from the ground shall die,
And Earth their tribe no more behold
Amidst her families inroll'd,   30
Who, impious, durst resistance give
To Thee, whom None resist and live.
In vain each hostile art they try;
Behold, as trembling back they fly,
Thy shafts, adjusted to the string,   35
Impatient wait upon the wing.
    Maker of All, through Earth and Skies
O let thy pow'r conspicuous rise,

And

And furnish to our grateful lays
A theme of everlasting praise.   40

PSALM XXII.

MY God, my God, O tell me, why
Unheeded still ascends my cry,
Why thus from my afflicted heart
Thy presence and thy health depart.
Eternal Lord, throughout the day   5
With fruitless plaint to Thee I pray;
Nor sleeps the anguish of my soul,
When night's dark shades involve the pole.
Yet unimpeach'd thy Faith appears,
Thy Sanctity my heart reveres,   10
O Thou, to whom in homage join
The Sons of *Jacob*'s chosen line.
Thee, Lord, our Sires their strength confest,
And found thee, as their stedfast breast
To Thee its full affiance gave,   15
Nor slow to hear, nor weak to save:
Secure thy wish'd for aid t' obtain,
In Thee they hop'd, nor hop'd in vain.
But what am I? A Man in form,
Yet brother to the trampled worm;   20
An outcast from the human kind,
To fierce derision's rage consign'd:
They shake the head, they shout, they gaze;
Each eye, each lip, contempt betrays:
" On God, they cry, thy hope was staid;   25
" Be God, if His thou art, thy aid."

Thine,

PSALM XXII.

Thine, mightiest Father, thine I am;
By Thee from out the womb I came,
From Thee my ev'ry comfort sprung,
While yet upon the breast I hung.
Hail, from my birth and to my end
My God, my Guardian, and my Friend.
O view me not with distant eye,
While various griefs await me nigh:
Thy aid withheld, what friendly pow'r
Shall shield me in the dang'rous hour?
See Bulls unnumber'd round me stand,
Bulls, nurs'd in *Basan*'s fertile land;
With wide-extended mouth they roar,
Nor rage the famish'd Lions more,
When nightly through the starless gloom
Along the howling Wild they roam.
My frame, disjoin'd, in swift decay
Wastes like the running stream away;
My heart in groans its grief proclaims,
And melts, as wax before the flames.
Fast to my jaws my tongue is chain'd,
My flesh, its vital moisture drain'd,
Dry as the clay-form'd vase appears,
And, while thy chastisement it bears,
Waits till thy hand resume my breath,
And lodge me in the dust of death.
Thou seest my soul by Dogs pursu'd,
Dogs fierce of kind, and train'd to blood;
Thou seest a throng, who Thee despise,
In dreadful siege against me rise,

And, while fast-issuing streams the gore,
My hands and feet relentless bore.
My starting bones to ev'ry eye
Expos'd, O Ye that, passing by,   60
In wonder (not in pity) join,
O say, was ever grief like mine?
My raiment each with each divides,
My vesture, as the lot decides,
Becomes some new possessor's spoil,   65
The prize that crowns his impious toil.
My God, my Strength, recede not far,
But haste, and make my soul thy care,
My soul, pursu'd by hostile hate,
Afflicted, helpless, desolate;   70
O turn th' impending swords away,
Nor yield it to the Dog a prey.
The foaming Lion's wrath assuage,
Nor let the Oryx, in his rage,
With headlong force against me borne,   75
Aim at my life the pointed horn.
So will I joy thy honour'd name
Amidst my brethren to proclaim,
And gath'ring Crouds shall hear my tongue
Thus to my God awake the song.   80
  " Exalt, ye Saints, the Pow'r divine,
  " Exalt him, All of *Jacob*'s line,
  " And let each tribe with duteous fear
  " His boundless Majesty revere.
  " 'Tis not in Him, with cold disdain   85
  " To hear the helpless Poor complain;

                              " He

PSALM XXII.

  " He (nor with unrelenting eye)
  " Each falling tear, each heaving sigh,
  " Regards, attentive to perceive
  " Their wants, and faithful to relieve."   90
Such Strains thy Mercy shall inspire,
While in the full-assembled Choir
To Thee the votive Song I raise,
And thankful-pay my debt of praise.
To You, ye humble, meek, and good,   95
Who ask from *Israel*'s Lord your food,
His hand indulgent from on high
Shall yield at full the wish'd supply:
Who seek like You their God, like You
To Him their praises shall renew,   100
Whose Love immortal life imparts,
And swells with joy their conscious hearts.
Maker of All! through ev'ry Land
Thy Deeds in full record shall stand,
And farthest Realms converted join   105
In homage to the Name divine;
Ev'n Kings in Thee their Mightier greet,
And lay their scepters at thy feet.
Earth's countless tribes the festal board
(Thy grace by sacrifice implor'd,)   110
Shall spread; and All, whose mortal frame
Th' insatiate Grave prepares to claim,
Thy Pow'r, immortal Judge, shall own,
And prostrate kneel before thy Throne.
See, while by Thee redeem'd I live,   115
A Race from Me their birth derive,

(A Race by just possession thine,)
Whose heart thy Spirit shall incline
The precepts of thy Will t' obey,
Whose tongue thy glory shall display, 120
And bid thy righteous Acts engage
The wonder of the future Age.

PSALM XXIII.

LO, my Shepherd's hand divine!
Want shall never more be mine.
In a pasture fair and large
He shall feed his happy Charge,
And my couch with tend'rest care 5
'Midst the springing grass prepare.
When I faint with summer's heat,
He shall lead my weary feet
To the streams that still and flow
Through the verdant meadow flow. 10
He my soul anew shall frame,
And, his mercy to proclaim,
When through devious paths I stray,
Teach my steps the better way.
Though the dreary vale I tread 15
By the shades of death o'erspread,
There I walk from terror free,
While my ev'ry wish I see
By thy rod and staff supplied,
This my guard, and that my guide. 20
While my foes are gazing on,
Thou thy fav'ring care hast shown;

Thou

PSALM XXIII.

Thou my plenteous board hast spread,
Thou with oil refresh'd my head;
Fill'd by Thee my cup o'erflows;
For thy Love no limit knows:
Constant, to my latest end
This my footsteps shall attend,
And shall bid thy hallow'd Dome
Yield me an eternal home.

PSALM XXIV.

EARTH, big with Empires, to thy Reign
Submits, great God, its wide domain;
Whate'er this Orb's vast bounds confine,
By just possession, Lord, is thine:
That Orb amid the watry waste
Thy hands, best Architect, have plac'd,
And bid th' unfathomable Deep
Beneath its firm foundations sleep.
Lord, who shall to thy Hill ascend?
Who suppliant at thine altars bend?
Whose hands and heart from guilt are free,
Who ne'er to idols bow'd the knee,
Nor, studious of deceit, would try
By oaths to consecrate a lye.
On such th' Almighty from above
Shall heap the blessings of his Love,
And, purg'd from sin's transmissive stain,
Admit them to his sacred Fane.
Such only form the chosen Choir,
Whose feet, with licens'd step, aspire

PSALM XXIV.

To visit *Sion*'s blest Abode;
Who seek the face of *Jacob*'s God.
Lift, lift your heads, each hallow'd Gate,
Aloft, with sudden spring, your weight,
Ye everlasting Portals, rear;   25
Behold the King of glory near.
And who this King of glory? say.
That Lord who bears th' eternal sway,
Who, cloth'd with strength, to war descends,
And conquest on his sword attends.   30
Lift, lift your heads, each hallow'd Gate,
Aloft, with sudden spring, your weight,
Ye everlasting Portals, rear;
Behold the King of glory near.
And who this King of glory? say.   35
The God, whom Heav'n's high Hosts obey:
In Him that King of glory view,
And yield to Him the homage due.

PSALM XXV.

TO Thee, great God, my soul shall rise;
On Thee my stedfast mind relies;
O save me, Lord, from shame and woe,
And blast the triumphs of my foe.
Nor shame nor woe the heart attends,   5
Whose trust on *Jacob*'s God depends:
But grief, confusion, doubt, and fear
In dire vicissitude shall tear
The guilty souls, whose love of ill
To rash transgression prompts their will.   10

Thy

PSALM XXV.

Thy paths, bleſt Source of light, diſplay,
And teach my doubting ſteps thy way.
God of my health, from morn to eve
In Thee my hopes have learn'd to live:
O lead me in thy truth, and ſtore 15
My heart with thy celeſtial lore.
Thy Mercy, Lord, recall to mind,
Whoſe beams from earlieſt age have ſhin'd,
And let oblivion's thickeſt veil
Th' offences of my youth conceal, 20
That I with Them my lot may bear,
Whoſe ſouls thy kind remembrance ſhare.
Good, Lord, and juſt art Thou; thy Love
Returning Sinners joy to prove,
And led by thy auſpicious ray 25
Correct the error of their way.
In Thee ſhall each of humble mind
The Friend and ſure Inſtructor find,
And, while the dictates of thy Law
His thoughts to full obedience awe, 30
With joy thy equal paths ſhall tread,
By Mercy and by Truth outſpread.
Thy wonted pity, Lord, impart,
While in the anguiſh of my heart
The burthen of my guilt I own, 35
And humbled bow before thy Throne.
   Ye Souls that to his fear incline,
Secure to God your ſteps reſign,
And learn from his directing hand
What path may beſt your choice demand. 40

How

PSALM XXV.

How blest, thy precepts, Lord, who knows!
As o'er Life's pilgrimage he goes,
See Peace and Safety nightly spread
Their tent around his favour'd head:
See, rang'd in fair descent, his line   45
The lot which thy Decrees assign
Divide, and, long as time shall last,
The blessings of thy Bounty taste.
Who bow to Thee th' attentive ear,
The secrets of thy will shall hear;   50
Thy Compact, Lord, to such reveal'd,
Shall light and heav'nly transport yield.
   Wrapt in the hostile snare I lie,
Yet lift to Thee th' expecting eye,
Till thou my full relief decree,   55
And bid my captive soul go free.
O turn thee, Lord, in pity turn,
Behold me helpless and forlorn;
See various griefs my heart oppress;
My wants supply, my wrongs redress;   60
O let me thy attention win,
And seal the pardon of my sin.
While factious Crouds around me wait,
Inflam'd with rage, and impious hate,
Stretch to my aid the arm of pow'r,   65
And guard me in the dang'rous hour,
Nor let my soul, on Thee reclin'd,
Its sorrows utter to the wind.
Let Truth and spotless Innocence
Their succours to my heart dispense;   70

Indulgent

Indulgent to my pray'r, with Mine
My Country's wish'd deliv'rance join;
God of my hope, thy Love disclose,
And heal, O heal, thy People's woes.

PSALM XXVI.

1.

BE Thou my Judge: thy searching eyes
   My guiltless life have known:
On Thee my stedfast soul relies,
   Nor fear of lapse shall own.

2.

O search me still; my heart, my reins,
   With strictest view survey:
Thy Love, great God, my hope sustains,
   Thy Truth directs my way.

3.

The house of guile, and seat of lies,
   With studious care I shun:
From Crouds that impious deeds devise
   My steps abhorrent run.

4.

In innocence I wash my hands,
   Thy altar compass round,
And grateful lead the sacred Bands,
   Whose hymns thy acts resound.

5.

How oft, instinct with warmth divine,
   Thy threshold have I trod!
How lov'd the Courts whose walls inshrine
   The Glory of my God!

PSALM XXVI.

6.

O let me not the vengeance share,
    That waits the guilty Tribe,
Whose murth'rous hands each mischief dare,
    And grasp the offer'd bribe:

7.

But pour, O pour, while thus I tread
    The path by Thee prepar'd,
Thy beams of mercy on my head,
    And round me plant a guard.

8.

Thou, Lord, my steps hast fix'd aright,
    And pleas'd shalt hear my tongue
With *Israel*'s thankful Sons unite
    To form the festal Song.

PSALM XXVII.

THOU, Lord, my safety, Thou my light,
    What danger shall my soul affright?
Strength of my life! What arm shall dare
To hurt whom Thou hast own'd thy care?
When erst, impatient to devour,
Against me rose each hostile pow'r,
Their fierce attempts successless found,
They stumbled, fell, and bit the ground.
Though adverse hosts the standard rear,
Thy servant shall without a fear
The gath'ring War around him see,
And fix, secure, his trust on Thee.
One wish, with holy transport warm,
My heart has form'd, and yet shall form;

PSALM XXVII.

One gift I ask; that to my end
Fair *Sion*'s Dome I may attend,
There joyful find a sure abode,
And view the beauty of my God.
For He within his hallow'd shrine
My secret refuge shall assign,
And, while the storms around me beat,
Fix on the rock my stedfast feet.
Behold his arm, beneath me spread,
High o'er my foes exalt my head.
For this, with grateful joy bestow'd,
My off'ring shall his altar load,
My tongue its note exulting raise,
And dictate to the harp his praise.
O hear me, Lord; on Thee I call,
And prostrate at thy footstool fall:
Propitious in my cause appear,
And bow to my request thine ear.
" Seek Ye my face with duteous care,
" And frequent to my Throne repair,"
Thus to my heart I hear thee speak;
Thy face, my heart replies, I seek:
Nor Thou to my desiring eye
Thy presence, heav'nly Lord, deny:
O let me, on thy aid reclin'd,
Thee still my great Salvation find,
Nor leave me, helpless and forlorn,
The absence of thy grace to mourn.
When, doom'd the Orphan's lot to bear,
No Father's kind concern I share,

Nor o'er me wakes a Mother's eye, 45
My wants attentive to supply,
Adopted by thy care, in Thee
The Parent and the Friend I see.
Instruct me, Lord, thy path to know,
And, while with secret art the foe 50
My doubting steps would turn aside,
Be Thou my Guardian and my Guide.
O save me from the hand of wrong;
My soul by each malignant tongue
With causeless insult loaded view, 55
And charg'd with guilt it never knew.
O how had grief consum'd my frame,
But that I hop'd, while yet my name
Amidst the living stands inroll'd,
Thy boundless Mercy to behold. 60

    With patient hope, with mind sedate,
On *Israel*'s God expectant wait;
Be strong, be stedfast: So thy heart
Shall feel his grace its aid impart:
Though press'd with sorrow's heaviest load, 65
O fix thy trust on *Israel*'s God.

PSALM XXVIII.

GOD my Strength, to Thee I pray;
    Turn not Thou thine ear away;
Lest, while to thy Suppliant's cry
Thou thy answer shalt deny,
Sudden I my place assume 5
'Midst the tenants of the tomb.

                          Gracious

PSALM XXVIII.

Gracious to my vows attend,
While the humble knee I bend,
And, inspir'd with holy fear,
Tow'rd thy shrine my hands uprear.
Give me not thy wrath to know,
Nor to feel the vengeful blow
By thy just decrees assign'd
To the Men of impious mind,
Who, their hearts intent on wrong,
Smooth with lies their venom'd tongue.
What shall guilt like theirs demand
From the Justice of thy hand?
Let whate'er their thoughts devise,
(Thus aloud that Justice cries,)
What their ruthless arm has dar'd,
Meet from Thee its full reward:
While thy wrath with steady pace
Step by step their feet shall trace,
And, though now their stubborn ear
Shun thy wondrous acts to hear,
Teach them to confess thy pow'r,
Shatter'd like some Heav'n-struck Tow'r,
That before th' astonish'd sight,
Stooping from its airy height,
'Midst the thunder's awful roar,
Falls, to be rebuilt no more.
   Let me (for with pitying ear
God my pray'r has deign'd to hear,)
Let me thanks perpetual yield;
He my Strength, and He my Shield,

On his long-experienc'd aid
See my hope for ever stay'd,
While my heart, with joy possess'd,
Dances in my throbbing breast,   40
And my tongue in grateful lays
Consecrates to Him its praise.
 Thou whose arm is o'er us spread,
Prompt to guard th' anointed head,
And from each invader's hand   45
Vindicate thy chosen Land,
Save thy People from distress,
And thy Patrimony bless!
Give them, Lord, thy Love to share,
Feed them with a Shepherd's care,   50
And their pow'r to latest days
O'er their foes triumphant raise.

PSALM XXIX.

SING, ye Sons of Might, O sing
 Praise to Heav'n's eternal King;
Pow'r and strength to Him assign,
And before his hallow'd shrine
Yield the homage that his Name   5
From a Creature's lips may claim.
" Hark! his voice in thunder breaks;
Hush'd to silence, while he speaks,
Ocean's waves from pole to pole
Hear the awful accents roll: 10
See, as louder yet they rise,
Echoing through the vaulted Skies,

Loftiest

PSALM XXIX.

Loftieſt Cedars lie o'erthrown,
" Cedars of ſteep *Lebanon*.
See, uprooted from its ſeat,   15
Lebanon itſelf retreat;
Trembling at the threat divine,
Sirion haſtes its flight to join:
See them like the heifer borne,
Like the beaſt whoſe pointed horn   20
Strikes with dread the ſylvan train,
Bound impetuous on the plain.
Now the burſting clouds give way,
And the vivid lightnings play,
And the wilds by Man untrod   25
Hear, diſmay'd, th' approaching God.
Cades, o'er thy lonely waſte
Oft the dreaded ſounds have paſt:
Oft his ſtroke the Wood invades:
Widow'd of their leafy ſhades   30
Mightieſt oaks its fury know;
While the pregnant Hind her throe
Inſtant feels, and on the earth
Trembling drops th' unfiniſh'd birth.
Proſtrate on the ſacred floor   35
Iſrael's Sons his name adore,
While his acts to ev'ry tongue
Yield its argument of ſong.
He the ſwelling ſurge commands;
Fix'd his Throne for ever ſtands;   40
He " his People ſhall increaſe,
" Arm with ſtrength, and bleſs with peace.

PSALM XXX.

TO Thee, great Ruler of the skies,
   Whose arm its constant aid supplies,
While vanquish'd foes confess my sway,
My heart its grateful vows shall pay.
As, press'd with woe, to Thee I cried,   5
Thy hand its healing pow'r applied,
And, while increasing languors gave
The signal to th' expecting grave
This mortal fabrick to receive,
Revers'd the doom, and bade me live.   10
Ye faithful Sons of *Israel*'s name,
Your Maker's sanctity proclaim,
And, while his mercies on your breast
In sweet memorial stand impress'd,
To Him in joyful accents raise   15
The song of gratitude and praise.
Behold his Wrath's avenging blast,
How slow to rise, how soon o'erpast,
How prompt his Favour to dispense
Its life-imparting influence.   20
Grief for a night, obstrusive Guest,
Beneath our roof perchance may rest,
But Joy, with the returning day,
Shall wipe each transient tear away.
   As pleas'd I cast my eyes around,   25
And view'd my life with blessings crown'd,
(While, safe in thy protecting hand,
High on the rock I took my stand,)

PSALM XXX.

In confidence of soul I said,
" What ills shall e'er my peace invade?" 30
But, instant, Thou thy face hadst turn'd,
And prostrate on the earth I mourn'd:
I mourn'd, and, O my Guard, my Guide,
(With humbler spirit thus I cried,)
Shall aught of profit, if the ground 35
My blood absorb, to Thee redound?
Or, vocal in thy praise, the Dust
Proclaim thy Counsels wise and just,
And wake thy wondrous Acts to tell
Amid Corruption's dreary cell? 40
Thy aid, my God, in pity lend,
And gracious to my plaints attend.

  Again the face of joy I wear;
Thy hand, indulgent to my pray'r,
The sackcloth from my loyns unbound, 45
With mirth's fair cincture wraps me round.
For this, my heart with zeal shall burn,
My tongue the bands of silence spurn,
And pleas'd, through life, in grateful verse
Thy Love, eternal Lord, rehearse. 50

PSALM XXXI.

LORD (for on Thee supported stand
   My hopes,) O let thy aiding hand
The justice of my cause proclaim,
And save me from impending shame.
Thy ear, thou Majesty divine, 5
Propitious to my pray'r incline;

PSALM XXXI.

Haste to my help, and let thy pow'r
My rock present and brazen tow'r:
That rock, that tow'r, my God, in Thee,
Snatch'd from surrounding ills, I see;   10
To life's last period (so thy Name
Shall praise and thanks perpetual claim,)
O let me, by thy counsel led,
Thy path with step unerring tread,
And, sav'd by thy preventive care,   15
Shake from my feet the broken snare.
God of my strength, the Wise, the Just,
To Thee my spirit I intrust;
From Thee, when terrors clos'd me round,
My soul its full redemption found.   20
My thoughts the self-deceiving train,
Enslav'd to superstitions vain,
Abhor, and 'midst increasing woes
Their confidence on Thee repose.
Thy Mercy shall my thanks employ,   25
My constant theme, my highest joy;
For Thou, my soul by griefs pursu'd,
My state with pitying eye hast view'd,
Confess'd me thine, and bid me share
The gifts of thy paternal care.   30
Thy hand, while rang'd in close array
Insulting hosts around me lay,
Gave to the wind their vain design,
And made the paths of freedom mine.
Once more, my sight with inward grief   35
Consum'd, vouchsafe me thy relief,

Doom'd,

PSALM XXXI.

Doom'd, while my soul its ceaseless pains
Deep through its inmost frame sustains,
Life's noon for eve exchang'd to bear,
And Age invited on by Care.   40
The guilt that in my thought revolves
My strength impairs, my joints dissolves;
The scorn of Foes, and, keener yet,
The scorn of Friends, my soul beset;
My lov'd Associates, that before   45
With frequent feet my threshold wore,
If now at distance in their way
Their eye my wasted form survey,
With horror struck the sight forgo,
And shun th' infection of my woe.   50
With lonely step the earth I tread,
Forgotten as the silent Dead,
Or as the vase of meanest clay,
In useless fragments cast away.
My fame opprobrious tongues invade,   55
While terrors wrap me in their shade,
And crouds with meditated rage
Against my life their pow'rs engage.
Yet see me, Lord, in Thee confide;
Thou art my God, my heart has cried;   60
From Thee my time its limit knows;
O save me from devouring foes,
And with resistless arm dispell
The clouds of wrath that o'er me dwell.
O let thy presence on me beam,   65
Thy clemency my life redeem,

Nor

PSALM XXXI.

Nor let me, Lord, the shame sustain
Thy aid to ask, and ask in vain.
Theirs be the shame, thy pow'r who brave,
Nor cease their insults, till the grave,   70
Absorbing quick the guilty throng,
In endless silence seal their tongue:
Such silence on their lips impose,
Whose words their pride-swoln heart disclose,
At Wisdom's Sons their malice aim,   75
And blast with lies the guiltless name.
O, how shall All who seek thy Love
The fulness of thy bounty prove!
How joy, while Thou thy treasur'd store
Indulgent in their lap shalt pour,   80
And teach th' admiring World to see
How blest the souls that trust in Thee!
Thy care their sure defence shall yield;
Within thy presence, Lord, conceal'd,
Thy Saints, while breath their life prolongs,   85
At distance from the strife of tongues,
Shall see thy tabernacle spread
Its awful splendors o'er their head.
  Blest be the name of *Jacob*'s God,
Whose Love, in happiest hour bestow'd,   90
Has giv'n within my lot to fall
The strong-built City's guarding wall,
That fix'd each adverse shock sustains,
And mocks the proud besieger's pains.
Awhile, with uncollected mind,   95
As banish'd from thy sight, I pin'd;

But

PSALM XXXI.

But Thou thy Servant's pray'r haſt heard,
In anguiſh of my heart prefer'd.
Ye Souls devoted to his fear,
With thankful love your God revere,   100
Who wakes your choſen Train to guard,
And deals to Pride its juſt reward.
Be ſtrong, be ſtedfaſt: So your mind
From Him its full ſupport ſhall find,
Ye Saints that in his care confide,   105
Nor own nor aſk a help beſide.

PSALM XXXII.

HOW bleſt the Man, whoſe conſcious grief
From Thee, great God, has found relief;
Whoſe guilt thy boundleſs Love has veil'd,
His fears compos'd, his weakneſs heal'd;
To whom th' offences of his hand   5
No longer now imputed ſtand,
Who learns thy precepts to revere,
Whoſe heart is pure, whoſe tongue ſincere.
While deep within my lab'ring breaſt
My mind its dire diſeaſe ſuppreſs'd,   10
Inceſſant groans, that ſhun'd controul,
Betray'd the anguiſh of my ſoul.
See Age-anticipating Care
My joints diſſolve, my ſtrength impair:
When Night extends its duſky cone,   15
Beneath thy terrors, Lord, I groan;
The ſhades anon retreating ſee;
And Day to All reſtor'd, but Me.

Behold

Behold my frame with drought confum'd,
That late with youthful vigour bloom'd;   20
Such drought the blafted fields betray,
Beneath the dog-ftar's burning ray.
My humbled Soul its crimes fhall own:—
Behold me bow before thy Throne,
To Thee my inmoft guilt difclofe,   25
And in thy bofom pour my woes.
But lo! while yet my hands I rear,
The voice of Mercy to my ear
Defcends, and whifp'ring peace within
Confirms the pardon of my fin.   30
For this fhall All who Thee adore,
E'er yet the day of grace be o'er,
To Thee with ftedfaft hope repair,
To Thee prefer th' unwearied pray'r:
So, when affliction's tempefts rife,   35
And heave the billows to the fkies,
They, fafe in Thee, the ftorm fhall brave,
And diftant view the madding wave.
When various griefs my foul furround,
In Thee my fure retreat is found;   40
Thy wifh'd Salvation meets my eyes,
And fongs of triumph round me rife.
  Come, from thy God inftruction learn;
While, prompt from error's path to turn
Thy feet, thy ev'ry ftep I fcan,   45
Let Reafon's ufe befpeak thee Man;
Nor imitate the Steed and Mule,
Whofe brutal mouth, averfe to rule,

To

PSALM XXXII.

To guard thee from their rage, muſt feel
The forceful rein, and curbing ſteel.　　　50
What pangs the impious Tribe await,
While hope and joy his heart dilate,
Who truſts in Thee, O King of Kings,
And Mercy round him ſpreads her wings!
Ye Saints, exulting lift your voice,　　　55
Ye pure of mind, in Him rejoice,
Whoſe preſence on the ſoul impreſs'd
With heav'nly tranſport fills the breaſt.

PSALM XXXIII.

YE Saints (to You the taſk belongs,
　　And Praiſe ſits comely on your tongues;)
Wake to *Jehovah*'s name the lute,
Nor let the ten-ſtring'd lyre be mute:
O ſing, in accents loud and ſtrong,　　　5
O ſing ſome new-invented ſong;
And let the finger's artful ſtroke
The pſalt'ry's various pow'r provoke,
And teach the praiſe of *Iſrael*'s Lord
To vibrate on the ſounding chord.　　　10
His words eternal Truth has ſeal'd;
His promiſes in act fulfill'd
Shall Equity and Judgement prove
The changeleſs objects of his love,
And bid the Earth's wide confines know　15
The gifts that from his bounty flow.
His Word yon azure vault outſpread,
E'er Time the Seaſons onward led;

Form'd

PSALM XXXIII.

Form'd by his Breath the starry host
Their unextinguish'd lustre boast; 20
While in their cavern'd storehouse sleep
The treasures of the watry deep.
Thy Maker's name, O Earth, revere;
And let thy Sons with holy fear
To Him in low prostration bend, 25
And duteous his decrees attend.
He spake: And Heav'n, and Seas, and Land,
Appear'd. He bade: And lo, they stand.
Their counsels vain the Heathen Tribes
Unite; but God th' event prescribes, 30
And blasts at will each hope that springs
Within the breast of haughtiest Kings.
Thy counsel, from controul secure,
Thy counsel only shall endure;
Thy thoughts to Time's remotest bound 35
With sure effect, great God, be crown'd.
How blest the People that have known
Thee, Lord, their God, and Thee alone;
The Flock thy heritage declar'd,
And objects of thy fix'd regard! 40
   Wide o'er the Sons of Earth his eye
The Pow'r eternal from on high
Extends, (that Pow'r, whose hand, with art
Mysterious, forms the human heart,)
Through life's wild maze their steps pursues, 45
Each act, each thought, attentive views.
Think not, ye Kings, (His aid resign'd,)
In well-arm'd Hosts your help to find:

In

PSALM XXXIII.

In vain with conscious pride the steed
Vaunts in the fight his strength and speed;
In vain the Warrior bold and young
His arm with active vigour strung:
Nor This shall promise from the sword
Himself to save, nor That his Lord.
Hail, sure Protector of the Just!
From Him who builds on Thee his trust
Thy arm averts with studious care
Each death that viewless wings the air;
Thy hand with food his life sustains,
When drought infests the blasted plains.
Our Souls by Thee, their Help and Shield,
With patient hope have stood upheld;
Thy sacred Name our trust, each mind
From Thee shall joy perpetual find:
That joy to our desiring heart
O let thy Mercy now impart;
And give thy Servants, Lord, to see
How just the hope that rests on Thee.

PSALM XXXIV.

THEE will I thank, and day by day
    Form to thy praise the joyful lay;
From morn to eve the song extend,
Thee boast my Father, Thee my Friend;
While pleas'd each heart of humble frame
Shall wake, great God, to hear thy fame.
O come, your voice triumphant raise,
And sing with Me your Maker's praise.

PSALM XXXIV.

To Him my Soul disclos'd its care;
He heard, and present to my pray'r   10
(His faithful buckler o'er me held,)
Each terror from my breast dispell'd.
The souls, that his decree regard,
Like Me his chearing light have shar'd,
And fearless of repulse or shame   15
The promise of his mercy claim.
Behold a heart with woes oppress'd;
Behold, its vows to God address'd,
His hand its healing pow'r display,
And chase each cloud of grief away.   20
His Angel, nigh the just man's tent
Encamp'd, each danger to prevent,
His sure protection round him throws,
Though harness'd Hosts his peace oppose.
O taste with Me, O taste and prove   25
The blessings of his boundless Love.
Hail, Saviour of the human race!
Hail, Fountain of exhaustless grace!
Thrice happy, who on Thee recline,
Nor own nor ask a help but thine.   30

   His fear preserve, ye just and pure,
And live from dread of want secure.
The strengthful Lion's tawny brood
With thirst and penury of food
Are stung; but who in God confide   35
Shall find their ev'ry wish supplied.
Ye Children, come; my precepts hear,
And learn the dictates of his fear:
                              O come;

PSALM XXXIV.

O come; if long extent of days,
With bleſſings crown'd, thy hope can raiſe, 40
Averſe from each injurious art,
Let falſehood from thy lips depart;
Be Good thy choice; from Evil ceaſe;
And plight the ready hand to peace.
Him ſerve, whoſe fav'ring eyes ſurvey 45
The hearts that his commands obey;
Him ſerve, whoſe ever open ear
With juſt regard their pray'r ſhall hear,
While terrors planted on his brow
Inſtruct the ſtubborn ſoul to bow, 50
And vengeance, kindled to a flame,
Blots from the earth the impious name.
With ſuppliant voice, in each diſtreſs,
His ſole ſupport, his ſole redreſs,
From God the Man of faithful mind 55
Shall ſeek, and what he ſeeks ſhall find.
He, ever watchful, ever near,
The meek and contrite ſoul ſhall chear;
And though the Juſt, by his decree,
Awhile a Man of griefs we ſee, 60
His Love ſhall ſoon its aid beſtow,
And deep oblivion of his woe:
To violence expos'd, his frame
Thy fix'd attention, Lord, ſhall claim;
Nor Hell's worſt rage one bone ſhall dare 65
To break, when Thou haſt bid to ſpare.
But ill on All who ill intend
In full proportion ſhall deſcend:

Who tow'rd the Juſt in hatred join,
Shall feel, great God, the weight of thine. 70
'Tis thine thy Saints from woes to free;
Nor Time throughout its courſe ſhall ſee
The ſoul, whoſe hope on Thee is ſtaid,
Neglected mourn thy abſent aid.

PSALM XXXV.

LORD, make my quarrel thine; my foes
   Let thy reſiſtleſs pow'r oppoſe;
Ariſe thy ſpeedieſt help to yield,
And reach the corſlet, reach the ſhield,
Graſp in thy hand the glitt'ring lance, 5
And obvious in the breach advance;
Say to my troubled Soul; "In Me
"Thy ſtrength and ſure ſalvation ſee."
Let ſhame their glowing cheeks o'erſpread,
Whoſe ceaſeleſs threats excite my dread, 10
And let them, ſtruck with wild affright,
Inglorious backward urge their flight,
Diſpers'd, as chaff before the wind,
Thy Angel preſſing cloſe behind,
Along the dark and ſlipp'ry way, 15
Whoſe paths their ſtagg'ring ſteps betray,
And from the arm ethereal find
The vengeance to their guilt aſſign'd.
Thou ſeeſt them, Lord, with cauſeleſs hate,
Beſide my path inſidious wait, 20
With cauſeleſs hate the pit prepare,
And plant before my ſteps their ſnare.

                        O let

PSALM XXXV.

O let destruction's sudden stroke,
While thus thy justice they provoke,
Descend, vindictive, on their head; 25
Fast in the net for Me outspread
Involv'd, let each repentant groan,
And reap the mischiefs he has sown.
But Thou, my Soul, with awful joy
On God thy stedfast thought employ, 30
And, his Salvation taught to prove,
Record the wonders of his Love.
Each bone whose strength supports my frame
With grateful transport shall exclaim,
Lord! Whom like Thee shall Mortals find, 35
For ever just, for ever kind,
Like Thee prepar'd th' afflicted poor
From lawless insult to secure,
And back their yielded life demand
From stern Oppression's iron hand? 40
Thus poor and thus oppress'd with wrong
Awhile was I: a hostile Throng
Against me urg'd, to falsehood prone,
The guilt my breast had never known,
And left me helpless and forlorn 45
The friendship ill repay'd to mourn,
That, when Affliction's weight they bare,
Had taught my heart their woes to share:
While sickness wrapt them in its chain,
And fix'd them on the bed of pain, 50
I knew their suff'rings to bewail,
And sunk with grief, with fasting pale,

To God, in sorrow's garb array'd,
With humblest intercession pray'd,
And find the pray'r their pride has spurn'd   55
With blessings on my head return'd:
Nor Friend for Friend sincerer woes,
Nor Brother for a Brother, knows;
Nor feels the Son his melting breast
With deeper sense of grief impress'd,   60
That grasps a dying Mother's hand,
And waits to take her last command,
Or o'er her loss in secret pines,
And wraps the sackcloth round his loyns.
Not such the pity shown to Me: 65
Ev'n abjects my abjection see
With scornful gaze, as round me stand,
In adverse league, a lawless Band,
These taught with well-dissembled art
To veil the purpose of their heart,   70
While Those in open hate engage,
And ceaseless vent their murth'rous rage,
Now furious grind their teeth, and now
Insulting aim the deathful blow.
How long wilt Thou, my God, how long   75
With patient eye behold my wrong?
How long shall I in vain attend
'Till Thou, my Guardian and my Friend,
The Lion's dreaded rage controul,
And rescue my deserted soul,   80
That, 'mid th' assembled Tribes, my tongue
May raise to Thee the thankful song?

                                         O let

PSALM XXXV.

O let not my uninjur'd foes,
With speaking eye, amidst my woes,
As round they stand in close array,   85
The triumphs of their heart betray:
Behold them, Lord, their arts address,
The friends of peace and truth t' oppress,
But chief my name with insults load:
" Thou wretch abandon'd of thy God,   90
" In vain, they clamour, what our eyes
" Attest, thy conscious tongue denies."
My God, (for Thou their rage hast seen,)
With timeliest succour intervene,
Nor silent long, Almighty Sire,   95
Remain, nor distant far retire.
Awake, thy aiding strength excite,
Awake, and vindicate my right.
Let Justice teach them, by thy stroke,
Their frantic triumphs to revoke;   100
Nor let their heart, its wish complete,
With secret joy transported beat,
Or boasting hail th' expected hour,
That gives me to the Murth'rer's pow'r.
Let All who make my grief their scorn   105
Their blasted hopes astonish'd mourn;
Let stern rebuke and foul disgrace
With shame perpetual clothe their face,
As, nigh me rang'd, with thankful voice
The friends of innocence rejoice,   110
And " Blest, they cry, be *Jacob*'s Lord,
" The God by Heav'n and Earth ador'd,

        " Who

PSALM XXXV.

"Who joys his Servant's cause to plead,
"And crowns with peace his favour'd head."
While, loudest in the choir, my tongue   115
To notes of praise shall tune its song,
And pleas'd through each revolving day
Thy Justice, mightiest Lord, display.

PSALM XXXVI.

BEHOLD the wretch, in error lost,
Whose stubborn heart with impious boast
His Law rejects, his Fear denies,
Who form'd the earth, and seas, and skies,
Nor self-abhorrent looks within,   5
To view the measure of his sin.
His tongue to falsehood train'd, his mind
No more to acts of good inclin'd,
Concerted mischiefs croud his breast,
And rob his midnight hours of rest.   10
Nor Wisdom to her paths his will
Can turn, or wean his soul from ill.
  Thy Mercy, Lord, to Heav'n extends,
Thy Truth the lofty clouds transcends;
Fix'd as the Mountain's solid base   15
Thy Justice stands; who seeks to trace
The counsels of the Will divine
By Reason's aid, with scanty line
(Prepost'rous,) would the Deep explore,
And measure with his span its shore.   20
Nor rest thy cares alone confin'd
To Us, the Sons of human kind;

Thy

PSALM XXXVI.

Thy hand th' unconscious Brute sustains,
And spreads his pasture on the plains:
But We, with pious trust, who know
What gifts we to thy Mercy owe,
(O, what that Mercy can excell?)
Beneath thy fost'ring wings shall dwell.
To each who seeks thy name behold
Thy House its richest stores unfold,
And bliss unintermix'd with woe
In fullest streams their breast o'erflow.
From out thy Seat, immortal King,
Forth issues Life's perennial spring;
Thy light with unextinguish'd rays
Shall o'er our heads auspicious blaze.
  Still may the Souls who Thee have known
The Blessings of thy Mercy own,
And each who bears a spotless mind
His refuge in thy Justice find.
Me let thy care, Almighty Friend,
From Pride's injurious foot defend;
Each impious hand that seeks my hurt
Let thy superior strength avert.
Lo, there they fall, their triumphs o'er,
And prostrate lie, to rise no more.

PSALM XXXVII.

LET not the Sinner's wealth or might
  The envy of thy soul excite:
Anon thine eye shall see him fade
Quick as the flow'r or vernal blade,

That now rejoicing lifts the head,
Now with'ring on the earth is spread.
But Thou thy will to Heav'n's high Lord
(His Faith thy trust, thy rule his Word,)
Submit, and nourish'd by his hand
Inherit from his gift the Land.
In Him delight, on Him depend;
Him chuse thy Guide, thy Way, thy End;
So shall his Love thy wishes grant,
His Care anticipate thy want,
And bid thy acts in light serene
Fair as the rising morn be seen,
Thy Justice as the noon of day
Diffusive pour its cloudless ray.
With patient hope await his will,
Nor let the sight of prosp'rous ill
Impell thee with disquiet vain
His wise disposals to arraign,
Lest wrath and doubt thy conscience blind,
And urge to acts of guilt thy mind.
See, from their dwelling torn, th' unjust
To those who fix on God their trust
(So wills the Majesty divine,)
Their forfeit heritage resign.
Wait but awhile; then look around:
No more the impious race are found;
Nor the proud roof nor wide domain
The mem'ry of their Lord retain.
But see the meek and pious Band
(Advanc'd by God's almighty hand

PSALM XXXVII.

The pow'r among them to divide, 35
To fierce Ambition's sword denied,)
Earth's bounds possess, and, Peace their care,
The fulness of its blessings share.
His wiles the Fool of Sin provides
To slay whom Wisdom's precept guides, 40
Now furious grinds his teeth, and now
Insulting aims the deathful blow:
But God his frantic rage derides,
And sees the Day, as on it glides,
Whose beams, with wrath uncommon red, 45
Shall stream in vengeance o'er his head.
On You, ye Poor, with dire intent,
The sword is drawn, the bow is bent;
But vain each wish, each effort vain,
To root from earth your chosen train: 50
The sword, with better aim impress'd,
Descends into its Owner's breast;
Reluctant to the Archer's will
Bursts the tough bow, and mocks his skill.
Exchange not Ye your scanty store 55
For heaps of guilt-polluted ore:
That God, ye Saints, whose Love ye seek,
The arm of lawless pow'r shall break,
And bid the Just protected stand
Beneath the shadow of his hand: 60
By Him your years determin'd flow;
The Lot, which his Decrees bestow,
From Sire to Son, till time shall end,
In sure succession shall descend:

When

When War's dire flames around you burn, 65
From You the darts their points shall turn;
Each blast that taints the red'ning sky
From Your exempted fields shall fly.
Who know not Thee, great God, to dread,
As Victims for the slaughter fed, 70
Consum'd by Heav'n's avenging fire
Shall perish and in smoke aspire.
While faithless These th' intrusted loan
With base ingratitude disown,
His plenteous alms the Just can give, 75
And pleas'd a Brother's wants relieve.
Earth's goods thy Blessing to the Pure
Shall grant, and what it grants insure;
While guilty souls the Curse divine
To full excision shall consign. 80
The Just, blest object of thy Love,
Thou, Lord, wilt lead, his path approve,
Thy faithful hands his steps sustain,
Nor falls he, but to rise again.
Once was I young, and now am old, 85
Yet ne'er the Righteous could behold
By God deserted, nor his seed
Requesting at my gate their bread:
His heart with gen'rous pity glows;
Inrich'd by what his hand bestows 90
He lives, and for his distant heirs
Prosperity and peace prepares.
    From Ill recede; to Good incline
Thy thought; and endless life be thine.

Delighted

PSALM XXXVII.

Delighted whom his Laws delight
Th' Almighty views; nor Day nor Night
The foul that bows to his Decree
Abandon'd from his Love shall see.
Behold, ye Just, th' eternal Doom
The Sinner's short-liv'd race consume,
While happier Ye to Yours assign'd
A heritage perpetual find.
How blest whom Thou, great God, hast taught!
His lips, with sacred science fraught,
The lessons of thy truth impart;
And, grav'd within his inmost heart,
Thy Law, the ever faithful Guide,
Forbids his stedfast feet to slide.
Each art the murth'rous tribe essay,
And mark the guiltless for their prey;
But God his rescue has decreed;
Himself will rise his cause to plead,
Refute th' Accuser's perjur'd tongue,
And save him from the hand of wrong.
Wait on thy God; observe his ways:
His pow'r aloft thy head shall raise;
Exerted in thy right his hand
Shall vindicate to Thee the Land,
And bid, before thy sight, his foe
The terrors of his vengeance know.
The prosp'ring Sinner once I view'd;
Strong as the healthful Tree he stood,
That, shadowing wide its native soil,
Nor knows, nor asks, the planter's toil:

H　　　　　　I went,

I went, I came, and look'd again; 125
I look'd, but sought his place in vain.
Behold the Juft, and mark his end:
See Peace his eve of life attend,
While on the Sinner's lateft hour
The ftorms of heavieft vengeance low'r. 130
To God the Juft his fafety owes,
Him owns his Strength amidft his woes,
Affur'd that He fhall each defend
Whofe conftant hopes on Him depend,
And, while his foes their peace invade, 135
Reach, in their caufe, his promis'd aid.

PSALM XXXVIII.

O Spare me, Lord, nor o'er my head
   The fulnefs of thy vengeance fhed.
Pierc'd by thy fhafts, great God, I ftand,
And feel the preffure of thy hand.
Thou feeft, from health eftrang'd, my frame 5
The terrors of thy wrath proclaim,
While confcious guilt alarms my breaft,
And robs my tortur'd joints of reft.
Whelm'd with a weight of fins I mourn,
A weight too heavy to be borne; 10
My wounds, whofe fmart thofe fins repays,
The wide-infected air betrays.
See! bow'd, from morn to eve, with woe,
And wrapt in fackcloth drear, I go;
My reins with hidden torments wrung, 15
Each limb difeas'd, each nerve unftrung,

Aloud

PSALM XXXVIII.

Aloud my suff'rings I bemoan,
And fainting pour the frequent groan.
But Thou, e'er yet my groans proceed,
My griefs and inmost wish canst read.   20
Behold my heart with anguish torn,
My strength with long affliction worn,
And stretch'd before my wasted sight
The shadows of approaching night.
Each Neighbour's eye with silent gaze   25
My alter'd lineaments surveys;
My Friends, and next Allies by birth,
(Once kind Companions of my mirth,
When wing'd with health the moments flew,)
My griefs with distant horror view.   30
With snares my foes beset my way,
Intent on death throughout the day
With fiercest rage my name revile,
And discipline their thoughts to guile:
Invented crimes, and taunts severe,   35
With steadiest patience, Lord, I hear,
Unmov'd, as One who deaf and mute
Nor censure feels nor can refute:
For Thou, best Advocate, art nigh;
On Thee, great God, my hopes rely;   40
O vindicate my fame from wrong,
And silence the reproachful tongue.
Thou know'st the tenour of my pray'r;
O let me not their insults bear:
Mark, when my steps have chanc'd to slide,   45
The shouts that rise on ev'ry side.

H 2   And,

PSALM XXXVIII.

And, echoing through the wounded air,
The triumphs of their heart declare.
Thou seest how prone to lapse my feet,
What woes my eyes incessant meet;   50
Nor shuns my soul its guilt to own,
But sorrowing bows before thy throne.
How strong, how num'rous, are the foes
That unprovok'd my peace oppose,
Their veins with health's full current warm,   55
And strung with active might their arm!
Ill for my Good return'd I find,
Nor know from aught (but that, inclin'd
To Good, their deeds I shun,) to date
The ground of their prepost'rous hate.   60
O let me, rais'd by Thee, no more
The absence of thine aid deplore;
God of my life, recede not far,
But haste, and make that life thy care.

PSALM XXXIX.

MY steps Discretion's rules shall guide;
   Nor error from my lips shall slide,
(Thus to myself resolv'd I said;)
Nor word, in Wisdom's scale unweigh'd:
While lawless crouds attend me nigh,   5
And mark me with insidious eye,
Behold me with the steady rein
Each effort of my tongue restrain.
   Awhile my soul its purpose keeps;
A stubborn silence seals my lips: 10
                            But

PSALM XXXIX.

But O! from themes of good withheld,
How oft my full-swoln heart rebell'd!
My thoughts in various tumult roll;
At length, impatient of controul,
Forth from my struggling bosom brake   15
The kindled flame; and thus I spake:
O let me, heav'nly Lord, extend
My view to life's approaching end,
And, lesson'd by thy Wisdom, learn
How soon my fabrick shall return   20
To earth, and in the silent tomb
Its seat of lasting rest assume.
What are my days? (a span their line;)
And what my age compar'd with thine?
Our life advancing to its close,   25
While scarce its earliest dawn it knows,
Swift through an empty shade we run,
And Vanity and Man are one:
With anxious pain this Son of care
Toils to inrich an unknown heir,   30
And, eying oft his heapy store,
With vain disquiet thirsts for more.
   Where, Lord, shall I my refuge see?
On whom repose my hope but Thee?
O purge my guilt, nor let my foe   35
Exulting mock my heighten'd woe.
Convinc'd that thy paternal hand
Inflicts but what my sins demand,
I speechless sate; nor plantive word,
Nor murmur, from my lips was heard.   40

But O, in thy appointed hour
Withdraw thy rod; left Nature's pow'r,
While griefs on griefs my heart affail,
Unequal to the conflict, fail.
O, how thy chaftifements impair 45
The human form, however fair!
How frail the ftrongeft frame we fee,
If Thou the Sinner's fate decree!
As when the fretting moths confume
The labour of the curious loom, 50
The texture fails, the dyes decay,
And all its luftre fades away.
Such, Man, thy ftate: then, humbled, own
That Vanity and Thou are one.
To Thee, great God, my knees I bend; 55
To Thee my ceafelefs pray'rs afcend;
O let my forrows reach thine ears,
And mark my fighs, my groans, my tears.
God of my Fathers! Here, as They,
I walk the Pilgrim of a day; 60
A tranfient Gueft, thy works admire,
And inftant to my home retire.
O fpare me, Lord, awhile, O fpare,
And Nature's ruin'd ftrength repair,
E'er, life's fhort circuit wander'd o'er, 65
I perifh, and am feen no more.

PSALM XL.

1.

WITH patient hope my God I fought;
   He to his Suppliant's want his thought
     In happiest hour applied:
He from the dark and miry pit
High on the rock has rais'd my feet;
     Nor fear my steps to slide.

2.

His praise inspires my grateful tongue,
And dictates to my lips a song
     In strains unheard before.
Admiring crouds his work shall see,
Their strength on Him repose with Me,
     With Me his name adore.

3.

Blest, who in Thee, great God, confide,
Nor madly trust the arm of pride,
     And helps that but betray.
Thy Mercies, Lord, all praise surmount,
Nor numbers can their sum recount,
     Nor words their worth display.

4.

Nor Sacrifice thy Love can win,
Nor Off'rings from the stain of sin
     Obnoxious Man shall clear:
Thy hand my mortal frame prepares,
(Thy hand, whose signature it bears,)
     And opes my willing ear.

                            5. And,

PSALM XL.

5.
And, since the Blood of Victims slain,
And hallow'd Gifts, attempt in vain
   T' avert th' Offender's doom,
Myself th' atonement will provide;
Lo! (touch'd with pity thus I cried,)
   I come, my God, I come.

6.
Thy Book, by sacred Bards unroll'd,
My full obedience has foretold
   To Thy mysterious Will.
His just assent thy Servant gives,
Thy words my Breast with joy receives,
   My Hands with zeal fulfill.

7.
The faithful Witness to thy fame,
Aloud thy Justice I proclaim
   To *Abraham*'s chosen Race:
My lips, Thou know'st, have ne'er declin'd
To preach the Theme by Thee injoin'd,
   The Wonders of thy Grace.

8.
With strong desire my bosom glows
Thy Truth and Mercy to disclose,
   In Man's relief display'd:
O let that Truth dispell my woe,
That Mercy, Lord, around me throw
   Its all-protecting shade.

PSALM XL.

9.
While griefs on griefs my cup have mix'd,
On earth my downward looks are fix'd;
   The Sins, whose weight I bear,
(Those Sins, that number'd by the eye
The hairs that shade my head outvie,)
   My heart with anguish tear.

10.
Haste to thy Servant's rescue, haste;
My Soul, by hostile numbers chas'd,
   To Thee directs its pray'r.
In wild confusion backward borne
Their wish defeated let them mourn,
   And lost in empty air.

11.
Be shame their just reward assign'd,
While round me with relentless mind
   Derision's shout they raise:
Thy Bliss let All who seek thee share,
And, taught thy Love, that Love declare
   In songs of ceaseless praise.

12.
While These in thy Salvation joy,
Increasing griefs my thought employ,
   And speediest aid demand:
My Helper and Redeemer, hear;
O, instant in my cause appear,
   And reach thy saving hand.

PSALM XLI.

BLEST, who with gen'rous pity glows,
Who learns to feel another's woes,
Bows to the poor man's want his ear,
And wipes the helpless Orphan's tear:
In ev'ry want, in ev'ry woe,   5
Himself thy pity, Lord, shall know;
Thy Love his life shall guard, thy hand
Give to his lot the chosen land,
Nor leave him in the dreadful day
To unrelenting foes a prey.   10
When languid with disease and pain,
Thou, Lord, his spirit wilt sustain,
Prop with thine arm his sinking head,
And turn with tend'rest care his bed.
  O let me, Lord, thy mercy share,   15
(Thus to my God I form'd the pray'r,)
Health to my fainting soul dispense,
That humbled owns its dire offence.
" When shall he perish?" Thus my foes
With ruthless tongue their wish disclose;   20
" Why lingers Death's appointed hour
" Oblivion on his name to pour?"
Beside my couch, dissolv'd in tears,
The hostile visitant appears,
Dissembling o'er my anguish mourns,   25
While with collected malice burns
His heart, and parted from my gate
Aloud proclaims his settled hate.

Now pleas'd they form some dark design,
Now whisp'ring thus in curses join: 30
" Still may the guilt unpurg'd remain,
" That binds him on the bed of pain;
" Nor let him from that bed arise,
" But close in endless sleep his eyes."
And Thou, the Friend, to whom my heart   35
Its inmost counsels wont t' impart,
For whom the social board I spread,
And broke with lib'ral hand my bread,
With lifted heel, severe return,
The partner of thy breast couldst spurn. 40
 Maker of All! be Thou my guard:
Give me, my strength by Thee repair'd,
Give me to teach the faithless band
To own the justice of thy hand.
So, while my pray'rs indulg'd approve   45
My Soul the object of thy Love,
My foes, with inward anguish torn,
Shall each his blasted triumphs mourn;
And I (for Thou thy aid shalt yield,)
In innocence of heart upheld   50
Thy Courts shall ever tread, and there
The fulness of thy presence share.
 O thankful bless th' Almighty Lord,
The God by *Jacob*'s Sons ador'd.
His fame, e'er Time its course began,   55
O'er Heav'n's wide region echoing ran;
To Him through endless ages raise
One song of oft-repeated praise.

PSALM

PSALM XLII.

AS pants the Hart for cooling springs,
   So longs my Soul, O King of Kings,
Thy face in near approach to see,
So thirsts, great Source of Life, for Thee.
When shall I reach thy blest abode?   5
When meet the presence of my God?
Tears, Lord, Thou know'st, have been my bread,
By day, by night, profusely shed,
While thus they urge me to despair:
" Where's now thy God, thou Outcast, where?" 10
While griefs like these beset my soul,
My busied thoughts tumultuous roll;
And oft in luxury of woe
Back to those happier hours I go,
When up fair *Sion*'s high ascent   15
The Tribes in long procession went,
And, while thy praise in grateful songs
Resounded from a thousand tongues,
I, rank'd amid the festive Train,
Exulting trod thy hallow'd Fane.   20
   Why thus, my Soul, with care oppress'd?
And whence the woes that fill my breast?
In all thy cares, in all thy woes,
On God thy stedfast hope repose;
To Him my thanks shall still be paid,   25
My sure Defence, my constant Aid.
   Thy mercies, Lord, before my eyes
Shall yet in sweet remembrance rise,

Though

PSALM XLII.

Though now with mournful step and slow
O'er *Jordan*'s lonely banks I go, 30
And, exil'd from thy much lov'd Dome,
On distant *Hermon* pensive roam.
Deeps to confed'rate Deeps aloud
Have call'd, and from the bursting cloud
Their licens'd rage the storms have shed, 35
And heap'd the billows o'er my head.
Yet 'midst the storm, and 'midst the wave,
Thy Love the beams of comfort gave;
Thy Name to rapture prompts my tongue,
My Joy by day, by night my Song; 40
To Thee my soul ascends in pray'r,
And in thy bosom pours its care.
God of my strength, attend my cry,
Say why, my great Preserver, why,
Excluded from thy sight I go, 45
And bend beneath a weight of woe;
Why sharper than the biting steel
Th' insulting Foe's reproach I feel,
While thus they urge me to despair:
"Where's now thy God, thou Outcast, where?" 50
  Why thus, my Soul, with care oppress'd?
And whence the woes that fill my breast?
In all thy cares, in all thy woes,
On God thy stedfast hope repose;
To Him my thanks shall still be paid, 55
My sure Defence, my constant Aid.

PSALM XLIII.

O Weigh me, Lord, in equal scale,
   And let my injur'd cause prevail:
O save me from an impious Throng,
The Sons of Violence and Wrong.
God of my strength, to Thee I cry;   5
Say why, by Thee rejected, why,
I bend beneath a weight of woe,
And bear the insults of the Foe.
O let thy Light attend my way,
Thy Truth afford its steady ray,   10
To *Sion*'s Hill direct my feet,
And bring me to thy hallow'd Seat:
Admitted to thy Altars there,
My hands to Thee the gift shall bear,
Whose Mercies, to my heart reveal'd,   15
A theme of endless transport yield.
Thy praise, O God, my God, the lyre
Shall wake, thy Love its song inspire.
   Why thus, my Soul, with care oppress'd?
And whence the woes that fill my breast?   20
In all thy cares, in all thy woes,
On God thy stedfast hope repose;
To Him my thanks shall still be paid,
My sure Defence, my constant Aid.

PSALM XLIV.

TAUGHT by our Sires, great God, our ear
   Thy wondrous Acts has wak'd to hear,
The Mercies to their Tribes reveal'd,
When Ages long o'erpaſt beheld
By Thee diſlodg'd an impious race   5
Yield to their choſen Seed a place,
And *Iſrael*'s Sons, thy foes o'erthrown,
Succeed to labours not their own.
There, planted by the hand divine,
With large increaſe their proſp'ring Line   10
Are bleſs'd, and nouriſh'd by thy care
The fulneſs of thy bounty ſhare.
For not the arm of human might,
Nor ſword of ſteel, upheld their right;
Thy pow'r exerted in their aid,   15
Thy preſence o'er their heads diſplay'd,
Proclaim'd them favour'd from on high,
And bde each force before them fly.
Thee, Lord, my King, and Thee alone,
Attentive to thy Laws I own;   20
Indulgent ſtill, Almighty Friend,
Thy Arm in *Iſrael*'s cauſe extend.
Through Thee our Hoſts unmov'd ſhall ſtand,
Strike with the horn each adverſe band,
Thy name invok'd, their fury meet,   25
And tread them breathleſs at their feet.
Not from my ſword or from my bow
My ſoul ſuch confidence ſhall know;

PSALM XLIV.

Thou, Lord, each adverse pow'r shalt quell,
Thy strength their gath'ring troops dispell: 30
That strength our boast, thy hallow'd name
Our hymns of loudest praise shall claim,
While Time shall roll its rapid tide,
And Day and Night thy works divide.

   But now, thy wonted aid withheld,   35
Repuls'd, asham'd, we quit the field;
No more we see, to battle led,
Th' Almighty Conqu'ror at our head,
But quick retreat in wild dismay,
Abandon'd to our foes a prey.   40
As Beasts for food decreed we die,
Or, spar'd, as worthless in thine eye
See! sold for nought our Lords we change,
And lost through distant climates range.
Each neighb'ring Realm with scornful gaze   45
Thy People's ruin'd state surveys;
Our name, amid the Nations round,
A proverb in each mouth is found;
Assembled Crouds insulting stand,
And fierce Derision claps the hand.   50
How feels my heart the dire disgrace!
How glows with ceaseless shame my face,
While thus, divested of thy fear,
With keen reproach they wound my ear,
And with revengeful hand fulfill   55
The dictates of their lawless will!

   Yet, torn with grief, with dread oppress'd,
Thy eyes can witness that our breast

Its

PSALM XLIV.

Its trust from Thee has ne'er remov'd,
Nor faithless to thy Compact prov'd.   60
No Lord but Thee thy Servants greet,
Nor wander from thy paths our feet,
Though 'midst the dragon's haunts we tread,
And death's dark shades are round us spread.
If e'er, averse to thy command,   65
To Stranger-Gods we lift the hand,
Say, shall our crime thy search elude,
Whose eyes our inmost thoughts have view'd?
Thy Cause we still avow; thy Cause
The hostile sword against us draws,   70
And numbers to the death our train,
As Sheep, whose blood the hallow'd fane,
Before the altar's kindled flames,
By regular allotment claims.
Arise, eternal God, arise;   75
Why sits this slumber on thine eyes?
Awake, nor from thy care expell
Thy once regarded *Israel*.
Why veils th' impervious cloud thy face?
Say why to our afflicted race   80
Thy ear its pity still denies,
Nor hears thy captive People's cries,
As sunk with sorrow's weight we bend,
And prostrate in the dust descend.
Arise, thy saving pow'r disclose,   85
And heal with pitying hand our woes.

PSALM XLV.

MY heart its noblest Theme has found:
O Thou, with regal splendor crown'd,
To Thee the grateful strains belong;
Thy Worth shall bid my willing tongue,
Quick as the pen of readiest art,   5
The dictates of my soul impart.
Hail, fairer than the Sons of Men!
Grace on thy lips and Beauty reign,
That speak thee honour'd from above,
And blest with God's eternal Love.   10
Hail, Thou whom Nations own their Lord!
Gird on thy thigh the glitt'ring sword;
By Mercy, Truth, and Justice led,
Ride glorious on, thy conquests spread:
Thy stubborn foes, a guilty race,   15
Thy hand with faithful search shall trace,
Mark, as their crimes for vengeance call,
And teach thy terrors where to fall:
While, edg'd with wrath, thy ev'ry dart
Shall pierce some proud Opposer's heart,   20
Assert the cause of *Judah*'s King,
And dip in impious blood its wing.
Through ages lasts, great God, thy Throne,
Thy Scepter Justice calls her own,
And (for thy heart his Law pursues,   25
And guilt with fix'd abhorrence views,)
Thy God, the God who rules the skies,
Has o'er thine Equals bid thee rise,

And,

PSALM XLV.

And, pleas'd, the oil of gladneſs ſhed
In large profuſion on thy head.   30
Myrrh, Aloes, Caſſia, to the ſenſe
Their all-reviving ſweets diſpenſe,
While, recent from the iv'ry cell,
Their mingled odours round thee dwell.
Their Daughters mightieſt Kings behold   35
Amid thy Virgin Train inroll'd;
And, ſeated on thy right, the Queen
In faireſt robes array'd is ſeen,
That ſtiff with gold, in *Ophir*'s mine
Matur'd, with fadeleſs luſtre ſhine.   40
Hear, Daughter, and attentive weigh
The precepts of the Heav'n-taught Lay.
Within thy thought retain no more
Thy Father's houſe and native ſhore:
So ſhall the King delighted ſee   45
Thy ſpotleſs Form; and O, be He,
That Lord whom Heav'n's high Hoſts revere,
Thy only Love, thy only Fear.
   Imperial *Tyre*, that, thron'd on high,
O'er ſubject ſeas extends her eye,   50
Her Gifts, O Prince, ſhall bring to Thee,
And ſuppliant Nobles ſtoop the knee.
The Virgin (Offspring of a King,)
Whom now thy happy Choice we ſing,
(Herſelf with each perfection bleſt)   55
E'er Thee ſhe greets, the various veſt
Aſſumes; where 'mid th' inwoven gold
A thouſand colours we behold,

                         That,

PSALM XLV.

That, kindled by the beams of day,
The needle's utmost art display.
By eminence of beauty known
Amidst her fair Associates, on
She moves, and joys with them to tread
The paths that to thy presence lead.
No more the Patriarchs of thy line
In Time's long records chief shall shine;
Thy greater Sons, to Empire born,
Its future annals shall adorn,
Thy Pow'r to Them deriv'd display,
And stretch through Earth their boundless sway.
That Earth, while thus to Thee I raise
A lasting Monument of praise,
With thankful voice shall join the strain,
And own the Blessings of thy Reign.

PSALM XLVI.

ON Thee, great Ruler of the Skies,
On Thee our stedfast hope relies:
When hostile pow'rs against us join,
What Aid so present, Lord, as thine?
By Thee secur'd, no fears we own,
Though Earth, convuls'd, beneath us groan,
Though tempests o'er her surface sweep,
And whirl her hills into the Deep:
Though, arm'd with rage, before our eyes
That Deep in all its horrors rise,
While, as the tumult spreads around,
The mountains tremble at the sound.

Behold

PSALM XLVI.

Behold fair *Sion*'s bleſt retreat,
Where God has fix'd his awful Seat:
No Tempeſts there licentious ſtray,
But ſoft along their level way
The ſacred Streams their courſe maintain,
And crown with health her happy plain.
God, ever watchful, ever nigh,
Bids ſtorms around her harmleſs fly;
His early care each foe withſtands,
And backward turns the yielding Bands.
See, rous'd by Diſcord's fierce alarms,
The headlong Nations ruſh to arms;
But God aloud aſſerts his ſway,
And Earth's whole fabrick melts away.
  On Heav'n's high Lord our truſt we build;
The God of *Jacob* is our Shield.
  O come, behold a ſcene of dread,
Behold a World with ſlaughter ſpread;
And know, 'tis God who bids each Land
Thus feel the terrors of his hand.
'Tis His, again the Earth to chear,
To break the bow, to ſnap the ſpear,
To wrap in flames the glitt'ring car,
And huſh the tumult of the war.
Bow then, ye Sons of Pride, and own
That I am God, and I alone:
Exalted o'er each Heathen Land,
Exalted o'er the Earth, I ſtand;
I bind all Nature to my Will,
And bid the factious World be ſtill.

On Heav'n's high Lord our trust we build;
The God of *Jacob* is our Shield.

PSALM XLVII.

1.

ARISE, ye People, clap the hand;
    Exulting strike the chord:
Let ev'ry Isle, and ev'ry Land,
    Confess th' Almighty Lord.

2.

How awful his mysterious Name!
    How high advanc'd his Seat!
Who bids the Nations own our claim,
    And casts them at our feet.

3.

He to our lot a Land assign'd,
    His favour'd *Jacob*'s boast,
And blest with gifts of various kind
    Her health-incircled coast.

4.

Hear, while the shouts wide-echoing round
    Th' ascending God proclaim,
The answ'ring trump through Heav'n resound,
    And shake its vaulted frame.

5.

Sing to our God; in loudest strain
    Perpetual praises sing:
O'er Earth's wide bounds extends his reign;
    O praise our God and King.

6. Prepare,

PSALM XLVII.

6.
Prepare, prepare, with tuneful art,
 In one assembled throng,
Your shares of harmony to part,
 And raise the Heav'n-taught Song.

7.
His sway the Sons of human kind
 With humblest homage own;
And Sanctity with Pow'r combin'd
 Supports his lasting throne.

8.
Kings from afar conven'd behold,
 Whose breasts with zeal have glow'd,
Among the tribes to stand inroll'd,
 That bow to *Abraham*'s God.

9.
For He, whose hands amid the skies
 Th' eternal scepter wield,
To Earth's whole race his care applies,
 And o'er them spreads the shield.

PSALM XLVIII.

1.
GREAT is our God: With warmest zeal
 O let his name be blest,
Within the precincts of his Hill,
 And City of his rest.

2.

Fair is that Hill; how wondrous fair!
  Imperial *Sion*'s Seat:
There centers, Earth, thy Joy, and there
  Its meafure owns complete.

3.

Her Walls, while there his lov'd recefs
  The Northern Heav'n furveys,
With fafety God vouchfafes to blefs,
  And pleas'd her fcepter fways.

4.

Earth's haughty Monarchs thither came;
  They came, they faw, they fled.
Amazement fhook their inmoft frame,
  And undiffembled dread.

5.

Such fears they fhare as Matrons find
  That feel th' increafing throe,
Struck by that God, whofe fhatt'ring wind
  Thy Ships, O *Tharfis*, know.

6.

Lord! what our ears long fince have known,
  Our eyes delighted trace,
Thy Love in long fucceffion fhown
  To *Salem*'s chofen race.

7.

Thrice bleft Abode! whofe ev'ry tow'r
  By Thee fupported ftands,
That God whofe wide-extended pow'r
  Th' ethereal Hoft commands.

8. When,

PSALM XLVIII.

8.
When, prostrate at thy hallow'd Shrine,
    Thy mercies each surveys,
Transported with the view, we join
    In wonder, love, and praise.

9.
Thy Name, through Earth's wide confines spread,
    Eternal honours crown;
Each sentence by thy hand decreed
    Fair Justice stamps her own.

10.
Let *Sion*'s Heav'n-devoted Mount
    With shouts of triumph ring,
And *Judah*'s Daughters pleas'd recount
    The Judgements of her King.

11.
Go, walk her sacred streets along,
    And let her tow'rs be told;
With curious eye her bulwarks strong
    And beauteous domes behold.

12.
So shall the fair description last,
    Preserv'd in full record,
And tell what glories once have grac'd
    The Seat of *Jacob*'s Lord.

13.
To Him our thankful hearts shall bow,
    Nor own a God beside;
To life's last period Him avow
    The ever faithful Guide.

PSALM XLIX.

Y E Nations, hear: Ye Sons of Earth,
    Of higheſt or obſcureſt birth,
Ye who from wealth's full board are fed,
And Ye who eat with toil your bread,
My words with juſt attention weigh,   5
And liſten to the hallow'd Lay.
My lips ſhall Wiſdom's leſſons yield,
My heart, with nobleſt ſcience fill'd,
Shall prompt me with obedient ear
The Heav'n-deſcending truths to hear,   10
While, touch'd with holy fire, my tongue
Forms to the harp the myſtic ſong.
   Why ſhould my ſoul with anxious dread
Behold the foes around me ſpread,
Who build on wealth their truſt, and ſtore   15
In boaſted heaps the glitt'ring ore?
Ceaſe, Mortals, ceaſe your pride; nor dream
That riches ſhall from death redeem,
Or from the all-diſpoſing hand
A Brother's forfeit life demand;   20
But, taught the Soul's juſt price to know,
At once the frantic thought forgo:
In vain would Friendſhip's zeal eſſay
The full equivalent to pay,
In vain the flitting breath to ſave,   25
And plead exemption from the grave,
Though envied *Ophir*'s wealthieſt mine
Its treaſures to the purchaſe join.

                         Thou

PSALM XLIX.

Thou feeſt the Man in Wiſdom's ſchool
Long tutor'd, like the untaught fool,   30
To death ſubmit, and leave his heir
His heaps of gath'er'd wealth to ſhare.
Though Art extends them all its aid,
Mortality's ſtrong graſp t' evade,
And bids them build the Dome ſublime,   35
Proof to the rage of eating Time,
While Lands ſubjected to their claim
Take from their haughty Lord a name,
Yet Man, with erring pride elate,
And high in pow'r, in honour great,   40
Shares with the Brute an equal doom,
And ſleeps forgotten in the tomb.
Their hope thus fond thus faithleſs found
Their Sons aſſume; in endleſs round
Another and another race   45
Their Fathers' wayward ſteps ſhall trace.
Together now behold them laid,
As Sheep, when Night extends her ſhade,
While Death within the vaulted rock,
Stern Shepherd, guards the ſlumb'ring flock.   50
Corruption there its work ſhall ply,
And, wrapt in darkneſs as they lie,
Each feature fair, each boaſted grace,
With unrelenting hand efface:
Ye Juſt, exulting lift your eyes;   55
Behold the promis'd Morn ariſe,
That bids you, o'er each haughty foe
Exalted, endleſs triumphs know.

My Soul, amidst your happy train,
The wish'd redemption shall obtain, 60
By God adopted, Death shall brave,
And mock the disappointed Grave.
Let not the Sight thy heart dismay,
If Man's proud Offspring thou survey
With growing wealth incircled round, 65
Or mark his house with honours crown'd;
Nor think his treasures, at his end,
Shall with him to the grave descend,
Or the vain pomp, that strikes thy view,
Through Death's dark shade its Lord pursue. 70
His life with each enjoyment fraught,
How bles'd his pamper'd Soul its lot!
And Thee, while pleasure crowns thy days,
Admiring Crouds perchance may praise;
Yet Thou, like Him, the way shalt tread, 75
Which, one by one, thy Sires have led,
And 'midst th' impenetrable gloom
Shalt find with Them thy lasting home.
For Man, with erring pride elate,
And high in pow'r, in honour great, 80
Shares with the Brute an equal doom,
And sleeps forgotten in the tomb.

PSALM L.

THE Lord, th' Almighty Monarch, spake,
And bade the Earth the summons take,
Far as his eyes the realms survey
Of rising and declining day.

Reveal'd

Reveal'd from *Sion*'s sacred bound, 5
The Seat with matchless beauty crown'd,
Our God his course shall downward bend,
Nor silent to his Work descend.
Devouring flames shall march before,
And mightiest tempests round him roar. 10
Heav'n from above shall hear his call,
And Thou, the vast terrestrial Ball;
While Man's whole race their Judge shall meet,
In countless throngs before his Seat
Assembled. " From the distant poles 15
" My Saints collect; the faithful Souls,
" With whom my compact firm has stood,
" Seal'd with the spotless Victim's blood."
Th' applauding Heav'ns the changeless Doom,
While God the balance shall assume, 20
In full memorial shall record,
And own the Justice of their Lord.
With humblest awe, my People, hear;
For God, thy God, his voice shall rear:
Myself, O *Israel*, will attest 25
The guilt that stains thy erring breast.
Not ritual Sacrifice withheld
My theme of just complaint shall yield:
Still let thy Stall the Steer detain,
Still let thy Goat untouch'd remain 30
Amidst his herd-mates: from thy hands
Nor Goat nor Steer thy Lord demands:
Mine are the Beasts that range the wood,
Mine all the tame or savage Brood

Whose train the Earth's wide pasture fills, 35
And wanders o'er her thousand hills.
Each fowl, that from its airy flight
Descends upon the mountain's height,
Each brute that o'er the champaign strays,
My all-observing eye surveys. 40
Admit, I hunger; shall thy God
Descend from Thee to ask his food,
Lord of the World and all its Store
Thy aid, thou Child of Earth, implore?
Shall Bulls to ease my want be slain, 45
Or blood of Goats my thirst restrain?
Go, suppliant at my altar bow,
And pay thy thanks, and pay thy vow:
(Be this thy Off'ring:) In thy woes
On Me with stedfast hope repose; 50
So shall my ear receive thy pray'r,
And, grateful, Thou my mercy share.

   Thou Wretch by discipline unaw'd,
(Thus to the Impious speaks my God,)
Thy secret crimes to Me are known; 55
I see my Laws behind thee thrown:
And Thou, dost Thou with lips profane
The precepts of my will explain,
And, rank'd thyself amid my foes,
My terms of offer'd grace propose? 60
Say, has the Thief to Thee applied,
And Thou thy wanted aid denied?
Or fail'd th' Adult'rer e'er to see
A partner of his guilt in Thee?

Thy

'Thy tongue to fraud has loos'd the reins,
And lye with lye connected feigns.
Haſt thou not ſat, with cruel aim
Reflecting on a Brother's fame,
And with invented ſcandal ſtain'd
Whom erſt one womb with Thee contain'd?
While ſilent thus thy crimes I ſee,
Thy folly pictures me like Thee:
But ſoon my op'ning lips ſhall yield
The juſt rebuke ſo long withheld,
And bid, before thy conſcious eyes,
Thy guilt in all its horror riſe.
Ye Souls forgetful of my fear,
With full regard my dictates hear;
Leſt, at my word, your life the Grave
Demand, and none be nigh to ſave.
Who yields the Sacrifice of praiſe,
His beſt-accepted homage pays:
Who forms his ſteps aright, ſhall know
What Joys from my Salvation flow.

PSALM LI.

LORD, let thy clemency divine
Conſpicuous in my pardon ſhine;
O let the fulneſs of thy grace
Each error of my life efface,
Its influence to my ſoul convey,
And waſh my ev'ry ſtain away.
My conſcious heart its guilt ſhall own;
My Deed to Thee, and Thee alone,

Obnoxious,

Obnoxious, nor the day nor night
Conceals from my abhorring sight.
Just is thy sentence, holiest Lord,
And Truth eternal seals thy word.
Thou from the birth my soul couldst view,
As shap'd in sin my breath I drew,
And seest me guilt's transmissive stain
Through life's revolving course retain.
But deep within my inmost frame
(Nor dares my soul contest thy claim,)
Thy just decrees, Almighty Sire,
Integrity and Truth require;
Thy hand, corrective of my will,
Shall wisdom in my breast instill;
With hallow'd hyssop sprinkled o'er,
My soul its spots shall mourn no more,
But, cleans'd by Thee, the whiteness know,
That clothes the new-descended snow.
How shall my ear thy pard'ning voice
Transported welcome! How rejoice
My bones, with vital moisture fill'd,
That, crush'd by Thee, by Thee are heal'd?
O turn, great Ruler of the Skies,
Turn from my Sin thy searching eyes,
Nor let th' offences of my hand
Within thy book recorded stand.
Give me a will to thine subdu'd,
A conscience pure, a soul renew'd,
Nor let me, wrapt in endless gloom,
An outcast from thy presence roam,

Or absent mourn th' ethereal Guest,
Whose visits chear th' afflicted breast. 40
O let thy Spirit to my heart
Once more his quick'ning aid impart,
My mind from ev'ry fear release,
And sooth my troubled thoughts to peace.
So shall the souls, whom Error's sway 45
Has urg'd from Thee, blest Lord, to stray,
From Me thy heav'nly precepts learn,
And humbled to their God return.
O would thy healing grace bestow'd
Absolve me from my debt of blood, 50
How should my tongue thy Justice sing,
Invisible, Immortal King,
And, long as breath extends my days,
The God of my Salvation praise!
Not Victims, Lord, in solemn rite 55
Presented, thy desire excite;
Else should my hand with zealous care
Th' exacted holocaust prepare.
A Spirit griev'd is sacrifice
Delightful to th' all-seeing eyes; 60
The heart, that, taught its guilt to know,
Repentant heaves with inward woe,
Shall find its pray'r, its groans, its sighs,
To Thee in full acceptance rise.

    Thy grace to *Sion*, Lord, extend, 65
And bid fair *Salem*'s walls ascend:
So shall the Sons of *Jacob*'s line
With purest offrings load thy Shrine,

                      And,

And, while in many a lengthen'd wreath
Their incense shall its odours breathe, 70
Before thy altar doom'd to bleed
The slaughter'd steer the flames shall feed.

PSALM LII.

1.

WHY, Tyrant, boasts thy heart the pow'r
    To work a Brother's woe;
While God his mercy bids each hour
    In streams unmeasur'd flow?

2.

With joy thy tongue, to falsehood prone,
    Its venom deals around;
Nor razor sharpen'd on the stone
    Inflicts so deep a wound.

3.

Thy lips far readier Ill than Good
    And Lies than Truth have sought;
Nor e'er has word that aim'd at blood
    Unwelcom'd met thy thought.

4.

But God, whose wrath thy crimes inflame,
    Shall pluck thee from thy home,
Root from the land of life thy name,
    And seal thy changeless doom.

5.

The Just, with thankful awe possess'd,
    Shall view thy blasted pride,

PSALM LII.

And, from their fiercest foe releas'd,
   Thy impious boasts deride.

6.
" Lo there the Wretch in trespass bold,
   " Who God's support disdain'd,
" And on his heaps of treasur'd gold
   " His frantic hope sustain'd."

7.
Fresh as the verdant olive, I
   Within thy Courts shall stand,
And, fix'd, indulgent Lord, rely
   On thy protecting hand.

8.
Thy Acts my praise shall ever claim,
   Thy Name, amidst my woes,
(How grateful to thy Saints that Name!)
   My ev'ry fear compose.

PSALM LIII.

BEHOLD the Fool, whose heart denies
   The God who form'd the Earth and Skies:
While, fearless, sin's worst paths he treads,
Mark how the dire example spreads
Through human race. Not one we find   5
To Virtue's Heav'n-taught rules inclin'd,
Who 'midst infectious times has stood
Unstain'd, and obstinately good.
Th' eternal Monarch from on high
Cast on the Sons of Earth his eye,   10
               If

PSALM LIII.

If haply some he yet might see
From error's baleful influence free,
Whose lives an impious Age might shame,
Who sought his Love, and own'd his Name.
He look'd: But Ah! not one could find   15
To Virtue's Heav'n-taught rules inclin'd:
Each, led from Wisdom's path astray,
Pursues the tenour of his way.
O say, what frenzy thus could blind
Their Souls, that with remorseless mind   20
As bread my People they devour,
Nor suppliant own their Maker's pow'r.
Yet see their thoughts tumultuous roll,
See causeless terrors shake their soul:
Wide o'er the field the bones are spread   25
Of Chiefs who by thy sword have bled,
And speak the doom that All must share,
Whom God abandons from his care.
 Who, mightiest Lord, to *Israel*'s eyes
Shall bid the wish'd Salvation rise,   30
From *Sion*'s hill its healing ray
Extend, and round us pour the day?
When Thou (Thy pow'r the Work demands,)
Shalt back recall our captive bands,
The blest event to *Judah*'s shore   35
Her songs of triumph shall restore,
And ceaseless shouts, through heav'n's wide frame
Loud-echoing, *Jacob*'s joy proclaim.

PSALM LIV.

1.

THY Name my stedfast heart avows;
Do Thou my injur'd cause espouse,
And be thy Strength my aid:
My plaints, eternal Monarch, hear,
And let them by thy pitying ear
With full regard be weigh'd.

2.

For Nations from thy fear estrang'd,
With Tyrants fierce, against me rang'd,
My guiltless soul pursue:
But 'midst my helpers Heav'ns high Lord
Shall stand, and faithful to his word
Each adverse pow'r subdue.

3.

O let my heart, their rage repell'd,
Itself a willing off'ring yield;
To Thee its praise shall flow,
While to my thought thy Mercies rise,
That gave me with exulting eyes
To see my prostrate foe.

PSALM LV.

O Hear my voice, All-potent Sire,
Nor distant from the pray'r retire,
Whose accents to thine ear impart
The anguish of my heaving heart.

PSALM LV.

A Croud, whose thoughts from Thee have stray'd, 5
With falsehood arm'd, my peace invade;
Oppression's shouts around me roar,
Death's blackest horrors whelm me o'er,
And griefs and fears, that shun controul,
Shake to its inmost depth my soul. 10
O who shall give me (thus my breast
Its vain inquietude express'd,)
The Dove's light wing, that through the air
A wretched fugitive may bear,
And grant me safe from harms to dwell 15
Within the rock's sequester'd cell?
How would I mount the wafting wind,
How leave the wrathful storms behind,
And in the Desert's lone retreat
Contented fix my lasting Seat! 20
Thy vengeance, Lord, inflict; their tongue
Divide; for Tumult, Strife, and Wrong,
Where'er I turn, before my eyes
In giant forms amid them rise;
Within their wall's unhallow'd bound 25
By day, by night, they take their round;
Nor cease their guilty streets to hear
The voice of falsehood, grief, and fear.
 Not threaten'd Rage, or Hate profest,
My fame insult, my peace molest; 30
My soul, when Foes had aim'd the wound,
Some safe recess perchance had found,
Or, disciplin'd by previous care,
Had learn'd th' expected ill to bear;
         But

But Thou, 'twas Thou, the Friend difguis'd, 35
The Man, whom chief of Friends I priz'd,
To whom, its Counfellor and Guide,
My foul in ev'ry doubt applied:
In bands of fweeteft union join'd,
Each wifh, each fecret of the mind, 40
We fhar'd, and 'midft th' affembled Train
Familiar trod the hallow'd Fane.
Let death (eternal Juftice cries,)
Let death their impious race furprize;
Let Earth its op'ning jaws extend, 45
While living to the grave defcend
The lawlefs Throng; whofe Land profane
Hell's worft-invented mifchiefs ftain.
But God my vows folicit; He
From each diftrefs my foul fhall free; 50
He, as with fervent lips I pray,
At dawn, at noon, at clofe of day,
Shall ftoop to my complaint his ear,
And inftant in my caufe appear.
He, when the battle round me bled, 55
From hoftile myriads fcreen'd my head,
Gave to my pray'r the wifh'd for peace,
And bade the dreadful tumult ceafe.
That Pow'r, who fate inthron'd above,
E'er Heav'n's vaft Orbs were feen to move, 60
Whofe Counfels, fix'd through ages paft,
Shall time's remoteft date outlaft,
That Pow'r my conteft fhall decide,
And humble to the duft their pride.

PSALM LV.

See, unprovok'd, the restless foe 65
Aim at thy Saints the deathful blow,
Thy fear, great God, behind him thrown,
And compacts oft confirm'd disown.
While War's fierce flames within him burn,
As milk new foaming from the churn 70
Smooth are his lips; as oil his words;
Yet wound they deep as keenest swords.
O cast thee fearless on thy God;
He, prompt to save, the grateful load
Within his fost'ring arms shall bear, 75
And feed thee with a parent's care.
   Author of good! beneath thy hand
Secure from lapse the Just shall stand,
While (such thy Mandate!) on his foes
Destruction's pit its mouth shall close. 80
Who thirst for blood, who falsehoods raise,
To death shall yield, e'er half their days
Be number'd, while, exulting, I
On Thee with stedfast hope rely.

PSALM LVI.

O Reach me, Lord, thy aiding pow'r,
  While hostile troops my strength devour;
My strength devour, and day by day
With fiercest threats my heart dismay:
Yet Trust in Thee my spirit chears, 5
And checks my sighs, and wipes my tears.
Thy promise, Lord, to notes of praise
In each distress my song shall raise:

God

PSALM LVI.

God in my cause his arm will rear;
And Man, shall Man excite my fear? 10
My words they torture; and, their thought
Each hour with deepest malice fraught,
In impious council nightly meet,
And watch, with murth'rous aim, my feet.
On wrong, and superstition vain, 15
Their hope the frantic tribe sustain;
But teach them, Lord, thy wrath to know,
And quell the insults of my foe.
My grief to thine observing eye,
As chas'd from realm to realm I fly, 20
In full display, great God, appears;
O treasure in thy vase my tears:
But see! already by thy hand
Recorded in thy book they stand.
Whene'er to Thee, my God, I cry, 25
Secure of aid the fight I try,
While hosts beneath my falchion bleed,
And back with headlong flight recede.
Thy word my breast with joy shall swell,
Thy promise, Lord, my woes dispell: 30
God in my cause his arm will rear,
And Man, shall Man excite my fear?
Their thanks, their vows, (thy just demand,)
My lips shall yield: Thy fav'ring hand
My feet from error, from the grave 35
My fainting soul, has deign'd to save,
And bids me still, to Thee allied,
Within the land of life reside.

PSALM LVII.

THY Mercy, Lord, amidst my woes,
   Thy Mercy to my eyes disclose;
Let me, my hope on Thee reclin'd,
Beneath thy wings a refuge find,
Till thy prevailing beams dispell   5
The clouds of grief that o'er me dwell.
   To Him, the God who reigns on high,
To Him with suppliant voice I cry,
Assur'd that He, indulgent still,
My plaint shall hear, my pray'r fulfill,   10
His timeliest aid from heav'n extend,
My fame from obloquy defend,
And bid his Truth and Mercy shed
Their kindest influence on my head.
   The Lions round me roar aloud;   15
And, fir'd with causeless rage, a Croud
Advance, (thy foes, eternal Lord,)
Whose teeth are spears, whose tongue a sword.
Inthron'd thyself above the skies,
O bid thy fullest glory rise,   20
And to the earth with cloudless ray
The wonders of thy pow'r display.
   Oft, as amid the snares I tread,
Each hour by hostile fraud outspread,
What fears, what woes, my bosom prove!   25
Yet, sav'd by thy preventing Love,
Th' artificers of death I see
Faln in the pit prepar'd for me.

PSALM LVII.

My heart is fix'd, Almighty Sire,
My heart is fix'd: To Thee aspire 30
My thoughts, and dictate to my lays
An argument of endless praise.
Awake (thou glory of my frame)
Awake, my tongue, to loud acclaim;
Awake my lute, and new-strung lyre; 35
Instinct, myself, with holy fire
I wake; and lo, the dawning sun
Already hears the strain begun.
From Me assembling crouds shall burn
The triumphs of thy Love to learn, 40
And, rapt with zeal, the Nations round
Catch from my lips the sacred sound.
Lo! to the clouds thy Truth extends,
Thy Mercy Heav'n's vast height transcends:
Inthron'd thyself above the skies, 45
O bid thy fullest glory rise,
And to the earth with cloudless ray
The wonders of thy pow'r display.

PSALM LVIII.

YE whose lips the cause decide,
   Say, does Truth your sentence guide?
Are your thoughts by Justice sway'd,
And in Reason's balance weigh'd?
Let your conscious tongues attest 5
What ye harbour in your breast.
Hearts ye bear, that deep within
Cherish each suggested sin,

And

And the dictates of your will
With remorseless hands fulfill.   10
From the womb, in error's way
See the infant sinner stray:
Nurtur'd in deceit and wrong
See him with advent'rous tongue
(Prompt his earliest skill to try,).   15
Lisp the meditated lye.
See their veins with venom swell;
Arm'd with such, the Adder fell
Stops her ear, in many a fold
'Mid the shelt'ring brake uproll'd,   20
While each note the Charmer tries,
And his utmost art defies.
 Smite, great God, the Lions' cheek,
And their fangs indignant break.
While they arm them for the war,   25
And their quiver'd stores prepare,
Let th' Oppressors feel thy pow'r,
Let thy sword their strength devour;
Let them waste in swift decay,
As the Torrents pass away,   30
As the earth-bred Snails consume,
As th' Abortions of the womb
(Life's short circuit scarce begun,)
Perish e'er they see the sun.
 E'er the Caldron learn to glow   35
From the kindling thorns below,
Let thy hotter wrath be shed
Quick on each rebellious head:

        Let

PSALM LVIII.

Let the Storms, that through the sky,
Minifters of vengeance, fly,   40
Inftant, Lord, at thy beheft,
Sweep from earth the living Peft:
While the Souls that truft in Thee
Pleas'd their caufe aveng'd fhall fee,
And, the dreadful conflict o'er,   45
Wafh their fteps in hoftile gore.
" Doubtlefs, each convinc'd fhall cry,
" Doubtlefs, there's a Judge on high;
" And who His commands regard,
" Reap at length their full reward."   50

PSALM LIX.

TH' impending ftorm, my God, affuage;
 High o'er the foes, that round me rage,
Exalt me, (foes, whofe ftubborn mind,
To wrong and violence refign'd,
Thy facred Laws has long withftood,)   5
And fave me from the Man of blood.
Affembling crouds the deadly fnare,
Without my crime, great God, prepare;
Without my crime, in fin allied,
To diff'rent paths their courfe divide: 10
O, obvious to my pray'r, arife,
Nor let their guilt efcape thine eyes.
Leader of Hofts, and *Ifrael*'s God!
Stretch o'er the Heathen tribes thy rod,
Nor let them, unchaftis'd, each hour   15
With mad prefumption brave thy pow'r.

        When

When eve's dark shades o'er heav'n are hung,
See! as the Dog with fury stung,
While hideous yells their wrath betray,
From street to street they urge their way.　　20
Swords in their lips, without a fear
Their threats they vent: for who shall hear?
By Thee, by Thee, those threats are heard;
Superior Thou each frantic word,
Eternal Monarch, shalt deride,　　25
And check with just reproach their pride.
Rock of my strength! To Thee on high
My Soul shall lift the stedfast eye,
Whose aid, e'er yet invok'd, each foe
Beneath my conqu'ring feet shall throw.　　30
Let not thy wrath, O God our shield,
Their name to full excision yield,
Lest, vanish'd from th' observing eye,
Th' example of the vengeance die;
But, arm'd with pow'r, through foreign lands　　35
Distribute wide their vanquish'd Bands.
Such vengeance from thine arm, great Sire,
Their tongue's repeated crimes require,
Their thoughts, inflam'd with impious pride,
Their oaths to guile's worst ends applied,　　40
And urge thee with impartial doom
Each bold transgressor to consume:
Strike, Lord, O strike the needful blow,
And teach an erring World to know,
That *Jacob*'s Sons thy pow'r obey,　　45
And Earth's wide confines own thy sway.

PSALM LIX.

When eve's dark fhades o'er heav'n are hung,
Still, as the Dog with fury ftung,
Still let them, clam'ring for their prey,
From ftreet to ftreet purfue their way, 50
Infatiate; while their deftin'd fpoil
Elufive mocks their fruitlefs toil.
I, Lord, fecure in Thee, thy might
Will praife, and with the rifing light
Thy Love, that in the dreadful day 55
Redeem'd me, on my harp difplay,
Thee own my Refuge, (heav'nly King!)
And Mercy's unexhaufted Spring.

PSALM LX.

REPULS'D, difpers'd, chaftis'd by Thee,
O grant us, Lord, thy face to fee,
And let the People, once thy care,
Again thy fav'ring prefence fhare.
How trembles this divided Land 5
Beneath the terrors of thy hand!
O Thou, the God whom we adore,
Its breaches heal, its peace reftore.
Thy juft Decrees to *Ifrael*'s eyes
Have bid a fcene of forrow rife, 10
And to his pallid lips the wine
Of dire Aftonifhment confign.
Yet fee, thy hands a ftandard rear;
Beneath it Each, who owns thy fear,
Engag'd in Truth's neglected caufe, 15
His fword, fecure of conqueft, draws.

Such,

Such, objects of thy tend'rest Love,
Defend propitious from above;
Let Me with Them thy Mercy share,
And hear, O hear, my ceaseless pray'r.   20
God with an Oath his purpose seals;
My hand with joy his word fulfills:
Behold me *Sichem*'s plain divide;
My line, to *Succoth's* vale applied,
Its bound describes; Thee mine I see,   25
O *Gilead*, and, *Manasses*, Thee.
Thou, *Ephraim*, art my strong defence,
Thou, *Judah*, sh'alt my Law dispense;
A diff'rent lot shall *Moab* find,
A Vase to vilest use assign'd;   30
A doom like his let *Edom* meet,
And wipe the dust from off my feet.
Philistia, pleas'd thy tribute bring,
And own in Me thy future King.
Who, as our troops in close array   35
To *Edom*'s forts direct their way,
Arm'd with resistless strength shall bid
Her gates unfold, her bolts recede?
Behold us, Lord, oppress'd with woe,
As exil'd from thy care we go: 40
Shall *Israel*'s hosts, thy aid withheld,
Still unsuccessful take the field?
Our hope, on Man repos'd in vain,
O let thy Strength, great God, sustain:
Thus arm'd, each adverse pow'r we dare,   45
And dauntless meet the rushing war,

                         While

While from thy sword our foes retire,
Or trampled in the dust expire.

PSALM LXI.

OPPRESS'D with grief, in exile lost,
To Thee from *Judah*'s utmost coast
My voice, eternal God, I send:
O hear my plaint; my pray'r attend.
High on the rock my footsteps rear; 5
There let me stand unmov'd, and hear
The storms, that now around me beat,
At distance roll beneath my feet.
Thee, Lord, I seek, whene'er my foes
With dire intent my path inclose, 10
And own thee in the dang'rous hour
My stedfast Hope, my strongest Tow'r.
Remote from fear, within thy shrine
Thou, Lord, my dwelling shalt assign;
Thy wings shall wrap me in their shade; 15
Thou, Thou hast heard me when I pray'd,
And yielded to my wish the joys
Of Those whose care thy Will employs.
Long Life shall *Israel*'s King behold,
And ages count on ages roll'd: 20
Safe in thy presence let him stand,
And share the blessings of thy hand;
His dwelling let thy Truth defend,
Thy Mercy on his steps attend.
So shall thy Love awake my song, 25
Thy Name the willing note prolong,

While, warm'd with zeal, my vows I pay,
And bless thee to my latest day.

PSALM LXII.

MY Soul in God its rest has found;
   When various griefs beset me round,
His Love shall sure deliv'rance yield;
By Him through life I walk upheld,
And safe from lapse my course maintain,   5
Or, falling, instant rise again.
How long, Artificers of ill,
Shall schemes of death employ your skill?
Behold the mischiefs ye intend
Retorted on your heads descend: 10
Your semblance see yon loosen'd Wall,
Yon Bulwark, nodding to its fall.
Vain are the wiles for Him prepar'd,
Whom Heav'n's high Lord vouchsafes to guard,
And, crown'd with honours from above,   15
Proclaims the object of his Love.
See, vers'd in fraud, the impious Throng
With blessings charge their guileful tongue,
While deep within the heart's disguise
The secret curse invelop'd lies.   20
But Thou, my Soul, on God reclin'd,
In Him thy wish'd for rest shalt find;
His Love shall sure deliv'rance yield;
By Him through life I walk upheld,
Superior brave the hostile Train,   25
And safe from lapse my course maintain.

Thee,

PSALM LXII.

Thee, Lord, my Glory, Thee alone
My Rock, my Health, my Strength, I own:
Ye Tribes, in God your help behold,
To Him, with me, your hearts unfold; 30
Each want confefs, each grief reveal;
For who, O who like Him can heal?
O Vanity, thy name is MAN:
Intent the human mind to fcan,
Come, try, if aught of weight there feem; 35
Sufpend the balance, fix the beam:
In vain.—With equal eafe were weigh'd
The flitting air, or empty fhade.
Truft not in Wrong and Fraud; no more
On Hope's light wing prefumptuous foar; 40
Let gather'd wealth before thee lie
Beheld with unretorted eye,
Nor let the glitt'ring heap impart
One wifh to thy deluded heart.
Once from his throne th' Almighty fpake, 45
And forth again the accents brake:
" I claim the univerfal fway,
" I mark if Man my will obey,
" And, where my Fear the mind impells,
" (For Pow'r in Me with Mercy dwells,) 50
" Each act obferve with kind regard,
" And pleas'd confer the juft reward."

PSALM LXIII.

THOU art my God; to Thee my eyes
   I lift, e'er yet the dawn arise:
With sacred thirst, O Lord, I burn,
My Heart, my Flesh, thy absence mourn,
As o'er th' unhospitable way   5
Amidst a barren waste I stray,
Yet here, by heav'nly Wisdom led,
Expectant wait, till o'er my head
Thy beams in mild effulgence play,
And turn my darkness into day;   10
Those beams which oft my eyes beheld
From *Salem*'s hallow'd Shrine reveal'd.
   Thy Love my lips shall ever tell,
(Can Life itself that Love excell?)
Nor cease, while breath prolongs my days,   15
In thankful notes the hymn to raise.
To Thee thy Servant, Lord, as now,
His hands shall rear, his knees shall bow.
For nought like this my soul can chear;
Nor marrow from the fatted steer   20
Could e'er to the luxurious sense
Such full delight, my God, dispense,
As what my satiate soul injoys,
Whene'er thy praise my tongue employs.
Thou Moon, be witness if my bed   25
Forgetful of my God I spread;
And Thou, revolving Sun, if e'er
I wake unconscious of his care.

PSALM LXIII.

Safe in the shadow of thy wings,
In Thee I joy, O King of Kings;   30
When dangers threaten to devour,
Superior to each adverse pow'r
Thy Arm extends the help divine,
And long Experience calls it mine.
Behold my foes in dread retire,   35
Or prostrate at my feet expire:
While to my conqu'ring sword they yield,
The Beasts that nightly range the field
Amid the slaughter'd heaps shall stray,
And rav'nous seize their licens'd prey.   40
By Thee exalted to the throne
Shall *Judah*'s King thy mercies own;
And blest be Each, my God, whose tongue
With Him shall raise the grateful song,
Who suppliant at thy shrine shall kneel,   45
While shame the Lyar's lips shall seal.

PSALM LXIV.

THY Suppliant's voice propitious hear;
My life, Blest Lord, from hostile fear
Secure, while Men of impious mind,
Their pow'rs in secret league combin'd,
With factious rage my soul pursue,   5
And hide, O hide me from their view.
Behold the slaughter-breathing Throng
Whet as a sword their baleful tongue,
And words, as arrows keen, prepare,
That edg'd with death shall walk the air,   10

Conceal'd from sight each fear disclaim,
And level at the Just their aim,
Nor rest, till in the blameless heart
Their hand has lodg'd the sudden dart.
Their dire designs, in guilt allied,   15
They form; secure, their snares provide;
" And who our aim shall thwart? What eye
" (They ask,) the hidden death descry?"
With future mischiefs teem their breasts,
(As each to each new wiles suggests,)   20
And seek in art's obscurest veil
Their guilty purpose to conceal.
Ah! Wretches, whither will ye fly?
Behold the arrow from on high
Descend, that bears upon its wing   25
The wrath of Heav'n's offended King:
The fatal shaft its errand knows,
And red with hottest vengeance glows.
   Their tongue, that seeks another's hurt,
Itself their footsteps shall subvert,   30
And passers by with inward dread
Behold them on the earth outspread.
Each heart shall own, with rev'rent thought,
That Thou the work, great God, hast wrought,
And, pleas'd, thy chastisements shall trace,   35
Inflicted on their guilty race,
While, rescu'd from their rage, the Just
Exulting fix on Thee their trust.

PSALM

PSALM LXV.

THEE *Sion*'s praife, O Lord, attends,
To Thee the frequent vow afcends
From each whom *Salem*'s walls behold
Among her faithful fons inroll'd:
To Thee, whofe ready ear the pray'r   5
Prevents, fhall Man's whole race repair:
Amidft them at thy footftool I,
Prefs'd with a weight of guilt, apply,
Affur'd from Thy free grace to win
The wifh'd atonement of my fin.   10
Bleft, who by fweet experience knows,
What Joys thy Prefence, Lord, beftows,
The Man, who, privileg'd by Thee,
Thy face in near approach fhall fee,
Behold thy beams effulgent play,   15
And in thy Dwelling fix his ftay.
Let *Ifrael*'s Tribes, their foes o'erthrown,
The terrors of thy Juftice own,
O Thou, the Hope of human race,
Of all whom Earth's wide arms embrace,   20
Of all who toft by tempefts fweep
The furface of the pathlefs Deep.
In Thee they truft, who girt with pow'r
Haft bid the Mountains heav'nward tow'r,
And, fix'd on ftrongeft bafe, defy   25
The warring blafts that round them fly:
In Thee — Who know'ft at will to rein
The infults of the foaming Main,

Check

Check the brute waves that roar aloud,
And still the madness of the Croud.   30
Remotest Realms with dire dismay
Thy wonders, mightiest Lord, survey;
And, as they walk th' ethereal Round,
The Morn and Eve thy praise resound.
Thy visits teach the grateful soil   35
To recompense the tiller's toil:
By unexhausted springs supplied
Thy River pours its copious tide,
And bids the strength-infusing grain
Earth's countless Family sustain.   40
The Clouds, in frequent show'rs distill'd,
Drop fatness on the pregnant field,
Break the tough glebe, the furrows chear,
And crown with good the gliding year.
The pastures of th' extended Waste   45
Thy gifts in rich profusion taste;
The hills around exulting stand,
And own the bounty of thy hand.
Nurs'd by thy care the fleecy train
Invests with white the rural plain,   50
While, as beneath the fav'ring skies
In crouded ranks the harvests rise,
The laughing Vale assumes a tongue,
And bursts triumphant into song.

PSALM LXVI.

YE Sons of Men, in God rejoice;
   Lift in one choir your thankful voice,
And spread through Earth's extended frame
The honour of your Maker's name.
How awful are thy Works, how great!   5
(Thus let the song his praise repeat,)
Thy late obdurate foes behold,
By thy superior strength controul'd,
With flatt'ring lip their homage pay,
And Earth's whole empire own thy sway.   10
Each tribe of human race to Thee
Shall suppliant bend the humble knee,
Each tongue in hymns of praise shall join,
And joyful bless the name divine.
O come, and view with rev'rent thought   - 15
The Acts by Heav'n's high Monarch wrought,
His wonders shown since Time began,
And friendlike intercourse with Man.
His word the Deep's vast channel dried,
And backward roll'd th' obedient Tide: 20
Now safe athwart its sandy bed
By Him our rescu'd troops are led,
Now lost in grateful transport stand,
And shouts of triumph shake the strand.
Time's latest period long o'erpast,   25
His pow'r shall self-supported last;
Each realm to his observing eyes,
From pole to pole, subjected lies,

And sees its rebel Sons in vain
With strength combin'd oppose his reign.   30
Ye Nations All of various tongue,
To *Jacob*'s God exalt the song;
Sing, sing aloud, that Nature's ear
His praise through all her bounds may hear,
Whose wakeful care within our breast   35
(Though countless foes our peace infest,)
Still gives the vital pulse to beat,
And guards from dread of lapse our feet.
Oft has thy hand, All-potent Lord,
By various proof our faith explor'd,   40
And bid the flame each heart refine,
As silver recent from the mine:
Now round us waves the net, and now
Beneath oppression's weight we bow,
While o'er our heads the Sons of pride   45
With hostile scorn exulting ride.
Through fires, through torrents, led by Thee,
At length th' expected Land we see,
Where streams irriguous cleave the soil,
And crown with wealth the tiller's toil.   50
Lo, to thy Dome, my God and King,
The sacred holocaust I bring,
That late, oppress'd by sorrow's cloud,
To Thee with fervent lip I vow'd:
Before thy Altar's kindled fire   55
The promis'd victims shall expire,
Here bleed the full-fed Goat, and here
The fleecy Ram, and stubborn Steer.

        O come,

PSALM LXVI.

O come, Ye Souls that fear your God,
And learn his grace on Me beſtow'd, 60
As, ſupplicating loud, my tongue
Wak'd to his praiſe the hallow'd ſong.
Had conſcious guilt my boſom ſtain'd,
How had his ear my pray'r diſdain'd,
That upward now through tracts of day 65
In ſure acceptance wings its way!
Bleſt be my God, who, thron'd on high,
Rejects not from his care my cry,
Nor, while afflictions round me riſe,
His mercy to my ſoul denies. 70

PSALM LXVII.

MAY God his fav'ring ear incline,
And bid his face on *Iſrael* ſhine,
That All thy counſels, Lord, may know,
Where Earth extends, or Oceans flow,
And, thankful, to their wondring eyes 5
Behold thy wiſh'd Salvation riſe.
To Thee, of Life th' eternal Spring,
Inviſible, All-potent King,
One chorus let the Nations raiſe,
One ſhout of univerſal praiſe. 10
Exult each Tribe, exult each Land;
Heav'n's mighty Lord with equal hand
The balance holds, and Earth's domain
Shall own to lateſt age his reign.
To Thee, of Life th' eternal Spring, 15
Inviſible, All-potent King,

One chorus let the Nations raise,
One shout of universal praise.
So, warm'd by genial suns, the field
With full increase its fruits shall yield, 20
And God, thy God, O *Israel*, shed
His choicest blessings on thy head.
   God shall on Us his blessings show'r,
And Man's whole Race revere his pow'r.

PSALM LXVIII.

LET God arise, and let his foes,
   His arm unable to oppose,
Back from the field, with wild affright
O'erwhelm'd, precipitate their flight.
Behold, great God, the impious Host 5
Like smoke in quick dispersion lost:
Behold them, at thy look, expire,
Dissolv'd, as wax before the fire;
While all who own thy just command
Exulting in thy presence stand, 10
And bid the shout of triumph rise
Loud echoing to the distant skies.
O, while his Acts your lips inspire,
And animate the vocal lyre,
A path for *Israel*'s God prepare, 15
Who, seated on his regal Car,
Triumphant o'er the Desert wide
In solemn state is seen to ride:
His Name JEHOVAH; Theme of praise
Exhaustless! in his presence raise 20

The grateful ſtrain, and joyous ſing
The Mercies of your heav'nly King.
Their Parent Him the Orphans hail;
He bids the Widow's cauſe prevail,
And, ſhrin'd above th' empyreal ſky, 25
Extends to All his equal eye,
A manſion to the Outcaſt gives,
The Captive from his chain relieves,
But bids the Sinner wear away
In barren wilds his ſhorten'd day. 30
When o'er the long-extended Waſte
Thy glory, Firſt of Beings! paſt,
And, beaming o'er thy People's head,
Their Bands to certain conqueſt led,
Earth, groaning, to its centre reel'd, 35
The Heav'ns, in clouds diſſolv'd, beheld
The footſteps of th' approaching God,
And *Sinai* own'd, with lowly nod,
Thy viſits, everlaſting Lord!
The Pow'r by *Jacob*'s Sons ador'd. 40
While yet the burning ſands they tread,
Thy kindlieſt rains, around them ſhed,
Beſpeak them fav'rites of thy care,
And Nature's wearied pow'rs repair.
Thus joy the Tribes whom Thou haſt lov'd, 45
Thus boaſt their lot by Thee improv'd,
Whoſe aid the humble and the poor
Shall ne'er with fruitleſs vows implore.

    Heav'n's mighty Monarch gave the word;
His mandate *Sion*'s Daughters heard, 50

And thus in one assembled throng
With sweet accordance form the Song:
" Kings with their hosts have fled; and We,
" Who sate from toils of battle free,
" (Content the houshold's care to guide,)   55
" The Victor's richest spoils divide."
Again (their form obscur'd awhile
By tasks of servitude and toil,)
Again the Sons of *Abraham*'s line
Array'd in spotless lustre shine,   60
As Doves, while obvious to the Sun
From plume to plume the splendors run,
Their wings in silver dipt unfold,
And necks that glow with living gold.
See Peace (for God thy wars has fought;)   65
See Peace, thy full deliv'rance wrought,
While back thy foes, O *Israel*, turn,
Present amid thy gloom a Morn,
Unsullied as the glitt'ring snow,
Diffus'd o'er *Salmon*'s ample brow.   70
No more, O *Basan*, vaunt thy height,
That strikes with awe the distant sight,
No more, ye swelling Mountains, rise
In haughty triumph to the skies:
On humbler *Sion*'s favour'd head   75
His tent th' eternal King has spread,
Her sacred Hill his choice confest,
And lasting mansion of his rest.
Ten thousand Cars, and yet again
Ten thousand Cars, in lengthen'd train   80

Along

Along her hallow'd way proceed,
While God the Pomp vouchsafes to lead,
And *Israel* views within her shrine
(Blest seat of Majesty divine,)
The scene that erst his Tribes beheld 85
On *Sinai*'s mystic top reveal'd.

 Admiring Crouds with upcast eye
Have seen thee, Lord, ascend on high:
Behind thee move a captive Train,
Fast fetter'd with the servile chain, 90
While gifts through Thee on All below
From Heav'n's high throne transmitted flow.
A Race, who shun'd thy Laws to own,
The Blessings of thy hand have known,
And, objects of thy tend'rest care, 95
With Us the heav'nly presence share.

 To God, our ever constant Aid,
Be thanks and ceaseless honour paid:
On Him thy wish'd salvation rests;
Him, *Israel*, praise; whose high behests 100
Death's dreaded march through Earth's domain
To paths by Him prescrib'd restrain.
To Each whose heart rejects his sway,
His terrors shall their guilt repay;
Intent on plans of future ill 105
His stroke the hairy scalp shall feel,
And share the vengeance, thus aloud
Denounc'd on the rebellious Croud.
 " Once more from *Basan*'s fertile plain,
 " Once more from the divided Main 110

" Thee, *Jacob*, my resistless hand
" Shall lead, and guard thy chosen Band.
" When foes thy sword presumptuous brave,
" Thy feet the sanguine stream shall lave,
" Thy dogs devour the slaughter'd throng,   115
" And tinge with impious gore their tongue."
 My God, my King, with joyful view
Thy steps our wond'ring eyes pursue,
While, rang'd in order's strictest line,
Before, (as onward to thy shrine   120
The Ark thy shrouded presence bears,)
The Singers walk, parting their shares
Of sacred harmony; Behind,
The Minstrels tread, in concert join'd,
While, in the midst, the Virgin train   125
Awake the timbrel's loudest strain.
" Your praises (thus begins the lay,)
" To Heav'n's eternal Sov'reign pay,
" Ye Tribes that boast your hallow'd Race
" From *Israel*'s fruitful source to trace."   130
Least of that Race, Thou, *Benjamin*,
With mightier *Judah* there art seen,
While *Naphthali*'s glad Chiefs conspire
With *Zebulon* to form the choir.
 Strong in thy God, O *Israel*, rise;   135
And Thou, great Ruler of the Skies,
Thy Work perpetuate; let thy Love,
Fair *Salem*'s shrine incircling, move
Assembled Kings her Courts to greet,
And cast their gifts before thy feet.   140

The Beast, that from his reedy bed
On *Nile*'s proud bank uplifts the head,
Rebuke, indignant; nor the Throng
Forget, from whose misguided tongue
The Heifer and the grazing Steer   145
The offer'd Vow unconscious hear,
While to the silver's tinkling sound
Their feet in solemn dance rebound.
Their thirst of war, great God, restrain,
And backward drive their scatter'd train: 150
So, summon'd from her farthest end,
Shall *Egypt*'s Lords to *Salem* bend
Their footsteps, and *Arabia*'s Land
Extend to Thee the suppliant hand.

 Ye various Realms that Earth divide,   155
O sing to *Israel*'s God and Guide,
Who o'er the skies, in awful state,
From earliest age, exalted sate;
Whose voice, in frequent thunders giv'n,
Tremendous shakes the vault of Heav'n.   160
To Him the pow'r ascribe, whose rays
To *Jacob*'s view conspicuous blaze,
Who downward from th' ethereal height
O'er subject Worlds extends his sight.
What terrors from thy presence flow!   165
O Thou, of *Israel*'s foes the Foe,
Whose strength his arm for toil prepares,
And crowns with sure success his wars.
To Thee, till Time shall reach its end,
Let songs of highest praise ascend.   170

PSALM LXIX.

O Reach me, Lord, thy hand, and save
My soul from the voracious wave.
In depths of mire behold me bound;
In vain my sinking feet the ground
Explore; while high above my head   5
The whelming floods their billows spread.
Faint are my limbs, my palate dry,
While ceaseless to my God I cry;
With wasting orbs my eyes attend
To see his promis'd grace descend.   10
Behold my Foes around me spread,
The hairs that shade my hapless head
Outnumb'ring; Foes, that, arm'd with pow'r,
My soul have labour'd to devour,
Though pure of each offence I stand,   15
Plight to their terms my willing hand,
Nor shun (Extortion's easy prey,)
The wrong-imputed debt to pay.
To Thee, my God, to Thee alone
The errors of my heart are known: 20
O let not, heav'nly Lord, thine aid
'Thus long to my request delay'd
.Their hope to hostile scorn consign,
Whose hearts on *Israel*'s God recline.
Thy Cause, by Me avow'd, my fame   25
To insult gives, my cheek to shame:
Domestick Wrath and kindred Hate,
In thy defence, my soul await;

The

PSALM LXIX.

The Brothers of my blood in Me
An Alien and an Outcaſt ſee.   30
With zeal devour'd my boſom burns,
While frequent to my thought returns
Thy Dwelling by an impious Train
Diſhonour'd, and each taunt profane,
That loud-tongu'd Rage for Thee intends,   35
On Me with fulleſt weight deſcends.
Diſſolv'd in tears, with faſting worn,
What obloquy my ſoul has borne!
My loyns with ſorrow's garb o'erſpread
With jeſts their cruel fancy fed: 40
I paſs the crouded gate, purſu'd
By laughter and reproaches rude,
The proverb of the Drunkard's tongue,
And theme familiar of his ſong.
O let me in th' accepted hour   45
In pray'r to Thee my ſpirit pour;
Thine ear in full accordance bend,
And pleas'd thy promis'd help extend.
Snatch from the miry depths my feet;
Back let my furious foes retreat;   50
And O! the ſwelling ſtorm aſſuage,
E'er yet the flood's remorſeleſs rage
In dreadful whirlpools wrap me round,
And plunge me in the dark profound.
Hear, Lord, and to my ſoul diſplay   55
Thy Mercy's all-enliv'ning ray;
Look down, eternal God, look down,
Behold me, but without a frown,

Nor to thy Servant's longing eye
Thy face, amidst my woes, deny.   60
Haste to my aid, O haste thee near,
Do Thou my soul from hostile fear
Release; thine ears each insult keen
Have heard; thine eyes my shame have seen,
And stedfast mark'd the adverse Band,   65
That leagu'd in guilt around me stand.
My soul, by evil tongues assail'd,
Unequal to the conflict fail'd:
In sad inquietude of thought
Some partner of my grief I sought,   70
And wish'd; in vain, the friend to find,
Whose voice might sooth my troubled mind.
These, 'mid the Croud that wait me nigh,
Gall to my lothing lips apply;
While These my thirst's afflictive rage   75
With juice of sharpest taste assuage.
Say, what requital from thy hand
Shall guilt like theirs, great God, demand?
While pleas'd the social board they share,
Let Death around it plant a snare,   80
And what should bliss and health bestow
With aim inverted work their woe.
Let blindness check their fell designs,
Bow with affliction's weight their loyns,
And let thy Wrath, with loosen'd rein,   85
Descending crush the rebel Train.
Let Horror and Destruction drear
Amid their tents the standard rear,

        Nor

Nor human habitant be found
Within their dome's capacious round: 90
Since, unprovok'd, with murth'rous view,
Whom Thou haſt ſmitten they purſue,
And ſeek, inſtinct with cruel joy,
The Man of ſorrows to deſtroy.
Let Each (for nought their hearts could bend;) 95
From depth to depth in ſin deſcend,
Ne'er, touch'd by healing Mercy, ſee
The path that leads to Bliſs and Thee,
Nor let them, 'mid thy choſen Band,
In life's fair page recorded ſtand. 100
And O! while preſs'd with ills I lie,
Caſt on my ſtate a pitying eye,
And let thy Mercy to my grief
In full ſufficience yield relief.
So ſhall thy name my tranſport raiſe, 105
And dictate to my lips thy praiſe.
To Thee my voice the ſong ſhall rear;
Nor ſhall the hoof'd and horned Steer,
New draughted from the fat'ning field,
A Sacrifice ſo grateful yield. 110
Ye humble Souls, that ſeek his aid,
His Love, in my releaſe diſplay'd,
His Love your dying hearts ſhall chear,
Who ſtoops the helpleſs poor to hear,
That, injur'd in his Cauſe, complain, 115
And captive drag the ſervile chain.
O praiſe him, Heav'n, and Seas, and Earth,
And All whom Nature wakes to birth:

Him

Him praise, who *Sion* deigns to shield,
Whose hand shall *Judah*'s Cities build, 120
And bid her Sons the Land divide,
Where unmolested shall reside,
Through rolling Time's extended Year,
A Race devoted to his fear.

PSALM LXX.

1.

HASTE to my aid, my Saviour, haste;
My Soul, by hostile numbers chas'd,
 To Thee directs its pray'r:
In wild confusion backward borne
Their wish defeated let them mourn,
 And lost in empty air.

2.

Be shame their just reward assign'd,
While round me with relentless mind
 Derision's shout they raise:
Thy Bliss let All who seek thee share,
And, taught thy Love, that Love declare
 In songs of ceaseless praise.

3.

While These in thy Salvation joy,
Increasing griefs my thought employ,
 And speediest aid demand.
My Helper and Redeemer, hear;
O, instant in my cause appear,
 And reach thy saving hand.

PSALM

PSALM LXXI.

ON Thee my Soul, with steady frame,
  (O blast not Thou my hope with shame)
On Thee my Soul its trust has staid,
And asks thy Justice to its aid:
Thy Servant, God of Gods supreme,   5
O hear, and hasten to redeem.
Be Thou my Rock, and safe Resort;—
My Rock thou art, my strongest Fort:
Thy lips my rescue have decreed,
And bid each threaten'd ill recede: 10
Haste then, thy promis'd help bestow,
And save me from th' invading foe,
Whose heart, with impious rage inflam'd,
Thy heav'nly precept has disclaim'd.
On Thee my hopes supported stand;   15
My Life from earliest youth thy hand
(That Life which first from Thee began,)
Preserv'd, and led me up to Man.
When lodg'd within the womb I lay,
Thy Care produc'd me to the day,   20
And, while that Care my years prolongs,
Thy Name shall animate my songs.
Though Crouds, with silent gaze, in Me
A spectacle of wonder see,
Amidst my grief, amidst my pain,   25
Thy Love shall still my faith sustain.
Thy arm in my relief employ,
That soon, my hope absorb'd in joy,

From op'ning dawn to clofing eve
Thy praifes on my tongue may live. 30
O let me not, Almighty Friend,
While with a weight of Age I bend,
And wearied Nature's fuccours fail,
The abfence of thine aid bewail.
" Behold (fuch words the ranc'rous heart 35
Suggefts, while, pleas'd, with fecret art
My foes the deathful fnare provide,)
" A Wretch whom God has caft afide:
" Purfue, and mark him for the grave;
" Purfue; for None is nigh to fave." 40
My God, my God, depart not far,
But hafte, and make my life thy care.
Let Shame, let Death their deeds repay,
Who wifh my guiltlefs foul their prey,
And black Difgrace their name o'erfpread, 45
Who aim their mifchiefs at my head.
My heart fhall ftill on Thee depend;
My thankful voice to Thee afcend,
And, through the day, my God and King,
Thy Juftice, thy Salvation, fing, 50
Yet ne'er, O ne'er, in equal ftrain
The meafure of thy Love explain.
Strong in thy Might I take my way,
Thy Righteoufnefs my only ftay,
Whofe Leffons on my youthful breaft 55
Fair Wifdom's facred lines imprefs'd,
And taught me, each advancing hour,
To fpeak the wonders of thy Pow'r.

Recede

Recede not now, while grey with years
His hands to Thee thy Servant rears,   60
Nor e'er thy wonted help withhold,
Till, pleas'd, my tongue thy Acts has told:
Such Acts as shall the ear invite
Of All who now th' ethereal light
Injoy, and oft rehears'd engage   65
The wonder of each future age.
Thy Pow'r, thy Justice, let my lay
To Nations yet unborn display.
How glorious are thy Works, how great!
Say, What in Earth, or Heav'n's high seat,   70
What shall the searching eye to Thee
Or equal, Lord, or second, see?
How hast thou bid my soul to know
A long vicissitude of woe,
Yet, back return'd, with quick'ning ray   75
Hast chas'd each cloud of grief away!
Thy hand, when Earth had clos'd me round,
Has snatch'd me from the dark profound,
My head with endless honours bless'd,
And sooth'd my anxious thoughts to rest.   80
O Thou, whom, wrapt in holy fear,
The Sons of *Israel*'s Line revere;
Thy Truth my psalt'ry shall inspire,
And tune to loudest notes my lyre,
My willing lips with praise o'erflow,   85
My rescu'd Soul with transport glow.
From morn to night, indulgent Lord,
My tongue thy Justice shall record;

     O   That

That gave the period to my woes,
And whelm'd in shame my vaunting foes. 90

PSALM LXXII.

INSTRUCT, great God, the kingly heart,
  Nor cease thy guidance to impart,
Till, pleas'd, the Heir of *Judah*'s throne
Thy precept's full extent has known.
So shall his hand dispense thy Laws, 5
Prompt to defend the poor man's cause,
Peace from the fort-clad Mountain's brow
Descending bless the plains below,
And Justice from each rocky cell
Shall Violence and Fraud expell. 10
In Him the Souls to scorn consign'd
The Advocate and Friend shall find;
His arm their injur'd race shall right,
And crush the proud Oppressor's might.
Thy fear succeeding Times shall own, 15
Long as the Sun and waxing Moon,
With varied light, in swift career,
Alternate guide the circling year.
Behold his influence downward pour,
Delightful as the copious show'r, 20
Whose drops refresh the new-shorn plain,
And swell with life the foodful grain.
His Care the Just aloft shall raise,
Nor fair Prosperity his days
Desist to crown, till round the pole 25
The measur'd Months shall cease to roll.

From

From Sea to Sea his wide Command
Shall reach, and from *Euphrates'* strand
Through Realms of various tongue extend
Far as to Earth's remotest end.   30
To Him the Desert's Tribes shall kneel;
His Foes, that on their conqu'ring steel
Repos'd e'erwhile their frantic trust,
Shall prostrate fall, and lick the dust.
From *Tharsis* and each distant Isle   35
See vassal Kings with willing toil
Their presents bring: Before him meet
The Chiefs, at whose imperial feet
Arabia's far-divided shores
Prolific spread their richest stores.   40
Each Prince to Him shall homage pay,
Each Nation own his equal Sway.
He, when the helpless Poor shall cry,
Shall hear propitious from on high,
Health to their fainting souls convey,   45
And challenge from the Grave its prey.
Nor Fraud, nor Rapine's iron hand
Shall dare to touch the pious Band;
For sacred is their blood, and high
Its price in his paternal eye.   50
Long shall he live, and *Sheba*'s gold
In tributary heaps behold
Display'd, while Crouds shall suppliant bow,
His health the subject of their vow,
And through the length of days his fame   55
Aloud with thankful voice proclaim.

PSALM LXXII.

    Lift to the Mountain's height your eyes;
And see the yellow harvests rise,
Wide-waving, as the verdure spread
On *Lebanon*'s exalted head.   60
Behold his Cities o'er the plain
Pour from their gates a num'rous Train,
And healthful as the vernal Birth,
That shades with green the joyous Earth.
From age to age the Orb of day   65
His brighter glories shall survey,
While Man's whole Race his Love confess,
And, blest in Him, his Name shall bless.
    Exalt, exalt your heav'nly Lord,
The God by *Jacob*'s Sons ador'd,   70
Whose wondrous Acts to Him alone
Assert the everlasting Throne.
To Him in loftiest praises join,
And bless the Majesty divine;
That Majesty whose cloudless rays   75
O'er Earth's capacious round shall blaze,
To Him again in praises join;
O, bless the Majesty divine.

PSALM LXXIII.

YES: mightiest Lord! My soul has known
    Thy Love to *Israel*'s Offspring shown,
And owns the Bliss by Thee ordain'd
To Each who bears a heart unstain'd.
Yet griev'd awhile thy paths, my God,   5
With hesitating step I trod,

And, but for Thee, the faithful Guide,
My erring feet had fwerv'd afide,
As fix'd in happieft ftate I fee
The foes to Virtue, Truth, and Thee.   10
Health ftrings their nerves; and Death, (their hour
Approaching,) with remitted pow'r
And flow advance his eafy doom
Inflicting, bows them to the tomb.
Forbid the gen'ral lot to fhare   15
Of pain, affliction, want, and care,
The lawlefs Tribe with cruel fkill
Augment the woes that others feel.
Pride on their neck its chain has bound,
And Violence invefts them round.   20
Their fwelling eyes and pamper'd frame
Their boundlefs appetite proclaim:
Their wifhes by fuccefs outrun,
Their headlong wills controulment fhun;
And words with fury wing'd impart   25
The genuine dictates of their heart.
Lo, train'd to infolence and wrong,
Againft the Heav'ns their impious tongue
Defiance and reproach has hurl'd,
And unrefifted walks the world.   30
 Untaught to fcan thy wife Decree,
With wonder, Lord, thy People fee
Life's choiceft gifts their want fupply,
Whofe breafts thy ev'ry threat defy:
Who afk, " Shall He our acts furvey,   35
" Whofe hands th' ethereal fcepter fway?

PSALM LXXIII.

"Who sits inthron'd above the stars,
"To Earth's low scene extend his cares?"
    While daring Mortals thus each hour
Thee, Lord, insult, and brave thy pow'r,　　40
Yet, sunk in ease, and blest with health,
Amass in heaps their growing wealth,
In vain, (thy Servant cried,) in vain,
I purge my breast from ev'ry stain,
My acts conform to thy commands,　　45
And wash in innocence my hands.
Each day opprest with fiercest pains,
Thy scourge my chasten'd Soul sustains;
Each Morn, that rising streaks the sky,
Awakes me but to misery.　　50
My heart, while thus by grief assail'd,
In silence long its thought has veil'd,
Lest Doubts like mine thy Saints betray
From thy Decrees, great God, to stray.
Thy Conduct weigh'd, awhile my mind　　55
Its hidden Cause essay'd to find;
That Cause, as deeper it inquires,
Still farther from its search retires.
Thy Fane at length I seek; and there,
(My anxious soul effus'd in pray'r,)　　60
Instructed by thy Spirit, read
The period to their guilt decreed.
I see thee on the slipp'ry seat
Of high Ambition plant their feet,
Then mark them as they downward bend,　　65
And headlong to the earth descend.

How

How swift, how sudden is their fate!
What horrors, Lord, their death await!
Wrapt in Oblivion's shade they lie,
Their image vanish'd from the eye,   70
As the light fabrick of a Dream,
Dissolv'd by day's intruding beam.

   Such woes, in error's fetters chain'd,
Such heart-felt anguish, I sustain'd,
Insensate, as the Brutes that rove   75
Th' extended Wild, or shady Grove:
Yet still thy Care confess'd me thine;
My hand within the hand divine
Was lock'd; and, by thy Counsel led,
Life's maze I yet, secure, shall tread,   80
And wait till thy appointed hour
The promis'd Glory round me pour.
O say, in Heav'n's capacious round
What Friend like Thee my Soul has found;
Or who, great God, on Earth resides,   85
Whose love with thine my breast divides.
My heart, my flesh, have fail'd; but Thee
My lasting heritage I see;
Thy strength my fainting spirit chears,
And checks my grief, and calms my fears.   90

   Who, taught to spurn his equal sway,
From *Israel*'s God adult'rous stray,
His Justice, with reverseless doom,
In Life's full vigour shall consume;
While, warm with holy transport, I   95
To Him with sure success apply,

Him trust, and, guarded by his Care,
To Man's whole race his acts declare.

PSALM LXXIV.

O Thou, whose hand has *Israel* led,
  His fold enlarg'd, his pasture spread,
Why hast thou doom'd us thus to bear
A long exclusion from thy care?
Why thus beneath thy anger groan   5
The Flock whom Thou hast seal'd thine own?
Call to thy thought the sacred Band
Once own'd the purchase of thy hand:
The Heritage by Thee redeem'd;
Fair *Sion*'s Mount, where copious stream'd   10
Th' eternal light, and spoke her Shrine
The Seat of Majesty divine:
Lift to that Seat thy steps again;
See Desolation spread her reign
Around it, and its wide extent   15
Each mark of hostile rage present.
With clamours fierce a lawless Train
The silence of thy Courts profane,
And bid their standard to the skies
Aloft in haughty triumph rise.   20
As when the Woodman's stroke invades
The lofty Grove's thick-woven shades,
So throu h thy Temple's awful bounds
Now here now there the axe resounds;
And down in shapeless ruins fall   25
The sculptures fair that grac'd its wall,

PSALM LXXIV.

Rich with the forest's noblest spoil,
And wrought by Heav'n-directed toil.
Along the violated Dome
Th' intruding flames licentious roam,   30
While spacious Courts, and Tow'rs sublime,
Whose roofs through long-revolving time
With holy wonder struck each eye,
Now heap'd in dire confusion lie.
" Come, (thus th' insulting foe has cried,)   35
" Come, deal the vengeance far and wide;
" And let the flames with equal doom
" Each House of *Israel*'s God consume."
They speak: and, instant, all around
The blazing ruins strew the ground.   40
No more thy wonders to our eyes,
Blest signals of thy presence, rise;
No more the Prophet's lips thy will
In mystic Oracles reveal,
Or to thy People's view disclose   45
The destin'd period of their woes.
But say, O say, great God, how long
Thus unchastis'd the hostile tongue
Shall mock thy pow'r, thy fear disclaim,
And load with loud reproach thy Name.   50
While Crimes like these redress demand,
Why in thy bosom sleeps thy hand?
O pluck it forth, and let the foe
Repentant feel th' inflicted blow.
Thee from of old my King I see,   55
Nor knows my heart a Friend but Thee:

Thine

Thine Arm alone, in *Jacob*'s right,
Has turn'd each adverse pow'r to flight.
At thy command, the watry Deeps
Asunder stood, in liquid heaps   60
Suspended; 'midst their waves, his head
Low to thy stroke submitted, bled
The proud *Leviathan*; his Train
Around their mighty King are slain,
While Rapine waits upon the strand,   65
And calls from far her hungry Band,
That scatter'd range the Desert wide,
The promis'd banquet to divide.
Thy stroke the rock's dark entrails clave;
Forth from its depth the foaming wave   70
Sprang instant, and with lengthen'd train
Irriguous lav'd the thirsty plain.
Thy Mandate *Jordan*'s channel dried,
And backward roll'd its wondring tide.
By Thee prepar'd, the Night and Day   75
Alternate walk th' ethereal way;
Thy Art the Light's thin texture spun,
And with it cloth'd the jocund Sun;
Thy hand the Earth's vast fabrick rounds,
Its balance fixes, marks its bounds,   80
With summer's show'rs its glebe unbinds,
Or warps it with the wintry winds.
Parent of Nature! God supreme!
While Folly's Sons thy acts blaspheme,
O vindicate thy Name from wrong,   85
And silence the reproachful tongue.

PSALM LXXIV.

Let not the fangs of cruel pow'r
Thy trembling Turtle's life devour,
Nor dark Oblivion's shade our pain
For ever from thy thought detain.   90
O give the Flock that bears thy Name,
Thy fed'ral mercy yet to claim:
Behold within each cavern'd cell
Fraud, Violence, and Rapine dwell:
Behold; and let th' afflicted Poor,   95
From terror and from shame secure,
With grateful heart, and joyous tongue,
Wake to thy praise the hallow'd song.
Rise, mightiest Lord; thy cause defend:
Wide o'er a guilty Race extend   100
Thy rod, and let the needful blow
Repress the licence of the Foe,
Whose mad presumption ev'ry hour
With heighten'd rage insults thy pow'r.

PSALM LXXV.

THY Name, immortal God, thy Name
    Our love and highest praise shall claim,
Whose Acts attest thee ever near,
And plant within each heart thy fear.
To Me, to Me the hour is known,   5
When, seated on th' eternal Throne,
My Justice shall assert its Laws,
And arbitrate each dubious cause.
Though Earth's wide Reign before mine eye
Dissolv'd in wide confusion lie,   10

Secure

Secure from lapse its pillars stand,
And rest on my supporting hand.
Lift not the horn, ye Sons of pride,
(Aloud with fierce rebuke I cried,)
Lift not the horn; nor thus in vain,   15
With stubborn neck, and lip profane,
My Rule oppose, or madly deem
That boundless Wealth and Pow'r supreme,
Their course to East or West inclin'd,
Float casual on the wafting wind,   20
Or issue from the Climes, that blaze
Beneath the Sun's meridian rays:
That God, who erst the Heav'ns outspread,
The regal crown from head to head
Transfers: Wealth, Honour, Pow'r, his Doom   25
At will shall grant, at will resume.
His hand the full-charg'd cup presents,
While red with wrath its wine ferments,
Whose mixture Earth's rebellious Train
Low to its utmost dregs shall drain.   30
But I, with sacred transport fill'd,
To *Jacob*'s God my praise will yield;
Through Life's continu'd round, my tongue
Shall wake to Him the joyous song.
Behold me, conqu'ring in his right,   35
Now crush the horn of impious Might,
Now bid the Just, that prostrate lies,
With lifted head triumphant rise.

PSALM

PSALM LXXVI.

THY Confines, *Judah*, God have known,
His greatness *Israel*'s Offspring own,
His glories *Salem*'s temple fill,
And rest on *Sion*'s sacred hill.
There broke his hand the sword and shield, 5
And cast them useless on the field;
There snap'd the arrows wing'd with fire,
And bade the raging War expire.
O cloth'd with Majesty divine,
O say, what strength shall equal thine; 10
Not such the Mountains boast, whose seat
To Rapine's Sons a safe retreat
Present, and, neighb'ring to the sky,
With awful wonder strike the eye.
Who wont with spoils the earth to heap, 15
Now spoil'd themselves have slept their sleep:
Amaz'd the Chiefs were seen to stand;
Nor knew the once resistless hand
Its task, but, summon'd to their aid,
Shrunk trembling back, and disobey'd. 20
At thy rebuke, O *Jacob*'s God,
The Steed, whose hoofs in hostile blood
Were dipt, the Car that o'er the plain
Rush'd headlong on, nor heard the rein,
With horror struck confess thee nigh, 25
And wrapt in iron slumber lie.
Thou, Thou alone our fear shalt claim:
O who, when, kindled to a flame,

Thy Vengeance shall its debt demand,
Shall dare within thy sight to stand? 30
    Earth heard, when God the judgement gave,
And rose his injur'd Saints to save,
In silent dread beheld his look,
And instant to her centre shook.
While impious Crouds oppose thy Reign, 35
Thou, Lord, their fury shalt restrain,
Thy stroke correct their stubborn will,
And teach them at thy shrine to kneel.
Low to our God, ye Nations, bow,
Yield to his Name the faithful vow, 40
Him serve with fear, and duteous bring
Your presents to the heav'nly King;
That King, whose sword, in wrath applied,
Lops in mid growth the Tyrant's pride,
And threatful bids each earthly throne 45
His mightier sway submissive own.

PSALM LXXVII.

TO God my suppliant voice I rear,
    With holy violence his ear
Solicit, and expectant kneel,
Till He my inward anguish heal.
With stretch'd out hand, and restless thought, 5
Beset with woes, his aid I sought:
When night's dark shades the earth invest,
And weary Nature sinks to rest,
Still, deaf to comfort, I complain,
And give my struggling griefs the rein. 10

Now fix'd on God, to Him in pray'r
My fainting spirit pour'd its care,
And words, in artless form compos'd,
The tumult of my soul disclos'd:
Now, dumb with sorrow while I weep,
My eyes their ceaseless vigils keep:
Anon my mind its search began;
And back to distant years I ran,
That, big with wonders, to my tongue
Had yielded themes of joyous song,
And deep inquiry to my breast
At midnight's thoughtful hour suggest.
Will God a heart oppress'd as mine
For ever to its griefs resign?
Has Mercy from his bosom fled?
His Word with vain assurance fed
My hope? Forgets he to be kind?
And shall his Love, in wrath confin'd,
No more its wonted aid bestow,
Or fix a measure to my woe?
  Now Reason's pow'rs collected rise,
And thus each anxious doubt chastise.
Though prest with various ills I stand,
And mourn the changes of his hand,
His Works, atchiev'd in ages past,
Shall fix'd in my remembrance last,
His Wonders on my thought shall dwell,
My tongue his Acts unwearied tell.
For Sanctity thy counsel guides,
And o'er thy paths, Blest Sire, presides.

Where finds, O where, the searching eye
A God, with *Israel*'s God to vie?
Maker of All! At thy command
Revers'd the Laws of Nature stand;
Stupendous scenes thy Acts afford,   45
And bid the Nations know their Lord.
Let *Jacob* and let *Joseph* say,
How strong thy Arm to chase away
Each woe that waits thy People near,
Each danger that excites their fear.   50
The Deeps beheld thee, heav'nly King!
The Deeps beheld thee; and each Spring,
That rose from out their sandy bed,
Tumultuous own'd its sudden dread.
Incessant from the bursting cloud   55
Down stream'd the bidden rain; aloud
Peal'd the big thunder; through the sky
Thy flaming shafts were seen to fly,
And, as thy voice around the pole
In awful threats was heard to roll,   60
Earth trembling groan'd, while o'er her head
Its livid sheet the lightning spread.
Wide yawn'd the Flood from shore to shore,
And op'd a path unknown before,
While *Israel*'s Guardian and his God   65
With trackless step its channel trod.
As sheep to distant pastures led,
Secure thy People march'd, convey'd
By *Moses*' and by *Aaron*'s hand
To promis'd *Canaan*'s happy Land.   70

PSALM LXXVIII.

YE Nations, to my Law give ear,
　　The dictates of my lips revere,
While Heav'n-taught Parables they yield,
And Truths in myſtic ſong conceal'd:
Truths, which, from earlieſt ages heard,　　5
To Us in ſacred truſt transfer'd,
From Sire to Son ſucceſſive flow,
That lateſt times his praiſe may know,
Whoſe pow'r preſides o'er *Judah*'s Land,
And own the wonders of his hand.　　10
He, bounteous Parent of Mankind,
His Law to *Jacob*'s Race conſign'd,
Th' appointed Theme of ev'ry tongue;
That Children from their Children ſprung
The Bleſſings of his Love might learn,　　15
And grateful yield the juſt return,
Truſt in his Aid, his Works record,
And mark the Precepts of his Word:
Unlike the Fathers of their line,
Who, Rebels to the Will divine,　　20
Turn'd from that Word their ſtubborn ear,
Nor ſought his Love, nor own'd his Fear.
Such *Ephraim*'s ſons; a heartleſs train,
That, arm'd for war, but arm'd in vain,
With bows unbended from the fight　　25
In wild diſorder urg'd their flight.
His ſacred League, and juſt Decrees,
Th' Almighty Lord forgotten ſees,

His wonders by their Sires beheld
On *Nile*'s wide banks, and *Zoan*'s field.　　30
What hand but His from side to side
Could bid the foaming Deep divide,
In liquid heaps suspended stand,
And safe transmit the chosen Band?
That hand the cloud around them threw,　　35
Day's kindled fervors to subdue,
And, lit by Him, with friendly ray
The fire nocturnal led their way.
He saw, when faint with thirst they stood;
And, fast as from the boundless Flood,　　40
Call'd from the op'ning Rock, the wave
Its streams in full effusion gave,
And onward pour'd with headlong haste
Luxuriant lav'd the burning Waste:
Strange to relate! Yet, stranger still,　　45
That Waste beholds them, to his Will
Oppos'd, in heighten'd sin conspire,
And dare to wrath the heav'nly Sire,
While Each, insatiate, from his hands
Meat for their fancied want demands.　　50
" Will God, to give his People bread,
" A table in the Desert spread?
" Our eyes have own'd the flinty Rock
" Obsequious to his mighty stroke,
" And seen the streams, with lengthen'd train,　　55
" Run copious o'er the thirsty plain;
" But can his stores, exhaustless still,
" With flesh our hungring myriads fill?"

　　　　　　　　　　　　　　He

PSALM LXXVIII.

He hears, and now in kindling flames
His vengeance dire at *Israel* aims,   60
And (for their speech a heart betray'd
Distrustful of his promis'd aid,)
Opes to their wish the doors of heav'n,
While back the parting clouds are driv'n,
And, downward pour'd, th' ethereal grain   65
In wide profusion fills the plain:
Their wants the full supply have known,
And Angels' food and theirs are one.
The Winds, that o'er the Desert fly,
New paths, by Him directed, try,   70
And onward, through th' aerial way,
In flocks the vagrant fowls convey,
Till o'er their tents the cloud impends,
And down the living show'r descends,
Thick as the dust, or as the sand   75
That lies upon the sea-beat strand.
Fed to the full, th' insensate throng
At will the joyous feast prolong,
While o'er their heads the vengeful sword
Hangs viewless, and but waits the word   80
To snatch their Princes to the tomb,
And *Israel*'s choicest strength consume.
Yet suff'rings still to suff'rings join'd
Fail to correct their faithless mind,
Though shorten'd in duration flow   85
Their years, and measur'd out by woe.
Scourg'd by his wrath, his pow'r they own,
And humbled bow before his throne:

With

PSALM LXXVIII.

With seeming gratitude possess'd,
His arm each tongue their shield confess'd; 90
And " who so strong to save, they cry,
" As Thou, great Ruler of the Sky ?"
Dissembling praise their lips prepare,
And solemn mockery of pray'r,
While, deep within, a mind they nurse 95
To Truth and to his Laws averse.
Yet He their trespass could forgive,
And bid th' obdurate Sinners live;
Oft arts of mild persuasion tried,
And laid th' uplifted bolt aside; 100
Ev'n wrath with mercy mix'd applies,
Nor lets his whole displeasure rise.
Indulgent He their frame survey'd,
Of flesh and frailty knew them made,
A Wind, that life's short passage o'er 105
Flits transient, and returns no more.
The conscious Wilderness shall tell
How oft the thankless Race rebel;
How oft, by mercies unsubdu'd,
Their Maker, wise, and just, and good, 110
(While, frantic, to their will they bind
The Counsels of th' eternal mind,)
They grieve, and challenge to the test
His Pow'r, so late their Aid confest,
When *Cham*'s proud offspring felt his Hand 115
Diffusing vengeance through their Land,
And Scenes, each hour, to Nature new,
In dreadful series met their view.

Their

Their *Nile* corrupted now they mourn,
And, though with fiercest thirst they burn, 120
Start back, affrighted, from the flood;
For Ah! its channel foams with blood.
Athirst for human gore, the Fly
In countless legions fills the sky,
And swarming Frogs, where'er they tread, 125
With dire intrusion round them spread.
The Beetle, clust'ring on their trees,
Now hastes the ripen'd fruit to seize,
While Locusts fell the tiller's toil
Consume, and riot in the spoil. 130
The frost-burnt fig-trees fade and die,
Their vines by hailstones ruin'd lie;
The sturdy tenants of the stall
Beneath the rattling tempests fall,
The flocks, by fire ethereal slain, 135
In heaps promiscuous strew the plain.
Wrath, horror, trouble, at his word,
Quick on the guilty Race were pour'd,
And Angel-Forms with dreadful haste
From door to door vindictive past. 140
With course direct his Vengeance flew,
Its path, by Him instructed, knew,
And Pestilence with noxious breath
Sow'd through the air the seeds of death.
Now to the grave, with anguish torn, 145
Each Mother yields her eldest-born,
And *Egypt*, through her wasted shores,
The first-fruits of her strength deplores.

Now,

Now, *Israel*, shines the Day to Thee,
That bids thy captive Sons go free.   150
Safe as beneath the shepherd's care
The flocks from waste to waste repair,
Each hostile fear by Him dispell'd,
Their destin'd course his People held,
While deep beneath the whelming wave   155
Their proud Pursuers found a grave.
Behold them, borne to seats of rest,
Seats by his hallow'd presence blest,
With joyful step the Mount ascend,
By his victorious arm obtain'd.   160
The Tribes whom *Canaan*'s tents confine
(A lawless Race!) to *Jacob*'s Line,
Themselves by Heav'n's high Doom expell'd,
Their forfeited possessions yield.
Yet, like their Sires, perverse they prove, 165
Reject the offers of his Love,
And, rebels to his just command,
Elude the guidance of his hand,
As starts aslant the Bow of steel,
And faithless mocks the Archer's skill.   170

   On interdicted Hills uprais'd,
With impious flame their altars blaz'd,
While figures by the Artist made
Thy honours, mightiest Lord, invade.
See, urg'd to wrath, th' eternal Sire   175
From *Silo*'s hallow'd Tent retire,
And quit the seat so lov'd before,
Resolv'd with Man to dwell no more.

His

His Ark, inviolated shrine
Of Strength and Majesty divine,   180
Now wanders captive o'er the plains,
Where Guilt in all its horror reigns.
Prevailing foes, conven'd from far,
On *Israel* pour the tide of war,
While God his Houshold from on high   185
Beholds with alienated eye.
No Virgins to the nuptial band
Assenting give the plighted hand,
While, snatch'd by the devouring fire,
Their Sons in early youth expire.   190
The sword destruction round them spread,
Nor spar'd the Priest's anointed head;
Nor lives the Widow to bemoan
Her Husband's fate, but meets her own.
His People's cry th' Eternal hears;   195
As wak'd from sleep, his strength he rears,
Shouts like a Giant chear'd with wine,
And wrathful lifts the Arm divine:
Th' averted Foe that Arm confest,
With shame and dire disease oppress'd.   200
But where, O *Israel*, shall thy God
Returning chuse his blest Abode?
Nor *Ephraim*'s Dwelling to his eyes,
Nor Thine, *Manasseh*, grateful rise:
On *Judah*'s Tribe he plac'd his care;   205
Thy Temple, *Sion*, founded there,
From age to age his Love demands,
Fix'd as the ground whereon it stands.

That

PSALM LXXVIII.

That Tribe a *David*'s birth has known,
Rais'd from a sheep-fold to a Throne. 210
As o'er the waste the teeming ewes
His eye with wakeful care pursues,
A Voice arrests the youthful Swain,
And calls him from the humble plain,
O'er *Jacob*'s realms to stretch the rod, 215
And feed the Heritage of God.
He hears, and, while each kingly art
Thy succours to his breast impart,
(All-potent Lord!) with faithful mind
Absolves the charge by Thee assign'd. 220

PSALM LXXIX.

O *Israel*'s Father and his God!
The Heathen Pow'rs thy lov'd abode
Rapacious seize; the Heathen Pow'rs
Thy shrine profane; and *Salem*'s Tow'rs,
That struck with sacred awe the eye, 5
Now whelm'd in wide confusion lie.
Each Beast, each Bird that wings the air,
Thy slaughter'd Saints insatiate tear,
Whose blood beneath the Victor's sword
Like water on the earth was pour'd: 10
While pierc'd they lay with many a wound,
And scatter'd *Salem*'s walls around,
None wept their fall, or pitying gave
The cheap indulgence of a grave.
See on our heads each neighbour Foe 15
Reproach and fierce derision throw;

See, Lord, and say how long thine ire
Shall blaze with unextinguish'd fire,
How long thy Flock are doom'd to prove
The sad suspension of thy Love.   20
On Nations who thy Laws disown,
Nor yet, with humbled heart, have known
Thy Pow'r to fear, thy Name invoke,
On These, great God, inflict thy stroke;
On These,—who *Jacob*'s strength devour,   25
And ruin on his Dwelling pour.
O let not our transgressions past
Within thy breast remember'd last,
But haste, while helpless thus we grieve,
Thy long-lost People to relieve.   30
Blest Saviour! Let thy pow'r divine
Conspicuous in our rescue shine,
And *Israel*'s trespass purg'd away
Thy boundless clemency display.
Say, why should the reproaching Foe   35
His triumphs build on *Judah*'s woe,
And ask, while thus thy scourge we bear,
" Where's now your God, ye Outcasts, where?"
Behold, behold thy Servants slain;
Nor let their loud-tongued blood in vain   40
The vengeance of thine arm demand,
But give us o'er each hostile Land
To see thy Wrath terrific rise,
And Folly's impious Brood chastise.
O hear the wretched Captive's groan;   45
The Souls whom Death has mark'd his own

Propitious save; the ceaseless wrongs,
By hands profane, and daring tongues,
Repeated, in thy balance weigh,
And sev'nfold to thy foes repay. 50
So shall the Flock acknowledg'd thine
To Thee in grateful praises join,
And, long as *Israel* boasts a name,
From sire to son transmit thy fame.

PSALM LXXX.

SHEPHERD of *Israel*, bow thine ear;
O Thou our pray'r indulgent hear,
Who *Joseph*'s pasture hast prepar'd,
His Guide by day, by night his Guard.
Betwixt the Cherubs seated high, 5
Glad with thy beams our longing eye:
With All who from *Manasses* claim
Their birth, and All of *Ephraim*'s name,
Each hostile pow'r by Thee o'erthrown,
Let *Benjamin* thy presence own; 10
Thine aid, great God, intreated give,
And teach our fainting hope to live.
O turn us, Lord, thy face display,
And grief and fear shall fly away.
How long shall *Israel*'s Offspring see 15
Thy wrath (while thus with bended knee
Their supplicating hands they spread,)
Smoke unextinguish'd o'er their head?
Her food the bread of tears, her draught
With sorrow's largest mixture fraught, 20

Sad

Sad *Sion* sees contending foes
Her sons, their destin'd prey, inclose,
And hears, with inward anguish torn,
The shouts of Obloquy and Scorn.
  O turn us, Lord, thy face display,
And grief and fear shall fly away.
  Transplanted by thy fost'ring hand,
Behold a Vine from *Egypt*'s Land
(Each Pow'r in adverse league combin'd
To just excision first consign'd,)
To *Canaan*'s shores convey'd: its bed
By Thee prepar'd, its root outspread
Far as the utmost coast extends;
While o'er the Hills its shade ascends,
And round the Cedar's loftiest boughs
Its cov'ring veil luxuriant throws.
Long cherish'd by thy care it stood;
Here, verging tow'rd th' *Assyrian* Flood,
In circuit wide the earth it crown'd,
And, There, the Ocean mark'd its bound.
But now, in sad reverse, (Ah! why?)
By Thee o'erthrown its fences lie,
Its fruits expos'd beside the way,
To each rapacious hand a prey.
The savage Boar with restless toil
Uproots it from the loosen'd soil,
And ev'ry Monster of the wood
Crops from its branch the obvious food.
Leader of Hosts, and *Israel*'s Lord!
Return: Thy succours oft implor'd

PSALM LXXX.

Extend: from Heav'n's high seat incline
Thy eyes, and visit this thy Vine.
Behold the offspring of thy hand,
'The Plant, which Thou hadst bid to stand,
And strengthen'd by thy pow'r defy   55
Each storm that rends the wintry sky:
The gath'ring flames its trunk surround,
Its ruin'd honours strew the ground.
Beneath the terrors of thine eye
We tremble, Lord, we faint, we die.   60
O let the Man whom, arm'd with might,
Thy hand ordains our cause to right,
By Thee, great God, supported stand;
And save, O save, a sinking Land,
So ne'er shall Sin our steps betray   65
Again in devious paths to stray,
But while, by Thee redeem'd, we brave
The threats of the devouring grave,
Each knee in pray'r to Thee shall bend,
Thy praise from ev'ry tongue ascend.   70
　O turn us, Lord, thy face display,
And grief and fear shall fly away.

PSALM LXXXI.

TO God our Strength exalt the song,
　To *Jacob*'s Lord the note prolong:
Come, take the Hymn, the timbrel ring,
Praise on the harp your heav'nly King;
Strike into life the trembling wire,   5
With loudest blasts the trump inspire;

For see the Moon with recent horn
Lead joyous on the festal Morn,
Whose hallow'd mirth to *Israel*'s Tribes
Thy Mandate, mightiest Lord, prescribes.　10
Its just observance *Joseph* learn'd,
When, pleas'd, with parting step he spurn'd
The ruthless soil, along whose shore
A tongue of sound unheard before
His ear had wounded.—I, his God,　15
I from his shoulders took the load;
I from the clay his toiling hands
Releas'd, and burst his stubborn bands.
O Thou, the voice of whose distress
From out the thunder's dark recess,　20
Propitious to thy pray'r, I heard;
In whose defence my arm I rear'd;
Whose faith my light inflictions tried
Near *Meribah*'s contentious tide,
O *Israel!*—with attentive ear　25
Thy Maker's just injunction hear.
Let none thy homage claim but Me,
Nor bow to foreign Gods the knee;
Jehovah only be thy Dread;
Thy footsteps He from *Egypt* led,　30
And gracious bids thee wide extend
Thy lap, while down his gifts descend,
And streaming copious from on high
Yield to thy wish the full supply.
Thus spake my Voice, but spake in vain;　35
Th' obdurate Race with fierce disdain,

Resolv'd their error to pursue,
Back from my yoke their neck withdrew.
No more their frenzy I restrain,
But give their wild desires the rein,   40
And leave them, guideless, to fulfill
The dictates of a headlong Will.
O had my People in their breast,
By heav'nly Discipline impress'd,
The lessons of my Love retain'd,   45
And trod the path by Me ordain'd!
When forth to War thy troops were led,
Myself, O *Israel*, at their head
Had met the Battle on its way,
And, while to time's remotest day   50
Each foe reluctant own'd thy pow'r,
To ease thy want, its purest flour
Th' augmented harvest had bestow'd,
And honey from the rock had flow'd.

PSALM LXXXII.

WHILE, cloth'd with pow'r divine, their bar
   Earth's Lords have fix'd, a mightier far
Amidst the Consistory stands,
And justice from their lips demands.
How long shall your unequal scale   5
Thus bid the impious cause prevail?
Let Law the Orphan's claim secure;
Lend to the helpless and the poor
Your willing ear; assert their right,
And save them from oppressive might.   10

PSALM LXXXII.

In vain I call: Their stubborn mind
To error's full excess resign'd,
'Through mazy glooms, to Wisdom's ray
Impervious, onward still they stray,
While Earth the dire confusion feels,   15
And, groaning, to her centre reels.
Gods Ye were nam'd; Earth's tribes in You
The Sons of Heav'n's high Monarch view;
But Death your frailty shall betray,
And mix with vulgar mould your clay.   20
   Rise, mightiest King, to judgement rise,
Th' oppress'd redeem, the proud chastise,
Till Man's whole offspring Thee alone
Their Lord and just Possessor own.

PSALM LXXXIII.

MY God, no longer silent stand;
No longer let thy pow'rful hand
Withhold its oft requested aid,
While thus thy foes our peace invade,
In mingled tumult round us rise,   5
And brave with lifted head the skies.
Behold them, Lord, their arts employ,
The Heav'n-rais'd People to destroy,
The Souls, whom with thy favour crown'd
Thy secret presence wraps around.   10
  " Come, (thus, by lawless fury led,
" Aloud they cry,) destruction spread
" Along their desolated shore,
" Till *Israel*'s name be heard no more."

Their

Their leagues, their plans, with frantic aim, 15
Against Omnipotence they frame;
And, fir'd to rage, with fierce alarms
The headlong Nations rush to arms.
The tents of *Edom* o'er the plain
Here vomit forth their impious train, 20
While with the Sons of *Ismael*'s line
The harness'd *Agaræans* join.
Here *Gebal*, *Moab*, *Ammon* stand,
And *Amalec*'s unconquer'd Band.
See, fearless, with imperial *Tyre* 25
Philistia's habitants conspire;
See *Assur* draw the hostile blade,
And lend to *Lot*'s vile Race his aid.
But give them, Lord, thine Arm to feel,
That Arm that made fierce *Midian* reel, 30
And to th' expecting Mother's pride
Her *Sisera*'s return denied;
That *Jabin*'s warlike troops subdu'd
Near antient *Kison*'s purpled flood,
While *Endor Israel*'s foes beheld 35
Inrich with slaughter'd heaps her field.
As *Oreb* and as *Zeeb* o'erthrown,
Beneath thy terrors let them groan;
What woes thy sin-chastising sword
On *Zebah* and *Zalmunna* pour'd, 40
Such let their Princes, Lord, endure,
Who vaunting to their arms insure
The Land by holy Patriarchs trod,
The Heritage of *Jacob*'s God.

As

PSALM LXXXIII.

As chaff, as stubble, let them fly, 45
That driv'n by winds obscure the sky.
Swift as the fiery deluge strays,
And wraps the forest in its blaze,
Or, furious, onward as it pours,
The mountain's shaggy waste devours, 50
Pursue them, mightiest Lord, pursue,
And let thy vengeance, to their view
Presented, whelm their souls in dread,
And burst in tempests o'er their head.
With wild confusion clothe their cheek, 55
And teach them, Lord, thy Name to seek,
While ruin, death, and shame, they see
To each ordain'd that errs from Thee.
" *Jehovah*, shall the Rebels cry,
" *Jehovah* only reigns on high, 60
" And o'er the Earth from day to day
" Asserts his everlasting Sway."

PSALM LXXXIV.

HOW sweet thy Dwellings, Lord, how fair!
What Peace, what Bliss, inhabit there!
With ardent hope, with strong desire,
My heart, my flesh, to Thee aspire;
I burn to tread thy Courts, and Thee, 5
My God, the living God, to see.
  Eternal King, within thy Dome
The Sparrow finds her peaceful home;
With her the Dove, a licens'd Guest,
Assiduous tends her infant nest, 10

And

And to thy Altar's sure defence
Commits th' unfeather'd innocence.
Blest, who, like these, from day to day
Within thy House permitted stay,
Whose joyous tongue thy Mercies raise   15
To Hymns of gratitude and praise.
Blest, who, their strength on Thee reclin'd,
Thy Seat explore with constant mind,
And, *Salem*'s distant tow'rs in view,
With active zeal their way pursue: 20
Secure the thirsty Vale they tread,
While, call'd from out their sandy bed,
(As down in grateful show'rs distill'd
The Heav'ns their kindliest moisture yield,)
The copious springs their steps beguile,   25
And bid the chearless Desert smile.
From stage to stage advancing still,
Behold them reach fair *Sion*'s hill,
And, prostrate at her hallow'd shrine,
Adore the Majesty divine.   30
O Thou, whom Heav'n's high Hosts revere,
God of our Fathers, bow thine ear:
Look down, our only Hope! look down;
Behold us, but without a frown,
And let thy beams, in mercy shed,   35
Stream copious on th' anointed head.
One day if in thy Courts I dwell,
That day a thousand shall excell:
Amidst the menial tribe to wait,
And guard th' approaches of thy gate,   40

Far

PSALM LXXXIV.

Far happier task my soul should find,
Than, mix'd with Men of impious mind,
To see the proud pavilion spread
Its dazzling splendors o'er my head.
Thou, Lord, art *Israel*'s Sun and Shield; 45
Thy Love shall grace and glory yield,
Nor e'er permit the pious train
Thy gifts to ask, and ask in vain.
Blest, who in confidence of pray'r
To Thee, great God, resign their care. 50

PSALM LXXXV.

OUR eyes, great God, have seen thy grace
Its beams effuse on *Jacob*'s race,
Loose from their chains the captive Band,
And call them to their native land.
Thy Mercy, Lord, their woes has heal'd, 5
Their trespass hid, their pardon seal'd,
Check'd in mid course thy dreadful ire,
And bid its kindled flames expire.
O grant us still thy Love to share;
God of our health! accept the pray'r, 10
That seeks thy clemency to win,
And cleanse, O cleanse us from our sin.
Say shall thy Wrath perpetual burn?
And wilt thou ne'er, appeas'd, return
Thy quick'ning influence to impart, 15
And wake to mirth each grateful heart,
While *Israel*'s rescu'd Tribes in Thee
Their Bliss and full Salvation see?

No longer, heav'nly Sire, delay
Thy wonted Mercy to display,   20
But let thy All-disposing Will
Thy People's stedfast hope fulfill.
Rev'rent I wait, nor silence break,
Till Heav'n's high Lord his purpose speak.
What shall he speak, but Peace, to Thee,   25
O *Israel?* What, but Joy, decree
To Each whose heart his precept learns,
Nor back to folly's path returns?
Behold, ye Souls that own his fear,
Behold your wish'd Redemption near;   30
See Glory, bursting from the Skies,
O'er *Judah*'s Land effulgent rise,
And fix amidst her coasts its seat;
There Verity and Mercy meet,
With mutual step advancing; There   35
Shall Peace and Justice, heav'nly Pair,
To lasting compact onward move,
Seal'd by the kiss of sacred Love.
Truth from thy furrows, Earth, shall spring,
And Righteousness, her healing wing   40
Expanded, downward cast her eye,
While Heav'n's great Monarch from on high
Shall crown th' expecting Lab'rer's toil,
And bless with full increase our soil:
She, as on earth thy feet shall tread,   45
Shall march direct, with lifted head
Preceding, and with duteous care
Thy path, eternal King, prepare.

PSALM

PSALM LXXXVI.

LORD! to my wants thy ear incline;
   Behold me, as with grief I pine;
My hope confirm, and guard from ill
A foul subjected to thy Will.
From rising to declining day
To Thee with fervent lip I pray:
Propitious, to thy servant's heart
Thy chearing influence impart:
To Thee, to Thee I vent my care;
I know thee, Lord, nor flow to spare,
Nor weak to vindicate from harm
The Souls with pure devotion warm.
My days with sorrow clouded o'er,
Thy wonted succours I implore:
Regard me, gracious; nor forbear
The voice of my request to hear.
For who, among the Seats divine,
Shall boast or Pow'r or Works like Thine?
Behold, their Maker taught to own,
Earth's future Sons before thy throne
In *Sion* suppliant kneel, and raise
To *Israel*'s God their joyful Lays.
Eternal Excellence! Thy hand
At will shall Nature's pow'rs command;
Thy wonders, through her confines wide,
She speaks, nor owns a God beside.
O give me, Lord, thy paths to tread,
And, while thy Truth my steps shall lead,

(The faithful Guide by Thee aſſign'd,)
Train to thy fear my willing mind. 30
My heart, by ſacred zeal impell'd,
To Thee the grateful ſong ſhall yield;
Long as I breathe the vital air,
Thy Love my loudeſt praiſe ſhall ſhare,
Whoſe aid my ſoul with health has crown'd, 35
And ſnatch'd me from the pit profound.
Thou ſeeſt, my God, the Sons of Pride,
In leagues of violence allied,
(Thy fear behind them thrown) my way
Surround, and mark me for their prey: 40
But well my great Preſerver knows
To weigh and to relieve my woes;
Long is thy patience, ſlow thine ire;
Eternal Mercy, mightieſt Sire,
Thy word (on that my truſt I build;) 45
And unrepenting Truth have ſeal'd.
My griefs with tend'reſt pity view,
With ſtrength thy Servant's heart renew,
And inſtant from th' expecting grave
The Offspring of thy Handmaid ſave. 50
O grant me, Lord, ſome fav'ring ſign,
Some pledge that may beſpeak me Thine,
That, ſtung with ſhame, my foes may ſee
What Aid, what Bliſs, I boaſt in Thee.

PSALM LXXXVII.

FIX'D on the holy Mountains stand
   Thy deep foundations: *Jacob*'s Land,
Throughout its wide-extended coasts,
No City, beauteous *Sion*, boasts,
Whose hallow'd gates have shar'd, like thine,   5
The favour of the hand divine.
Thee God the Mansion of his rest,
And Seat of Empire has confess'd,
While thus aloud to latest days
His heav'nly Edict speaks thy praise.   10
   Amidst the Souls that own my sway,
And learn my precepts to obey,
Thy Sons, O *Nile*, shall find a place,
And *Babylon*'s accepted Race;
Nor thine, O *Tyre*, nor, *Midian*, thine,   15
Nor whom *Philistia*'s bounds confine,
Excluded from my thought shall stand,
But mix with *Sion*'s sacred Band.
Each tenant of the peopled Earth
Shall claim from Her his happy birth: 20
Aliens no more, within her Seat
Behold th' united Myriads meet,
And joyous tread her blest Abode,
The *Israel* and the Heirs of God:
That God, whose pow'r upholds her State,   25
And seals to endless time her date.
When on the page, whose wide extent
Shall *Adam*'s num'rous Line present,

Each Kindred, Family, and Tribe,
Th' eternal Cenfor fhall infcribe, 30
His hand th' adopted Names fhall there
Thy Natives, *Solyma*, declare,
And bid them with thy Sons refide,
In concord's ftricteft bands allied.

   Hark, how the trump, and tuneful tongue, 35
The facred Jubilee prolong,
To notes of loudeft triumph rife,
And echo to the diftant fkies:
While I (thy Maker, God, and King,)
I, *Salem*, bid the living Spring 40
Amid thee yield its copious ftore,
And crown with health thy happy fhore.

PSALM LXXXVIII.

GOD of my health! To Thee by day,
   To Thee by night, aloud I pray:
O bend thine ear, and let my cries
Accepted to thy throne arife.
Satiate of griefs, with downward feet 5
I feek the hollow grave's retreat,
And, ftrengthlefs, mingle with the train,
That fill its melancholy reign.
A Gueft familiar of the Dead,
Lo, in the duft I make my bed, 10
As One, on whom thy ftroke its aim
Directs, and blots from earth his name.
As, loft to ev'ry human eye,
Deep in the loweft pit I lie,

PSALM LXXXVIII.

Thy wrath incumbent whelms me o'er, 15
And all thy billows round me roar.
No friendly feet approach me nigh,
But backward, each, abhorrent fly;
While, in my prison faſt immur'd,
My eye with ſorrow's miſt obſcur'd, 20
With ceaſeleſs moan my ſuppliant hand
To Thee, great Monarch, I expand.
Shall, whom the bands of death infold,
The wonders of thy pow'r behold,
And, ſtarting from the tomb, thy Name 25
In hymns of joyful praiſe proclaim?
Shall echo on thy Mercies dwell
Amid the dark ſepulchral cell?
Or through Deſtruction's vaults profound
Thy Truth, eternal God, reſound? 30
Shall regions that exclude the day
Thy miracles to view diſplay,
And pale Oblivion's confines drear
The records of thy Juſtice hear?
To Thee I call; to Thee in pray'r 35
At earlieſt dawn diſcloſe my care:
Lord! why haſt Thou my ſoul repell'd?
Why thus thy quick'ning beams withheld?
E'er yet to manly years I grew,
My fainting heart thy terrors knew, 40
And through ſucceeding life ſuſtains
A long viciſſitude of pains.
While thus beneath thy wrath I groan;
While countleſs woes come rolling on,

PSALM LXXXVIII.

And o'er me, as a swelling Sea, 45
Hang imminent; remov'd by Thee,
Each Friend, that wont my board to share,
Each kind Consoler of my care,
As round I look, my sight evade,
And seek concealment's thickest shade. 50

PSALM LXXXIX.

MY grateful tongue, immortal King,
Thy Mercy shall for ever sing,
My verse to time's remotest day
Thy Truth in sacred notes display.
That Mercy (thus thy Voice mine ear 5
Bespeaks,) on firmest base I rear;
That Truth in Heav'n my lips command
From age to age confirm'd to stand.
My Love to *Jesse*'s Son reveal'd
Th' irrevocable Oath has seal'd. 10
Blest Object of my choice! Thy Line,
Protected by the hand divine,
In long descent thy Throne shall heir,
Nor rolling years their pow'r impair.
   Thy Acts, great God, Heav'n's lofty Seat 15
With awful wonder shall repeat;
And, while within thy hallow'd shrine
Thy Saints in humblest homage join,
Thy Truth to thankful mirth shall raise
Each heart, each tongue incite to praise. 20
O say, what strength shall vie with Thine?
What Name, among the Seats divine,

Of

PSALM LXXXIX.

Of equal excellence poſſeſs'd,
Thy ſov'reignty, great God, conteſt?
Ye Tribes, that form his choſen Choir,
Let *Iſrael*'s God your fear inſpire,
Ye Natives of each neighb'ring ſhore,
With proſtrate hearts his pow'r adore.
Thee, Lord, Heav'n's Hoſts their Leader own;
Thee Might unbounded, Thee alone,
With endleſs majeſty has crown'd,
And faith unſullied veſts thee round.
'Tis thine the Ocean's rage to guide,
And calm at will its ſwelling tide:
From Thee the deep-inflicted wound,
Her guilt's juſt portion, *Egypt* found;
When, rang'd in fight, the lawleſs Band
Thy pow'r, preſumptuous, durſt withſtand,
Each foe thine Arm beheld with dread,
And back in wild confuſion fled.
The Heav'n above, and Earth below,
Thee, Lord, their great Poſſeſſor know;
By Thee this Orb to being roſe,
And All that Nature's bounds incloſe.
From Thee amid th' aerial ſpace
The North and South aſſume their place;
While *Tabor*'s brow, with ev'ning red,
And Eaſtern *Hermon*'s unſhorn head,
Wide through their echoing groves thy name
In ſongs of grateful joy proclaim.
Strong is thy Arm; thy ſtedfaſt Will
Thy Hands with ſure effect fulfill;

While

While Justice, 'mid th' ethereal plain,
And Equity thy Throne sustain,
And white-rob'd Truth and Mercy fair   55
Thy steps precede, thy path prepare.
O, Blest the Tribes, whose willing ear
Awakes the festal shout to hear;
Who thankful see, where'er they tread,
Thy fav'ring beams around them spread.   60
How shall they joy from day to day
Thy boundless Mercy to display,
Thy Righteousness, indulgent Lord,
With holy confidence record,
Thy Strength their surest refuge deem,   65
Thy Grace their dignity supreme!

   Behold, ye Saints, behold a Shield
In *Israel*'s aid by God upheld;
Behold exalted to the Throne
A King, whom He has seal'd his own.   70
   Thy Visions, Lord, from Heav'n reveal'd,
The raptur'd Prophet has beheld;
And thus thy Voice in awful strains
The purpose of thy Love explains.
To One selected from thy Line   75
Thy safety, *Jacob*, I consign,
And, cloth'd with strength, before thy eyes
High o'er his Equals bid him rise.
See *David*, prompt my Will t' obey:
On Him th' important charge I lay,   80
And copious on his favour'd head
The consecrating unction shed.

PSALM LXXXIX.

My hand shall hold him fast; my care
From each assault, from ev'ry snare,
Shall guard him: with resistless stroke,   85
When hostile Crouds his wrath provoke,
My Arm shall crush the impious train,
And load with slaughter'd heaps the plain.
On Mercy and on Truth divine
Behold him (nor in vain,) recline   90
His trust, and, by my strength upborne,
Aloft, exulting, lift the horn;
While (such my Will;) o'er subject Lands
In wide extent are stretch'd his hands;
Beneath his left the Ocean rolls,   95
His right th' *Assyrian* Flood controuls.

    Thou art my Father, (thus my Name
His lips, instinct with grateful flame,
Aloud shall hail;) My God in Thee,
And Rock of sure defence, I see.   100
    Him, pleas'd, my Firstborn I avow,
Bid mightiest Kings before him bow,
And Blessings to his reach expand,
Insur'd by Compact's sacred band.
Transfer'd by Me from Sire to Son,   105
To Heav'n's extremest date his Throne
Shall last: If from my Laws his Line,
Ingrateful, shall their steps decline,
Fond (while their hearts reject my sway,)
In interdicted paths to stray,   110
My rod their trespass shall pursue,
My scourge their stubborn will subdue.

                              Yet

PSALM LXXXIX.

Yet never, never, shall my Love
From Him its steady beams remove;
Ne'er shall my Truth forget to guard 115
The promise by my lips declar'd.
To *David*, once, (nor need I more,)
Once by my Sanctity I swore,
That, cherish'd by my care, his Race
Thy Throne, O *Judah*, long shall grace; 120
Long as the Sun, with welcome ray,
Shall warmth and life to Earth convey,
Or Thou, O Moon, in circuit wide
The witness of my Compact glide.
Yet Ah! repuls'd, contemn'd, by Thee, 125
Th' Anointed of thy hand we see
No more thy plighted mercy share,
But, doom'd thy wrath, just God, to bear,
With countless woes contend: His Crown
Low in the dust by Thee is thrown; 130
No more his Forts ascend on high,
But, fal'n, in heapy ruins lie;
No more his Walls the War exclude;
But passers by with insult rude
His rights invade, and Nations round 135
His ear with keen reproaches wound.
Their hand by Thine uprais'd, each foe
Aims at his head the deathful blow;
With fiercest joy their bosom burns,
While back with edge rebated turns 140
His sword, and, thy support withheld,
His vanquish'd legions quit the field.

PSALM LXXXIX.

His pow'r extinct, his lustre gone,
On earth, subverted, lies his Throne:
Age on his Youth has stoln; and shame
With thickest cloud obscures his fame.

 How long shall I, with anguish torn,
Thy face, my God, averted mourn?
How long behold, in dire amaze,
Thy wrath with flames incessant blaze?
O weigh within thy thought my State!
How frail my life! how short its date!
Nor leave me, Lord, to deem (my mind
To dark inquietude resign'd,)
Thy plastic Art employ'd in vain,
Or Man created but to pain,
While thus through varied scenes of woe
With hast'ning step to death we go.
For Who shall boast, of human frame,
Exemption from his doom to claim,
Or, arm'd with native might, withstand
The Sepulchre's rapacious hand?

 Say, where is now the Love, O where,
Which erst thy lips to *David* sware?
That Love, by Truth eternal seal'd,
Again to view, great Father, yield:
O think what wrongs thy Servants bear,
Wrongs pour'd on Me in largest share,
As deep within my silent breast
Each offer'd insult I digest,
While impious Crouds his steps revile,
Whom Thou hast touch'd with sacred oil.

O wise

O wise in all thy Works! thy Name
Let Man's whole Race aloud proclaim,
And, grateful, through the length of days, 175
In ceaseless songs repeat thy praise.

PSALM XC.

THEE, Lord, their refuge, Thee alone,
   From earliest age thy People own:
E'er yet the Mountains rose to birth,
E'er yet their form the Heav'ns and Earth
Assum'd, Thou cloth'd in light divine 5
Hast shone; and shalt for ever shine.
Thou to the sons of human kind
In short extension hast assign'd
Their term, and bid them, at its end,
Low to their native dust descend. 10
To Thee as Yesterday appears
The prospect of a thousand Years;
And Ages, roll'd successive on,
Quick as the circling Watch are gone,
That, 'midst the hours of soft repose, 15
With silent lapse unheeded flows.
As plants that drink the nightly show'r,
Refresh'd by sleep's irriguous pow'r
(Thy gift,) at Morn the mortal Race
With joyous bloom, and vernal grace, 20
Exulting flourish: Ev'ning nigh,
Cropt like the plant, they fade and die.
Thy hand with unremitted force
In mid progression stops our course,

While

While storms of vengeance round us roll,
And whelm in dread our conscious soul.
Thy eyes our inmost guilt can read;
Thy presence, Lord, on each misdeed,
That studious shuns the sight of day,
Resistless darts its searching ray.
See, fast as words dissolv'd in air,
While crimes on crimes thy Justice dare,
Our days in rapid flight consume,
And bear us onward to the tomb.

 Its date to sev'nty years confin'd,
If aught of life remain behind,
If Nature yet a ten years' day
Indulge us, e'er her debt we pay,
Our strength but weakness then we know,
And added Age but lengthen'd Woe.
Strip'd of our pride, we close our span,
And vanish from the eye of Man.

 O, who thy terrors justly weighs?
Who to thy pow'r submissive pays
Proportion'd homage? Teach us Thou
To count life's moments as they flow,
And, while its end our thoughts survey,
By Wisdom's line to guide our way.

 Return, All-potent Lord, return:
How long shall we thy absence mourn?
Return, and let thy wonted Love
With speediest aid our griefs remove:
Thy Mercy, to our Souls reveal'd,
Satiety of bliss shall yield,

And, while thy breath our life prolongs, 55
With grateful mirth inspire our tongues:
That Mercy, mightiest Lord, display;
And bid at length some happier day
Compensate with its joys the years
Consign'd to sorrow, groans, and tears. 60
Author of Good, thy Work mature;
Let *Israel*'s Tribes, in Thee secure,
From age to age the Blessings trace
Intail'd on their distinguish'd Race.
O may the Majesty divine 65
On Us its mildest beams incline,
And while, new Scenes of hope to view
Disclos'd, our labour we pursue,
Thy fav'ring hand with full success
That hope confirm, that labour bless. 70

PSALM XCI.

WHO makes Omnipotence his Aid,
    Who rests beneath *Jehovah*'s shade,
And joyful cries, " My God, in Thee
" My Fortress and my Hope I see,
" And, stedfast, on the Arm divine 5
" My trust in each distress recline,"
How blest that Man!—Thy Maker's care
Shall snatch thee from the hunter's snare:
When sick'ning Nature's pow'rs shall fail,
No fatal stroke shall Thee assail: 10
His wings around thee shall be spread,
His pinions guard thy favour'd head.

His

His Truth thy shield, nor terror pale
By night shall o'er thy soul prevail,
Nor shaft, that aims its flight by day, 15
Thy guiltless bosom shall dismay;
Nor Plague, that with gigantic stride
In darkness walks its circuit wide,
Nor sultry blast, whose dreaded breath
Taints the meridian air with death. 20
Though thousands by thy side are slain,
And myriads round thee press the plain,
No dart shall thy destruction dare,
Or wound whom God has bid to spare.
Each foe before thine eyes o'erthrown, 25
Still shalt thou pass in triumph on,
And, since thy heart, to God resign'd,
In him its refuge boasts to find,
Behold him on each impious head
The fulness of his vengeance shed. 30
No dangers shall thy path await,
Or touch thine interdicted gate.
While, round thee plac'd, th' Angelic Train
Thy steps with tend'rest care sustain,
Safe shalt thou walk through ways unknown, 35
Nor strike thy foot against the stone.
Go, fearless on the Dragon tread,
And press the prostrate Lion's head:
Behold the Tyrant of the wood
(In vain with youthful strength indu'd,) 40
Behold the Serpent (in his veins
Though half the poison of the plains

Be lodg'd,) before thee vanquish'd lie,
And close in death their languid eye.
  Thy duteous Zeal, thy filial Love, 45
I mark, and all thy Acts approve:
For this, thy head aloft I rear,
Bow to thy pray'r the willing ear,
Thy fears avert, thy griefs attend,
(Thy God, thy Guardian, and thy Friend,) 50
Thy years prolong; and to thy heart
My health-dispensing grace impart.

PSALM XCII.

HOW blest the task, with fervent heart
    To summon from the tuneful Art
Its succours, and thy Name record,
O Thou, whom Nature owns her Lord!
Thy boundless Mercies, heav'nly King, 5
At morning's earliest hour to sing,
And, rapt in praise, thy Truth to tell,
When night's dark shades around us dwell:
While with the ten-string'd instrument
The psaltry's measur'd strains consent, 10
And o'er the harp each liquid note
With solemn sound is taught to float.
How have thy Acts my wakeful breast
With rapt'rous gratitude impress'd!
How joys my tongue, with holy flame 15
Inspir'd, thy Wonders to proclaim!
Great are the Works thy hand has wrought,
And deep beyond all search thy Thought.
                                    Thy

PSALM XCII.

Thy Acts the minds of brutish mould
With unregarding eye behold,
And, strangers to thy wise design,
In erring censure madly join;
Nor know, that, when the impious Band
In guilty pomp conspicuous stand,
Fresh as the flow'r, or verdant blade,
In summer's fullest pride array'd,
Mature for death their heads they rear,
And swift destruction waits them near.
But Thou, above the starry plain,
In endless Majesty shalt reign:
Thy foes, eternal God, thy foes
In death's long sleep their eyes shall close,
And all, whose hearts thy pow'r defy,
In wide dispersion backward fly:
While I, by heav'nly Might upborne,
Strong as the Oryx lift the horn;
And o'er my head in copious show'rs
Thy Oil its richest fragrance pours.
When factious Crouds against me rise,
With scenes of triumph Thou my eyes
Shalt satiate, and their full defeat
My ears with happiest tidings greet.
Fair as amidst their native bed
The stately Palms their branches spread,
Or Cedars, tow'ring to the skies,
On *Lebanon*'s broad summit rise,
Within thy Courts the Just shall stand;
And, nourish'd by thy fost'ring hand,

Each adverse blast by Thee repell'd,
To latest age their fruits shall yield   50
In large increase, through life's whole round
With health and youthful verdure crown'd.
Thy Goodness shall their lips record,
(God of my strength!) thy ev'ry Word
In Truth's unvarying balance weigh'd,   55
Thy ev'ry Act by Justice sway'd.

PSALM XCIII.

1.

THE Lord th' eternal scepter rears,
　　And Nature's pow'r observant hears
　　　Whate'er his Will injoins:
His head with purest splendors crown'd,
With majesty he vests him round,
　　And girds with strength his loyns.

2.

Encircled by th' ethereal space,
And fix'd by Him on firmest base,
　　The Earth's vast Orb appears:
From earliest age, great God, thy Throne
Aloft in Heav'n prepar'd has shone;
　　Nor numbers Time thy years.

3.

A scene of horror strikes my eyes;
The Floods, my God, the Floods arise,
　　And lift their voice on high:
What pow'r shall curb the headlong tide?
What bid the swelling waves subside,
　　And clear the stormy sky?

4.

Thee, o'er all height exalted, Thee
The Deeps revere; at thy Decree
    The Waves their rage refign:
Fix'd are the Laws by Thee ordain'd;
And Truth and Sanctity unftain'd
    Adorn thy awful fhrine.

PSALM XCIV.

THOU God with vengeance arm'd, appear;
    Thou God with vengeance arm'd, whofe fear
The Earth (for Thee her Judge fhe knows,)
Submiffive owns, thy pow'r difclofe,
And inftant from thy feat arife,   5
Each proud tranfgreffor to chaftife.
How long fhall impious Crouds, how long,
With haughtieft infult arm their tongue?
How long in bitt'reft gall each word
Infufe, and boaft their conqu'ring fword?   10
Thy Flock, great God, their fury own;
Beneath their ftroke thy People groan:
Their hands, remorfelefs, to the tomb
The Widow and the Stranger doom;
Nor innocence nor tend'reft age   15
Can fhield the Orphan from their rage.
" Ne'er fhall our deeds in Heav'n be known,
" Or reach (they cry,) the diftant Throne
" Of *Ifrael*'s Lord."—Ye fools and blind!
Return, and feek a better mind.   20

Say

Say when shall Wisdom's light serene
Your souls from error's childhood wean?
Who knew to plant the ear, shall HE
Not hear? Who form'd the eye, not see?
Shall aught of guilt his search evade,   25
Who bids the Nations he has made,
Inform'd by his paternal care,
The gifts of various Science share,
Who Reason in the bosom pours,
Its growth improves, its fruit matures,   30
Each counsel of the human brain
Weighs in his scale, and stamps it vain?
 O, Blest the Man, for ever blest,
Whose faithful heart, by thee impress'd,
Eternal Teacher, from thy Laws   35
The lessons of his conduct draws;
Who shelter'd from the evil day
Its distant dangers shall survey,
And wait, till Thou the pit prepare
For Each whose crimes thy vengeance dare.   40
 Ne'er from the Children of his Love
Shall Heav'n's high Lord his care remove,
Or to the foes of *Israel*'s Line
His purchas'd Heritage resign:
For Judgement shall its seat assume,   45
Triumphant; while its equal doom
Each heart to Virtue's cause a friend
With conscious transport shall attend.
 Say, who with Me will plight the hand,
With Me the sons of guilt withstand?   50

Had

PSALM XCIV.

Had God his aiding pow'r withheld,
How had my soul in silence dwell'd!
But when my foot with fault'ring tread
Suggested to my thought a dread,
Thy Love, its speediest care applied, 55
Forbade my dubious steps to slide.
While deepest woe my bosom tries,
And thoughts with thoughts conflicting rise,
Thy comforts, Lord, my soul sustain,
And calm my fears, and sooth my pain. 60
Shall proud Oppression's lawless Chair
In thy Alliance find a share,
Whose Mandates to the impious Tribe
Their tasks of cruelty prescribe?
See willing Myriads, at its word 65
Assembled, grasp the hostile sword,
In guiltless blood their thirst allay,
And mark the Righteous for their prey.
But God, my refuge and my shield,
Firm on himself my trust shall build; 70
That Lord, whom *Israel*'s Sons adore,
Their sin shall in their lap restore,
Their steps with certain vengeance trace,
And root from earth th' offending Race.

PSALM XCV.

O Come, and to th' eternal King
  New songs of triumph let us sing;
With holy transport Him alone
The strength of our Salvation own;

Admitted

Admitted to his presence pay 5
The tribute of the grateful lay,
And, while his Acts our mirth inspire,
Wake to his praise the vocal lyre.
Extended wide beyond all bound,
Beyond all height, his pow'r is found, 10
Nor Lords, with Him, nor Gods beside
The honours of his Throne divide.
Earth's stores, throughout its inmost frame,
He, great Proprietor, shall claim;
Your Range, ye cloud-transcending Hills, 15
His pow'r commands, his presence fills.
Inrich'd by his prolific hand
In Him the All-productive Land,
In Him the Sea, that rounds its shore,
Their Maker and their Lord adore. 20
O come, and let your knees with mine
To Him in lowliest homage join;
In Him your God, your Father, see,
The People of his pasture Ye,
The Flock that guided by his care 25
The blessings of his bounty share.
O *Judah*, if in this thy day
My Will thou purpose to obey,
Steel not thy breast to truths divine,
As erst the Fathers of thy line; 30
Whose Bands th' inclosing Desert saw,
Rebellious to the Heav'n-taught Law,
With mad presumption from my hand
The signals of my pow'r demand;

       Indulg'd,

PSALM XCV.

Indulg'd, the wish'd for sight obtain;
And, seen, demand them yet again.
Through forty years the circling sun
Beheld their date of mercy run,
As, griev'd, I strove, but strove in vain,
Their growing frenzy to restrain:
Behold a Race, at length I cried,
Whose heart from Me has swerv'd aside,
(By Error's pow'r subdu'd,) nor known
That Wisdom's paths and Mine are one.
My Oath, for by Myself I swear,
My kindled anger shall declare,
And bar them from my Rest, decreed
To faithful *Abraham*'s chosen Seed.

PSALM XCVI.

SING to the Lord some new-taught Song;
   Earth, to his praise the note prolong:
Bless, bless his Name; from day to day
Let His Salvation prompt the lay,
Till Realms remote his Acts have known,
And Man's whole Race his Wonders own.
Great is the Lord, and great his Praise:
What God like Him our fear can raise?
Not such as Heathen Lands afford,
Created first, and then ador'd:
Creation Him its Lord avow'd,
When erst the arch of Heav'n he bow'd;
And Light and Majesty divine
With fadeless splendor grace his shrine.

Let

PSALM XCVI.

Let ev'ry People, ev'ry Tribe, 15
Pow'r, glory, strength, to Him ascribe:
Yield to his Name the honours due;
Oft to his Courts your way pursue
With solemn step, and joyful bring
The off'ring to your heav'nly King. 20
Before the Beauty of his shrine,
Ye Saints, in low prostration join:
Ye Natives of each distant shore,
His Pow'r revere; his Name adore.

O tell to All whom Earth sustains, 25
O tell them, that *Jehovah* reigns,
That, fix'd by His Almighty hand,
Its pond'rous Orb unmov'd shall stand,
And All who issue from its womb
Receive from Him th' unerring doom. 30
Exult, ye Heav'ns; exult, O Earth;
And, partner in the sacred mirth,
Let Ocean in its fulness rise,
And thunder to the distant skies.
Rich in his gifts, ye Fields, rejoice; 35
While in his praise the Woods their voice
Exalt, and hail with lowly nod
The presence of th' approaching God.
He comes, in awful pomp array'd,
He comes, to judge the World he made. 40
Truth shall with Him the cause decide,
And Equity his sentence guide.

PSALM XCVII.

To God belongs th' eternal Sway;
Let Earth with joy his Will obey:
Exult, ye Isles that crown the Main,
Blest in his mild auspicious Reign.
The station'd Clouds around him meet, 5
And Darkness rolls beneath his feet;
While Equity and Truth combine
To rear aloft his awful shrine.
Before him walks the wasting Fire;
Wrapt in the blast his foes expire; 10
While Earth, convuls'd, in dire dismay,
Beholds the forky lightnings play,
And down, like wax before the flame,
Down flows the Mountain's solid frame,
That late, ambitious, met the sky; 15
For God, the World's great Lord, is nigh.
His righteous Acts the Heav'ns display,
His fame from pole to pole convey,
And bid the Majesty divine
To ev'ry eye conspicuous shine. 20
Shame to the Wretch that wood and stones
The Objects of his homage owns,
And frantic to the Creature pays
The Maker's interverted praise.
Ye Gods, his sov'reign Might avow, 25
And rev'rent at his footstool bow.
 Well-pleas'd thy Counsels, Lord, to hear,
Imperial *Salem* bows the ear;

And *Judah*'s happy Daughters sing
The Mercies of th' eternal King.   30
Thou, Lord, in Majesty serene
Exalted o'er the Earth art seen:
What Pow'r, great God, shall boast a Name
Like Thine? Like Thee our homage claim?
 Ye Souls with Love divine impress'd;   35
Just to its precepts, Sin detest:
Each fear deliver'd to the wind,
In God your certain refuge find,
Whose pow'r protects the pious Band,
Though Myriads, leagu'd, against them stand.   40
To You, ye Good, to You alone
The seeds of heav'nly light are sown,
That wake within the human breast
Joys ne'er by human tongue express'd.
O crown'd with Mercies from above,   45
To God your grateful zeal approve:
His Sanctity revere; his Name
In hymns of loudest praise proclaim.

PSALM XCVIII.

SING to the God whom we adore;
 So sing, in lays unheard before,
The Mercies shown us from above,
The Wonders of redeeming Love:
His Hand, exerted in our aid,   5
His Hand those Wonders has display'd;
His holy Arm Salvation sends,
And Conquest on its stroke attends.

His

His Justice through the World has shin'd;
His Truth, with endless Mercy join'd, 10.
Now seals the promise of his Grace
To faithful *Abraham*'s chosen Race;
And Earth, to just obedience aw'd,
Has own'd her Saviour and her God.
Ye distant Realms, your voice employ 15
In shouts of gratitude and joy:
Let hymns of rapture swell each throat;
Call from the harp th' according note;
On the shrill trump your mirth prolong,
And sound the cornet to the song. 20
To Him who claims th' eternal sway,
To Him the vocal tribute pay:
Him let the hoarse-resounding Tide,
With All that in its depths reside,
Praise, thank, and bless, in loudest strains; 25
Him Earth, and All whom Earth sustains.
Ye Floods, triumphant clap the hand;
Ye cloud-topt Hills, exulting stand;
See, thron'd aloft in awful state,
While Man's whole Race his sentence wait, 30
The Judge supreme his scale assume;
And Equity directs the Doom.

PSALM XCIX.

I.

JEHOVAH reigns: Ye Nations own,
  With prostrate hearts, his sway:
Betwixt the Cherubs stands his Throne;
  Earth! tremble and obey.

PSALM XCIX.

2.

His Rule, in *Sion* long confeft,
    O'er All extends; his Name
Shall hallow with its fear each breaft,
    Each tongue with zeal inflame.

3.

Thy Pow'r with Equity allied
    Through time's long courfe has ftood:
Thy Judgements *Jacob*, Lord, has tried,
    And knows them juft and good.

4.

Let Each, with humble joy elate,
    Before thy footftool bow;
Thee, ceafelefs, praife: For who fo great,
    So holy, Lord, as Thou?

5.

By God with facred honours crown'd,
    See *Mofes*, *Aaron*, fee,
And *Samuel*, ever faithful found,
    To Him incline the knee.

6.

To Him the favour'd Three aloud
    The frequent Vow prefer'd,
And inftant from the pillar'd cloud
    His awful Anfwer heard.

7.

With wakeful zeal their bofoms burn'd;
    Obfervant of his Will,
With joy the heav'nly precept learn'd,
    And haften'd to fulfill.

PSALM XCIX.

8.

To Thee, great God, their ev'ry pray'r
  In full acceptance rose:
Thy hand their weakness knew to spare,
  And, pitying, heal'd their woes.

9.

Yet could thy Wrath, when Sin had dar'd
  Their erring breast to stain,
Deal to their guilt its just reward,
  And vindicate thy Reign.

10.

Let Each, with humble joy elate,
  On-*Sion*'s Mountain bow;
Thee, ceaseless, praise: For who so great,
  So holy, Lord, as Thou?

PSALM C.

YE Tribes of Earth, in God rejoice,
His presence hail with thankful voice;
To Him your willing homage pay,
And wake the tributary lay.
Submissive to his Will, in Him   5
Behold the God of Gods supreme:
With conscious wonder oft survey'd,
He, not Ourselves, our frame has made:
The subjects of his pow'r we stand,
The sheep that own his guiding hand.   10
" O, enter then his gates with praise,
To Him your loudest accents raise,
With grateful hearts his Love proclaim,
And bless, O bless, his awful Name.

For Truth in Him and Mercy live: 15
That Truth shall time itself survive;
That Mercy through the length of days
Unclouded pour its healing rays.

PSALM CI.

MERCY, Judgement, now my tongue
   Makes the subject of its Song:
Lord! to whom then shall I sing,
But to Thee, th' eternal King?
Wisdom shall my footsteps guide, 5
Nor permit my feet to slide,
Or from Thy All-perfect Way,
Lost in paths of Sin, to stray.
When, O when, celestial Guest,
Shall my roof with Thee be blest? 10
Lo! my heart with studious care
For thy presence I prepare,
And my Dwelling's full extent
Spotless to thy view present.
Ne'er shall my presumptuous hand 15
Dare to break thy just Command;
Ne'er within me shalt thou find
Aught that speaks a faithless mind.
Serv'd by none who serve not Thee,
Let me not the Impious see; 20
Let the wretch of froward heart
From my gate repuls'd depart;
And the Man of lofty eye,
Scornful mien, and stomach high,

And

PSALM CI.

And the Tongue to slander bred, 25
Learn my heaviest wrath to dread.
Come, ye Good and Just, O come,
Sure with Me to find a home:
Pleas'd I see the pious Band
Round my throne attendant stand, 30
And in sacred homage join
To their own great Lord and mine.
Hence ye Children of deceit,
From my threshold turn your feet:
Let the soul that dares a lye 35
Instant from my presence fly.
Soon, O *Judah*, shall my hand
Root th' offenders from thy Land;
Wrathful seize the rebel train;
And from sin's infectious stain 40
By my guilt-avenging rod
Purge the City of my God.

PSALM CII.

HEAR, Lord, my pray'r, and let my cries
   Accepted to thy throne arise:
O turn not Thou thy face away,
Nor longer my relief delay;
But mark my sorrows from on high, 5
And pitying to my call reply.
Fast as the mounting smoke decays,
On time's light pinion flit my days:
My bones the hearth's fierce heat sustain;
My heart the herbage of the plain 10

Resembles, o'er whose leaves have past
The fervors of the southern blast.
For ah! forgetful of my food,
Incessant o'er my griefs I brood,
While struggling groans their weight proclaim, 15
And waste with toil my languid frame.
Not the wide Desert's confines drear
Laments of louder accent hear,
When, 'midst its fens, with dismal note
The Pelican distends her throat, 20
Or to the winds in lengthen'd strains
The self-sequestring Owl complains;
Nor vents its sister-bird a moan
So deep, when on the roof alone
She sits; whose woes, like mine, affright 25
The silence of the tedious night.
From Morn, till Eve extend its veil,
Reproaches keen my ears assail;
And, leagu'd by mutual oaths, my foes
With fierce intent my steps inclose. 30
See ashes, scatter'd o'er my head,
Mix, undistinguish'd, with my bread;
See mingled tears my cup supply;
Since first thy wrathful Arm on high
Caught me amaz'd, and swiftly round 35
Reverting hurl'd me on the ground.
As fades the shadow of the sun,
With quick decline my moments run,
Just verging to their close: my face,
Its vernal bloom and youthful grace 40

Ex-

PSALM CII.

Extinguish'd, withers on the eye,
As plants beneath a hostile sky.
But Thou, Blest Guard of *Israel's* fold,
Shalt ages see on ages roll'd,
And, thron'd above, to endless days   45
Extend thy honour, name, and praise.
O rise, (th' appointed hour is come;)
Rise, mightiest Lord, thy Charge assume;
And let sad *Sion's* seat no more
The absence of thine aid deplore.   50
How lovely to thy Servants' eyes,
How lovely ev'n in ruin lies
Her hallow'd Wall! a pensive Throng,
They walk her fenceless courts along,
And, as her scatter'd wastes appear,   55
Drop on her dust the pitying tear.
How shall thy Name, great Sire, its dread
Through Earth's awaken'd regions spread!
How shall her Kings with deep dismay
Thy boundless Majesty survey,   60
When *Salem's* structures from their fall
Thy hand, propitious, shall recall,
While down th' eternal Glory pours,
Incircles with its blaze her tow'rs,
And speaks thy favour (oft implor'd,)   65
To *Israel's* exil'd Tribes restor'd!
Thy Acts the faithful pen shall trace,
And Myriads of the human Race,
Yet strangers to the birth, thy fame
In Songs of loudest note proclaim.   70

For

For He, beneath whose sacred seat
The starry Orbs their course repeat,
Th' eternal Ruler of the sky,
Has cast on Earth his equal eye,
Intent the injur'd cause to own,   75
To hear the helpless Captive's groan,
The Souls to death consign'd to save,
And snatch them from the greedy grave.
For this, through *Sion's* ample bound
Jehovah's Name shall oft resound,   80
Thy shouts, distinguish'd *Salem*, raise,
And wake thy tongue to hymns of praise:
See to thy Courts the Nations flow,
His just dominion taught to know,
And, Each with Thee in compact join'd,   85
Their hearts to his obedience bind.
'Twas He, whose unresisted force
In mid progression stop'd my course;
My healthful vigour reft away;
And hasten'd to its eve my day.   90
Spare, mightiest Lord! nor thus, I cried,
My brittle chain of years divide,
O Thou, of Life th' exhaustless Spring,
Invisible, Immortal King!
Thy hand the Earth's foundation laid,   95
Thy hand the Heav'n aloft display'd,
E'er yet along the vast profound
The restless Months began their round:
That Earth, that Heav'n's stupendous frame,
Corruption with permitted claim   100
Shall

PSALM CII.

Shall seize: But Thou, from Age secure,
Shalt self-existent still endure.
These, as the labours of the loom,
Shall Time with gradual force consume;
Till Thou, whose hand their texture spun, 105
When Time its stated course has run,
Again that pow'rful hand apply,
And fold them up, and lay them by;
While brighter Scenes, disclos'd to view,
Creation's varied face renew. 110
But varyings Thou hast none: Thy rays
With undiminish'd lustre blaze;
Thy years shall circumscription spurn,
And back upon themselves return,
In endless course revolving. Thee 115
Thy Saints their strong Support shall see,
And, rang'd in long succession, share
The gifts of thy paternal Care.

PSALM CIII.

AWAKE to praise, my Soul, and sing
The Mercies of th' eternal King:
O deep throughout thine inmost frame
Bless, bless the great *Jehovah*'s Name;
Nor cease with studious thought to trace 5
The Acts of that stupendous Grace,
That blots from Heav'n's record thy sin,
That, while thy passions war within,
Assuasive calms their furious strife,
And rescues from the pit thy life; 10

Bids countless blessings round thee rise;
Thy ev'ry wish with Good supplies;
Thy years renews in their decline;
And makes the Eagle's vigour thine,
That, stript of age, exulting springs, 15
And heav'nward spreads his recent wings.
'Tis God's, the friendless and the poor
From proud Oppression to secure.
His Ways to *Moses* stood reveal'd;
Thou, *Israel*, hast his Works beheld, 20
His breast with mercy fraught hast known,
To anger slow, to pity prone.
He ne'er with erring mortals knew
A ceaseless contest to pursue,
But, when their crimes his vengeance raise, 25
His wrath in mid effusion stays.
If e'er our trespass he chastise,
Not to its weight proportion'd rise
The just corrections of his hand,
But bounded by that Mercy stand, 30
That high as to the starry pole
Extends, and, far as from its goal
The Sun in daily circuit roves,
The humbled sinner's guilt removes.
What fondness for his infant Care 35
A Father's bosom learns to share,
Such from th' eternal Monarch claim
The Souls that rev'rent own his Name.
For well his eye our texture knows;
Sees that the dust's light grains compose 40
Our

PSALM CIII.

Our frame; and marks the days of Man
Contracted to the narrow span,
That measures to the herb its date,
Or bids the flow'r, in vig'rous state
Exalted, now the field adorn,   45
Now, by the passing tempest shorn,
At once its vernal pride resign,
And with'ring on the earth recline:
In swift decay behold it waste;
Nor knows the soil, whose bed it grac'd,   50
To witness to th' inquirer's view,
Where late the short-liv'd wonder grew.
But Thy Compassions, Lord, the Just
From age to age with stedfast trust
Shall own; Thy Righteousness their Race,   55
In long descent, shall joy to trace,
While pleas'd thy Compact they fulfill,
And frame to thy Decrees their will.
 His Seat above th' empyreal plain
Our God has fix'd; his equal Reign   60
Creation's utmost bounds confess:
His Name, ye Tribes Angelic, bless;
Who, cloth'd with might, his word obey,
And wing, as He directs, your way.
Him praise, ye bright ethereal Band,   65
That rang'd beneath his banner stand,
And Ye who round his Throne of State
With duteous zeal ministrant wait.
Ye Works of God, where'er his sway
Extends, your Maker's fame display;   70

Nor Thou, my Soul, forget to sing
The Mercies of th' eternal King.

PSALM CIV.

AWAKE, my Soul, to hymns of praise;
To God the song of triumph raise.
O cloth'd with majesty divine,
What pomp, what glory, Lord, are thine!
Light forms thy robe, and round thy head   5
The Heav'ns their ample curtain spread.
Thou know'st amid the fluid space
The strong-compacted beams to place,
That proof to wasting Ages lie,
And prop the chambers of the sky.   10
    Behold, aloft, the King of Kings,
Borne on the Wind's expanded wings,
(His Chariot by the Clouds supplied,)
Through Heav'n's wide realms triumphant ride.
Around him rang'd in awful state   15
Th' assembled Storms ministrant wait;
And Flames, attentive to fulfill
The dictates of his mighty Will.
On firmest base uprear'd, the Earth
To Him ascribes her wondrous birth.   20
He spake; and o'er each Mountain's head
The Deep its watry mantle spread:
He spake; and from the whelming flood
Again their tops emergent stood;
And fast adown their bending side   25
With refluent stream the Currents glide:

Aw'd

Aw'd by his ſtern rebuke they fly,
While peals of thunder rend the ſky,
In mingled tumult upward borne
Now to the mountain's height return,　　30
Now lodg'd within their peaceful bed
Along the winding vale are led,
And, taught their deſtin'd bounds to know,
No more th' affrighted Earth o'erflow,
But obvious to her uſe (their courſe　　35
By Nature's ever copious ſource
Supplied,) refreſh the hilly plain,
And life in all its forms ſuſtain.
Here ſtooping o'er the river's brink
The herds and flocks promiſcuous drink;　　40
There, 'mid the barren Deſert nurs'd,
The Wild-Aſs cools his burning thirſt:
While faſt beſide the murm'ring ſpring
The feather'd minſtrels ſit and ſing,
And ſhelter'd in the branches ſhun　　45
The fervors of the mid-day ſun.
His ſhow'rs with verdure crown the hills;
The earth with various fruits he fills:
Preventive of their wants, his aid
Yields to the Brute the ſpringing blade;　　50
For Man, chief object of his care,
His hands the foodful herb prepare,
The glad'ning wine, refreſhing oil,
And bread that ſtrings his nerves for toil.
By Him with genial moiſture fed　　55
The Trees their ſhades luxuriant ſpread;

The Cedars, nurtur'd by his hand,
On *Lebanon*'s high summit stand,
And weave their social boughs, design'd
A refuge for th' aerial kind: 60
While on the Fir-tree's spiry top
The vagrant Stork is seen to stop,
Where, cradled in their waving nest,
Her infant brood in safety rest.
See from the hills the Goats depend, 65
Or bounding from the cliff descend:
The lesser tribes, in furry pride
Array'd, the rock's dark caverns hide.

   Her way by Him prescrib'd, the Moon
Our seasons marks, and knows her own; 70
And taught by Him the Orb of day
Slopes in the West his parting ray.
Now Night from Ocean's bed ascends,
And o'er the earth her wings extends;
While favour'd by the friendly gloom 75
The sylvan race licentious roam:
The Lions chief with hideous roar
From God their needful food implore,
And eager for the wonted prey
Along the echoing Desert stray; 80
Till now, as Morn approaches nigh,
Back to their cavern'd haunts they fly,
Where, satiate with the bloody feast,
The lordly savage sinks to rest.
His care sufficient to the day, 85
Man to his labour takes his way,

His task at earliest dawn begun,
And ended with the setting sun.
Eternal Ruler of the Skies,
How various are thy Works, how wise! 90
Nor Earth alone beholds her shores
Inrich'd from thy exhaustless stores;
Alike, throughout their liquid reign,
Th' extended Seas thy gifts contain:
Beneath, unnumber'd reptiles swarm, 95
Of diff'rent size, of diff'rent form;
Above, the ships enormous glide,
Incumbent on the burthen'd tide;
And oft, the rolling waves between,
The huge Leviathan is seen, 100
There privileg'd by Thee to stray,
And wanton o'er the watry way.
Thy care, great God, sustains them All;
As, urg'd by hunger's furious call,
Expectant of the known supply, 105
To Thee they lift the asking eye,
And reap from thy extended hand
Whate'er their various wants demand.
If Thou thy face but turn away,
Their troubled looks their grief betray; 110
If Thou the vital air deny,
Behold them sicken, faint, and die;
Dust to its kindred dust returns,
And Earth her ruin'd offspring mourns:
But soon thy breath her loss supplies; 115
She sees a new-born race arise,

And, o'er her regions scatter'd wide,
The blessings of thy hand divide.
Thy Glory, fearless of decline,
Thy Glory, Lord, shall ever shine,   120
Thy Works in changeless order lie,
And glad their great Creator's eye.
Earth at thy look shall trembling stand,
" Conscious of sov'reign pow'r at hand,
And, touch'd by Thee, Almighty Sire,   125
The cloud-topt Hills in smoke aspire.
To God in ceaseless strains my tongue
Shall meditate the grateful song,
And, long as breath informs my frame,
The wonders of his Love proclaim,   130
Assur'd that his paternal ear
With full regard my voice will hear;
His Acts its unexhausted theme,
His Favour my Delight supreme.
Behold his wrath on Sinners shed;   135
Behold them number'd with the dead:
But Thou, my Soul, the hymn of praise
In loudest notes triumphant raise;
And let consenting Nations join
To bless with Me the Name divine.   140

PSALM CV.

COME, celebrate your God and King;
   Awake the song, awake the string;
His pow'r invoke; his praise proclaim;
And, faithful Heralds to his fame,

Aloud

PSALM CV.

Aloud declare, through ev'ry Land,
The Wonders of his mighty hand.
O let his Name your thought employ;
His Name, fit theme of highest joy:
Such joy may each for ever share,
Whose steps to *Salem*'s Fane repair:
O frequent seek that blest Abode,
O seek the face of *Jacob*'s God.
   The Acts of Heav'n's Almighty Lord
Let *Israel*'s thankful Sons record;
Ye Seed of *Abraham*, his Friend,
With joy to his Commands attend.
To You his presence stands confest;
His judgements Earth's wide Realms attest:
His Promise kind, and wise Decree,
Though Man forget, yet will not He;
The Oath confirm'd through periods past,
And doom'd to latest times to last;
To *Terah*'s Son, to *Isaac*, sworn,
And seal'd to Nations yet unborn.
The Compact to his Fathers made
See thus to *Jacob*'s hands convey'd:
" Arise, thou favour'd of thy God,
" And claim the Gift by Him bestow'd:
" Behold thy Sons their wide command
" Extend o'er *Canaan*'s fertile Land."
But when? or how? Their number view;
(It asks no toil;) a helpless Few,
Yet Strangers in its coast, their seat
Of future rest with weary feet
                       Ordain'd

Ordain'd to traverſe, long they roam, 35
And ſeek through diſtant climes a home.
Yet, privileg'd by Him from wrong,
Secure the Exiles march along:
Kings hear his dread reproof, nor dare
To hurt whom God has bid to ſpare. 40
" Touch, touch not Theſe; for on their heads
" My hand the ſacred unction ſheds:
" Your eyes in Them my Prophets ſee;
" And what they ſpeak, they ſpeak from Me."

He calls; and on the cultur'd ground 45
Life's needful ſtaff no more is found,
While Drought, incumbent o'er the plain,
Checks in mid growth the rip'ning grain.
Yet Mercy ſtill his Wrath outran;
Thy ſhores, O *Nile*, receive the Man, 50
Ordain'd the choſen Race to ſave,
Thy future Lord, though now thy Slave.
What though, his feet in fetters bound,
His ſoul th' afflicting irons wound,
Yet, *Joſeph*, patient bear thy lot: 55
Thy lips, with heav'nly ſcience fraught,
Shall ſoon the myſtic Dream explain,
That ends thy woes, and breaks thy chain.
The Monarch bids; the priſon door
Detains the injur'd Saint no more: 60
New honours now his wrongs repair;
The regal Palace to his care
Its wealth conſigns; and *Egypt*'s land
Bows to her Captive's wiſe command.

Ev'n Princes own'd with rev'rent awe 65
The dictates of his will their Law,
And Senates on his youthful tongue
In silent wonder list'ning hung.
But who is He, that, bow'd with years,
Now first on *Mizraim*'s Coast appears? 70
'Tis *Jacob:* joy'd, that now his eyes
Have seen his *Joseph* e'er he dies,
Th' illustrious Pilgrim's wearied feet
In *Egypt* fix their last retreat.
With large increase his Line is blest, 75
And *Zoan* in th' adopted Guest
With hostile eye beholds up-grown
A strength superior to her own.
See hence the woes on *Egypt* pour'd!
(But Thou, O Monarch, shouldst thy word 80
Absolve, nor thus with impious rod
Oppress the Servants of thy God.)
See *Moses*, pleading, stretch the hand;
See *Aaron* lift the sacred wand,
And lead th' invited vengeance on 85
In scenes to Nature's Laws unknown.
But O, what terrors, *Cham,* are thine,
While quick on thy devoted Line,
Far as thy utmost coasts extend,
Thou seest the various pest descend! 90
If Fear their stubborn hearts may melt,
Let Darkness, Darkness to be felt,
Inclose them.—Thus th' Almighty spake:
As forth the awful accents brake,

                      Darkness

Darkness the high behest obey'd,   95
And round them wrapt its thickest shade.
The Heav'n-struck *Nile*'s extended flood
Now rolls a current black with blood;
While breathless on their oozy bed
In heaps the finny tribes are spread.   100
The loathsom Frog, a num'rous Birth,
Springs instant from the teeming earth,
Nor walls that guard a Monarch's rest
Know to exclude the hideous guest.
He bids; and through the darken'd air   105
In troops th' assembling Flies repair,
And swarms of Reptiles, scatter'd wide,
Rebuke the faithless Tyrant's pride.
In league against them now conspire
The rushing Hail, and bick'ring Fire: 110
And, instant, by the tempest torn,
Their ruin'd shades the forests mourn:
No more array'd in native green
The fig-tree and the vine are seen,
No more with flow'ring honours crown'd,   115
But useless load th' incumber'd ground.
He bids; and join'd in close array
Th' embattled Locusts take their way:
Before them plains with verdure grac'd
Appear; behind, a barren waste: 120
While the dun Beetle through the sky
With eager speed is seen to fly,
And, partner in the offer'd spoil,
Consumes th' astonish'd planter's toil.

                         Now

Now to the grave, with anguish torn, 125
Each Mother yields her eldest-born;
And *Egypt*'s land, along its shores,
The first-fruits of its strength deplores.
Rise, *Israel*, rise; for in their ear
Thy Sons the voice of Freedom hear: 130
The wealth of their relenting foes
Earth's sov'reign Lord on Them bestows,
And bids them leave the hostile soil
Each strong for travel, strong for toil.
As now their destin'd path they tread, 135
Egypt, yet pale with recent dread,
Exulting sees the sacred Band
With parting footsteps press her strand.
Expanded wide above their heads
The shadowing Cloud its curtain spreads; 140
Before them walks th' embodied Fire,
And bids the shades of Night retire.
Quails on their appetite bestow'd,
And Bread ethereal, gave them food;
While, at his word, from out the rock 145
Th' imprison'd streams luxuriant broke,
And onward pour'd, with lengthen'd train,
Ran murm'ring o'er the thirsty plain.
Such Mercies, All-indulgent Lord,
Thy changeless promises afford, 150
Such Blessings thy remembrance kind
Of *Abraham*'s ever faithful mind.
Redeem'd from stern Oppression's seat,
With grateful joy their bosoms beat;

Joy,

Joy, yet enlarg'd, when *Canaan*'s Land 155
Resigns her scepter to their hand,
And bids them reap from off her soil
The harvest of another's toil.

 Behold the Love to *Israel* shown,
That We, great God, thy pow'r might own, 160
And each with stedfast heart fulfill
The dictates of thy mighty Will.

 Awake the song, awake the string,
And thankful praise th' immortal King.

PSALM CVI. *Hallelujah.*

LET songs of joy to God ascend,
 Whose Love nor limit knows nor end.
But O, what tongue in equal lay
His acts can speak, his praise display?
Thrice happy, who with stedfast will 5
The dictates of his Law fulfill!
With These, thy chosen Flock, assign'd
May I my lot for ever find:
O grant me, Lord, with These to prove
The pow'r of thy redeeming Love, 10
And, while thy Mercy on our heads
The fulness of its blessing sheds,
With Them th' accepted hymn to sing
To Thee, my Saviour and my King.

 Too faithful followers of our Sires, 15
Our Life with theirs, great God, conspires
Thy wrath on *Judah*'s Realm to call,
And teach thy terrors where to fall.

         O say,

O say, thou *Erythræan* Main,
(Thy Waves beheld the rebel Train;)   20
How soon Oblivion could efface
Each act of God's stupendous Grace,
The wonders by his mighty hand
Perform'd in *Cham*'s affrighted Land.
Yet, still, that Man his Pow'r might own,   25
Conspicuous in their aid it shone:
Aw'd by his voice the briny Flood
In gath'ring heaps suspended stood,
While, safe as o'er the sandy waste,
Th' admiring troops betwixt them past: 30
Freed from the ruthless Tyrant's hand
Soon as they reach the adverse strand,
Its strength resum'd, th' impetuous wave
Their foes within the watry grave
Absorbs; nor one exempted Man   35
Back with the dreadful tidings ran.
Convinc'd they now (What could they less?)
His words the words of truth confess,
Yield to his Name th' extorted praise,
And songs of grateful triumph raise;   40
But soon rebellious as before
(His Works remember'd now no more,)
To times by Them prescrib'd confine
The counsels of the Will divine.
    By lawless appetite impell'd,   45
As o'er the Wild their course they held,
Fierce rise their Bands, in evil hour,
And challenge to the proof his Pow'r:
        X   That

That Pow'r the wifh'd for Ill fhall grant,
And fatiate their imagin'd want: 50
That Pow'r alone their outrage fell
From Thee, O *Mofes*, could repell,
And unconteſted rev'rence claim
To confecrated *Aaron*'s name.
Wide, difcontinuous, yawn'd the ground, 55
And *Dathan* in the dark profound,
With proud *Abiram*'s frantic Train,
Receiving inſtant, clos'd again;
While fires impetuous, roll'd along,
Wrapt in the blaze th' apoſtate Throng. 60
But, *Horeb!* What is wrought on Thee?
Bluſh, confcious Earth, O bluſh to fee
A figure from the grazing herd
To God, the living God, prefer'd:
That God, their Glory late confeſt; 65
But Ah! within their thankleſs breaſt
No longer now recorded ſtand
The wonders of his faving hand,
In vain on *Egypt* fhown, in vain
Repeated on the bord'ring Main. 70
See, as in awful threatnings heard
Eternal Juſtice gives the word,
The fummon'd Storms the heav'nly Throne
Surround, impatient to be gone:
But *Mofes* in the breach appears, 75
And, as his fuppliant voice he rears,
Averts, yet waiting on the wing,
The vengeance of th' almighty King.

As

As now in near approach they stand
To promis'd *Canaan*'s fertile Land, 80
That promise, seal'd by Truth divine,
They doubt, and at the gift repine:
From tent to tent the murmur runs,
While each the heav'nly counsel shuns,
That bids them safe in Him confide, 85
Their God, their Guardian, and their Guide.
Their guilt mature for vengeance found,
Th' uplifted sword, in act to wound,
Hangs imminent; and myriads slain
In heaps promiscuous load the plain. 90
The conqu'ring Foe through unknown ways
The scatter'd Fugitives conveys;
Their names *Bel-phegor*'s fanes behold
Amidst his Votaries enroll'd,
While pleas'd the impious board they spread, 95
And eat the off'rings of the Dead.
New crimes new chastisements provoke;
And forth the Pest wide-wasting broke,
Unseen the furious onset gave,
And swept them to the crouded grave; 100
Till, *Phineas*, thy prevenient care
Purg'd from its taint the deathful air.
The pious deed to latest days
Shall consecrate the Hero's praise.
Nor *Meribah*'s yet thirsty ground 105
Unconscious of their guilt is found;
Till, summon'd from the rock, the wave
Her plain in full effusion lave.

Nor *He, great Leader of their Bands,
From touch of blame exempted stands: 110
While murmurs, heard on ev'ry side,
And loud reproach, his patience tried,
Resentment quick his bosom stung,
And words unweigh'd escap'd his tongue.
The Nations round, with error blind,   115
To just excision long design'd,
Rebellious to their God they spare,
Nor shun th' accursed rite to share,
That bids them bow to sculptur'd stone,
And frenzy's deepest influence own.   120
To *Dæmons* rear'd their altars stand,
And scenes of blood pollute the Land;
While with untrembling hands the Sires
Their Son, their Daughter, to the fires
A victim yield: to lifeless Gods   125
(Such, *Canaan*, shame thy dire abodes;)
Streams on the knife the filial gore,
And, guiltless, stains th' unhallow'd floor.
What, *Israel*, now shall wash thee clean,
While Lessons of inventive Sin   130
Have prompted thy adult'rous heart
Thus from thy Maker to depart?
Fierce o'er thy head his anger burns;
From his own Heritage he turns,
Abhorrent: Now let *Jacob*'s foes   135
At will th' abandon'd race inclose.
Behold them by oppression torn,
And fix'd the mark of hostile scorn.

* *Moses.*

Oft

PSALM CVI.

Oft were they fav'd, and oft again
Rebellious fpurn'd his equal Reign,   140
Again their ruin'd ftate deplor'd,
And bow'd beneath a foreign Lord.
Yet He with pity from on high,
True to his Compact, heard their cry,
Beheld them drag the fervile chain,   145
And, ftudious to relieve their pain,
Compaffion's tend'reft fenfe imprefs'd
On the ftern Victor's iron breaft.

   O ftill our Father, ftill our Friend,
To *Ifrael*'s woes, great God, attend: 150
From diftant climes, and hoftile lands,
Collect once more our fcatter'd Bands;
That *Sion* with delighted ear
The hallow'd ftrains again may hear;
Thy Name the fubject of each fong,   155
Thy Praife the boaft of ev'ry tongue.

   O thankful hail th' Almighty Lord,
The God by *Jacob*'s Sons ador'd:
His fame, e'er Time its courfe began,
O'er Heav'n's wide region echoing ran;   160
To Him through endlefs ages raife
One fong of oft-repeated praife;
And let confenting Nations join
To blefs with Us the Pow'r divine.   *Hallelujah.*

PSALM CVII.

1.

TO God above from All below
    Let hymns of praise ascend;
Whose Blessings unexhausted flow,
    Whose Mercy knows no end.

2.

But chief by Those his name be blest,
    To whom his aid he gave;
Beheld them by the Foe oppress'd,
    And reach'd his arm to save.

3.

To East, to West, to South, to North,
    Condemn'd awhile to roam,
His hand in pity brought them forth,
    And call'd the Wand'rers home.

4.

Behold them o'er the Desert stray,
    A helpless, hopeless, Train:
Some City, where their steps to stay,
    They seek, but seek in vain.

5.

Ah! what shall chear their fainting mind,
    Or what their woes assuage,
To thirst's afflictive pain consign'd,
    And famine's fiercest rage?

PSALM CVII.

6.
Diſtreſs'd, to God they make their pray'r:
    He guides, direct, their feet;
And, ſafe in his protecting care,
    They reach their deſtin'd ſeat.

7.
O then that All would bleſs his Name,
    Whoſe Mercy thus they prove,
And pleas'd from age to age proclaim
    The wonders of his Love:

8.
That Love, whoſe gifts with thankful breaſt
    The Sons of want divide,
And find their ev'ry grief redreſs'd,
    Their ev'ry wiſh ſupplied.

9.
Theſe erſt he bade th' Avenger's hand
    In Death's dark ſhades detain;
And added to the iron band
    Affliction's heavier chain.

10.
Such is the Doom to thoſe aſſign'd,
    Who, frantic, durſt withſtand
The Counſels of th' Almighty Mind,
    And ſpurn his juſt Command.

11.
O'erwhelm'd with deepeſt woe they lie,
    And ſinking to the grave:
No pitying ear attends their cry;
    No hand is nigh to ſave.

12.

Distress'd, to God they make their pray'r;
  He, instant, near them stands,
Dispells the gloom of black Despair,
  And breaks their stubborn bands.

13.

O then that All would bless his Name,
  Whose Mercy thus they prove,
And pleas'd from age to age proclaim
  The wonders of his Love:

14.

That Love, that oft its succour gives,
  The Captive's woes to heal,
The gates of brass in sunder cleaves,
  And bursts the bars of steel.

15.

Beneath his terrors bid to groan,
  Behold the impious Band
The fruits of Folly reap, and own
  The Justice of his hand.

16.

Estrang'd from food, their languid soul
  The needful meal forgoes:
Life feels its current faintly roll,
  And hastens to its close.

17.

Distress'd, to God they make their pray'r;
  And Nature, joyous, sees
His Word her ruin'd strength repair,
  Her fiercest tortures ease.

18. O

PSALM CVII.

18.
O then that All would bless his Name,
    Whose Mercy thus they prove,
And pleas'd from age to age proclaim
    The wonders of his Love:

19.
That Realms of various tongue would sing
    His Acts in frequent lays,
And yield to Heav'n's eternal King
    The sacrifice of praise.

20.
Who o'er the Waves from shore to shore
    The gifts of Commerce bear,
The wonders of the Deep explore,
    And own that God is there.

21.
By These his Works are seen; his Ways
    By These are understood:
He speaks the word; the Storm obeys,
    And rising lifts the Flood.

22.
Now high as Heav'n the Bark ascends,
    Now seeks the depth below:
Each heart beneath the terror bends,
    And melts with inward woe.

23.
As gorg'd with wine, in wild amaze
    They reel from side to side:
Nor Hope survives, their souls to raise,
    Nor Reason wakes to guide.

24. Distress'd,

24.

Diſtreſs'd, to God they make their pray'r;
    Obedient to his Will,
The Storms that rag'd their rage forbear,
    The Seas that roar'd are ſtill.

25.

Each grief, each fear, at once reſign'd,
    They ſee their labour o'er;
Then led by Him their haven find,
    And touch the wiſh'd for ſhore.

26.

O then that All would bleſs his Name,
    Whoſe Mercy thus they prove,
And pleas'd from age to age proclaim
    The wonders of his Love:

27.

That *Salem* in her ſacred ſhrine
    His praiſe with thankful tongue
Would utter; while her Elders join
    To ſwell the feſtal ſong.

28.

He bids; and lo a burning Waſte,
    Where roll'd the floods before;
And, touch'd by the deſcending blaſt,
    The ſprings are ſeen no more.

29.

Sad witneſs of ſome dire offence,
    Behold the fertile ſoil
No more its wonted gifts diſpenſe,
    But mock the tiller's toil.

PSALM CVII.

30.
He bids; and o'er the Defert wide
    The liquid Lake is fpread:
New fprings the thirfty earth divide,
    And murm'ring lift the head.

31.
There Myriads, late with hunger wan,
    By Him affembled, meet;
There pleas'd the future City plan,
    And fix their fure Retreat.

32.
And now they fow the foodful grain,
    The tender vine they rear;
Now waves the harveft o'er the plain,
    And plenty crowns the year.

33.
Bleft in his care, the Sires with joy
    A num'rous race behold;
Nor dares Difeafe their herds annoy,
    Or wafte the peopled fold.

34.
Anon, if, funk with heavieft woe,
    They feel oppreffion's pow'r;
If civil rage, or conqu'ring foe,
    Their boafted ftrength devour;

35.
Though, humbled from their ftate, awhile
    Their Princes feel his rod,
And wander o'er a barren foil,
    By human ftep untrod,

PSALM CVII.

36.

His hand affords the wish'd release;
  Collects their scatter'd train;
And bids them like the flocks increase,
  That fill the verdant plain.

37.

Such Truths his Servants shall attest,
  And, joyful, wake the song;
While shame the impious shall invest,
  And chain their speechless tongue.

38.

His Works attentive while it sees,
  The Heav'n-instructed Mind
Shall own how equal his Decrees,
  His Providence how kind.

PSALM CVIII.

MY heart is fix'd, eternal Sire;
  My heart is fix'd: To Thee aspire
My thoughts; to Thee my joyous tongue
Preluding forms the grateful song:
That tongue, whose highest praise shall be   5
The pow'r it boasts of praising Thee.
Awake, my lute, and new-strung lyre;
Instinct, myself, with holy fire
I wake; and lo, the dawning Sun
Already hears the strain begun.   10
From Me assembling Crouds shall burn
The triumphs of thy Love to learn,

And,

PSALM CVIII.

And, rapt with zeal, the Nations round
Catch from my lips the sacred sound.
Lo! to the clouds thy Truth extends; 15
Thy Mercy heav'n's vast height transcends:
Inthron'd thyself above the skies,
O, bid thy fullest Glory rise,
And to the earth with cloudless ray
The wonders of thy pow'r display. 20
The Just, blest Objects of thy Love,
Defend propitious from above:
Let Me with Them thy Mercy share,
And hear, O hear, my ceaseless pray'r.
God with an Oath his purpose seals; 25
My hand with joy his word fulfills:
Behold me *Sichem*'s plain divide;
My line, to *Succoth*'s vale applied,
Its bound describes; Thee mine I see,
O *Gilead*, and *Manasses*, Thee. 30
Thou, *Ephraim*, art my strong defence,
Thou, *Judah*, shalt my Law dispense:
A diff'rent lot shall *Moab* find,
A Vase to vilest use assign'd;
A doom like his let *Edom* meet, 35
And wipe the dust from off my feet.
Philistia, pleas'd thy tribute bring,
And own in Me thy future King.
Who, as our troops in close array
To *Edom*'s forts direct their way, 40
Arm'd with resistless strength shall bid
Her gates unfold, her bolts recede?

Behold us, Lord, oppress'd with woe,
As exil'd from thy care we go:
Shall *Israel*'s hosts, thy aid withheld,   45
Still unsuccessful take the field?
Our hope, on Man repos'd in vain,
O let thy strength, great God, sustain:
Thus arm'd, each adverse pow'r we dare,
And dauntless meet the rushing war,   50
While from thy sword our foes retire,
Or trampled in the dust expire.

PSALM CIX.

GOD of my praise, thy silence break;
  Thy timeliest aid my woes bespeak,
While tongues to falsehood train'd prepare
To wrap me in the deathful snare:
Now words of deepest art they try;   5
Now hostile threats around me fly;
And Crouds, inflam'd with causeless rage,
Wars, fiercest wars, against me wage.
While stedfast Hate my Love repays,
To Thee my Soul incessant prays: 10
But O, what anguish rends my mind!
What keen regret! condemn'd to find
(As gifts on gifts my hands bestow,)
In each expected friend a foe.

  On Him whose heart, with malice fraught,   15
Against my peace has bent its thought,
Thus let thy Justice, Lord, by Me
Aloud proclaim its fix'd Decree.

Arraign'd

Arraign'd at stern Oppression's bar,
Some dread accuser let him share,   20
That, planted on his right, may stand,
And vengeance from his Judge demand:
Nor let his deprecation win
The wish'd for pardon to his sin,
But witness of his guilt become,   25
And seal, beyond reverse, his doom.
Let death's accelerated day
To worthier hands his Charge convey,
His roof a weeping Widow see,
Her Orphans hanging at her knee;   30
Let These, by thy inflictions won
Th' example of his deeds to shun,
(While, as from morn to eve they roam,
Some ruin'd Cell their casual home,
Each night, affords,) by hunger led,   35
Seek at the rich man's gate their bread.
His wealth let fell Extortion spoil;
The gather'd harvest of his toil
Let Rapine's greedy hand surprize,
While Each his woes unpitying eyes;   40
And let his Race, no succour near,
Corrected, lesson in thy fear
This Age; and, one succession o'er,
Be seen by human eye no more.
Let what of sin his Sires have done,   45
What guilt his Mother's heart has known,
On records uneffac'd by time
In Heav'n be noted, and their Crime

(Its measure by himself fulfill'd,)
Their name to just extinction yield.   50
Such vengeance on the miscreant rest,
Who, when with heaviest woes oppress'd
The helpless innocent he view'd,
With murth'rous hate his soul pursu'd.
In Curses (for in them his heart   55
Delighted,) let him bear his part,
Dread Spectacle! a foe profest
To Blessing, and himself unblest.
His tongue with Hell-enkindled fire
Inflam'd, in Execration dire   60
He veils him o'er, and at thy word
Its influence within him pour'd
Like water shall his bowels rend,
Like oil into his bones descend:
Fast as his vesture to his side   65
Still let it cleave, by Thee applied,
And, o'er his loyns for ever bound,
In painful cincture wrap him round.
   Such recompence my Foe shall claim;
Such All who blast with lies my fame.   70
But let thy Grace on Me bestow'd
Thy Name exalt, immortal God;
Thy Love (how sweet that Love!) reveal,
And stretch the hand my heart to heal,
That fainting pours th' incessant groan,   75
And sorrow's deepest wounds has known.
To Life's last verge, impell'd by woe,
Fast as the flitting shade I go;

Chac'd

PSALM CIX.

Chac'd as the Locust see me roam;
My knees, by hunger's force o'ercome, 80
Sink fault'ring; in my wasted frame
While, half extinct, the vital flame
Its due supplies in vain demands,
Reproaching foes, their num'rous bands
In scornful gaze around me spread, 85
With haughtiest triumph shake the head.
Thy wonted Clemency bestow;
And give them, mightiest Lord, to know
Thy Care extended to my aid,
Thy Pow'r in their repulse display'd. 90
Though curs'd by Them, yet bless me Thou;
O teach their stubborn hearts to bow;
And let their rage by Thee suppress'd
With grateful transport fill my breast.
On each who calls himself my foe 95
Let shame its thickest mantle throw,
While I, amid th' assembled Throng,
Raise to my God the ceaseless song,
Who, constant at his side, the Poor
From lawless judgement shall secure. 100

PSALM CX.

THUS to my Lord th' Almighty said;
  In awful Majesty array'd
Come, seat thee at my own right hand,
Till, at my word, the hostile Band,
As low with prostrate necks they lie, 5
A footstool to thy steps supply.

Y 3   Thy

PSALM CX.

Thy God from *Sion*'s lofty tow'r
Shall bid thee stretch the rod of pow'r:
Victorious o'er the rebel train,
Arise, and vindicate thy reign.   10
Behold the long-expected day,
When willing Crouds their homage pay,
And, while from out the mystic shrine
Thy beams in mild effusion shine,
To Thee their sacred off'rings bring,   15
And hail their Saviour and their King.
Thy future Offspring view, a Birth
More num'rous than the Dews, on earth
(Beneath the twilight's dubious gloom)
Diffus'd from Morn's prolific womb.   20
Th' irrevocable Oath is sworn:
" My Best-belov'd, my Eldest-born,
" Charg'd with th' eternal Priesthood see,
" And rank'd, *Melchizedec*, with Thee."
Thine arm th' anointed Prince shall shield,   25
Thou, Lord, beside him tread the field,
While Kings shall feel th' inflicted wound,
And hardiest Warriors press the ground.
His Name the subject World shall awe,
His sword to distant Lands give law;   30
By him their scepter'd Chiefs are slain,
And heaps of carnage load the plain.
   While with advancing step his feet
The Conflict yet prepare to meet,
The Streams, that glide along the way,   35
New vigour to his heart convey,

And

And bid him, 'mid the scene of dread,
Secure of conquest, lift the head.

PSALM CXI. *Hallelujah.*

1.

MY Soul, with sacred zeal inspir'd,
　Shall wake to God the thankful strain,
In secret with his Saints retir'd,
And 'midst fair *Sion*'s crouded fane.

2.

Great are his Works: With studious aim
Each faithful heart those Works has trac'd;
His Act shall highest honour claim,
His Equity for ever last.

3.

His Wonders to the grateful sense
In sweet memorial stand confest:
For boundless grace his hands dispense,
And tend'rest pity warms his breast.

4.

His Love the Souls to Him allied
With food of heav'nly growth has fill'd,
Nor suffers from his thought to slide
The Promise to his People seal'd.

5.

Thy Pow'r that People, Lord, have known,
Blest Heirs of *Canaan*'s fertile Land:
Thy Precept Truth and Justice own,
And bid thy Deeds reverseless stand.

6. Salvation

6.

Salvation from our God defcends;
His Faith fhall *Ifrael*'s blifs infure:
Majeftic Awe his Name attends,
And Sanctity from blemifh pure.

7.

His Fear th' obedient heart refines,
And Wifdom's path to view difplays:
In brighteft beams array'd it fhines,
And prompts each tongue to endlefs praife.

PSALM CXII. *Hallelujah*.

1.

HOW bleft the Man, his God who fears!
   Thy Precept, on his thoughts imprefs'd,
Eternal King, his Spirit chears;
And peace perpetual fills his breaft.

2.

His Sons the reins of pow'r fhall hold,
Tranfmiffive Bleffings on their Line
Be pour'd, his treafures fwell with gold,
His Righteoufnefs for ever fhine.

3.

How to thy Saints, juft, kind, and good,
Has light amidft the gloom upfprung!
Their hands have ampleft gifts beftow'd,
And fair Difcretion guides their tongue.

PSALM CXII.

4.
Secure from fall the Juſt ſhall ſtand,
Nor e'er from thy remembrance ſlide:
No rumour'd ills his fear demand,
Whoſe hopes in Thee, great God, reſide.

5.
Without a dread (Thy ſtrength his truſt,)
He meets the battle on its way,
Nor turns, till proſtrate in the duſt
His eyes the vaunting Foe ſurvey.

6.
Inrich'd by what he gives, his hands
Deal to the ſons of want his bread:
His Innocence unſullied ſtands;
And laſting honours crown his head.

7.
His bliſs Tranſgreſſors ſhall behold,
And grind their teeth, and inly groan,
Their impious toil by Thee controul'd,
Their ev'ry wiſh by Thee o'erthrown.

PSALM CXIII. *Hallelujah.*

YE faithful Servants of your God,
   On Him be all your praiſe beſtow'd;
Through time's extended courſe, his Name
Shall praiſe, and thanks, and homage, claim:
Its circuit from the Eaſt begun,   5
To fartheſt Weſt his fame ſhall run,
His glory Earth's wide realms o'erflow,
Nor higheſt Heav'ns its limit know.

O whom

O whom to Him ſhall Mortals dare
To equal? Whom to Him compare? 10
Who ſits aloft, o'er Gods a God,
Eternity his dread Abode,
Yet ſtoops to view, and, view'd, records
The ſcenes that Earth's low ſeat affords;
Lifts from the duſt the helpleſs Poor, 15
And gives the abject and obſcure,
The dunghill for a throne exchang'd,
To ſit with mightieſt Monarchs rang'd.
'Tis His the barren houſe to bleſs;
His gift let Each the Babes confeſs, 20
That, long to her requeſt denied,
The joyful Mother's care divide. *Hallelujah.*

PSALM CXIV.

1.

WHEN *Jacob*'s Sons through paths unknown
    From *Egypt* took their way,
In *Judah*'s Tribe his preſence ſhone,
    And *Iſrael* own'd his ſway.

2.

Old Ocean ſaw them, as they came;
    He ſaw, and backward fled:
Recoiling *Jordan* turn'd his ſtream,
    And ſought his fountain-head.

3.

The Mountains feel the ſudden ſhock;
    As rams, from off the ground
They ſpring: As younglings of the flock,
    The Hills affrighted bound.

PSALM CXIV.

4.
Thou Ocean, fay, why, as they came,
    Thy billows backward fled:
And what, O *Jordan*, urg'd thy ftream
    To feek its fountain-head?

5.
Ye Mountains, whence the fudden fhock?
    Why leap ye from the ground
As rams? As younglings of the flock,
    Say why, O Hills, ye bound.

6.
Earth, inftant, to thy loweft bafe
    Convuls'd, avow thy fear,
While Heav'n's high Lord reveals his face,
    While *Jacob*'s God is near:

7.
Diffolv'd beneath whofe potent ftroke
    The flint a torrent gave;
Who fpake; and from the yielding rock
    Gufh'd forth the bidden wave.

PSALM CXV.

O Let not Us, Thou God of Hofts,
   O let not Us with frantic boafts
The glory claim: To Thee alone
Thy Truth and Grace, to *Ifrael* known,
Shall ceafelefs honour yield, and raife   5
Each heart to Love, each tongue to Praife.
Why fhould the heathen tribes demand,
" Where's now the God of *Ifrael*'s Land?"

In Heav'n our God has fix'd his throne,
That Lord whose Will and Act are one.　　10
Not such the Gods whom Ye adore,
That, once a mass of shapeless ore,
Now crown'd with furtive honours stand,
The creatures of the Artist's hand;
Of sense-belying parts possess'd,　　15
In useless imag'ry express'd;
Of mouth, but not for speech design'd;
Of ears and eyes, yet deaf and blind:
Whose nostrils, as along the fane
It breathes, the incense greets in vain;　　20
Whose hands th' imprinted kiss ne'er feel,
While suppliant crouds before them kneel;
Whose feet have never step essay'd;
Whose throat has never sound convey'd:
Unvisited by Wisdom's ray　　25
Their breast: nor less insensate They,
Who made their mimic forms, or, made,
With fruitless pray'r invoke their aid.
Ye happier Sons of *Israel*'s Line,
Conducted by the Light divine,　　30
On God your firm reliance build;
Him own your refuge, Him your shield.
Ye who from vested *Aaron* trace
The honours of your chosen Race,
On God your firm reliance build;　　35
Him own your refuge, Him your shield.
Ye Souls with pure devotion warm,
Whose Lives to his Decrees conform,

On

On God your firm reliance build;
Him own your refuge, Him your shield. 40
Behold his beams around us shine:
He, *Jacob*, He shall bless thy Line,
You, who from vested *Aaron* trace
The honours of your chosen Race,
And You, with pure devotion warm, 45
Whose Lives to his Decrees conform,
From Him whose hand the scepter guides,
To Him who in the cot resides.
To You, to Yours, till time shall end,
His Love its blessings shall extend, 50
Heirs of the changeless promise giv'n
By Him who form'd the Earth and Heav'n:
That Heav'n, within whose awful bound
Himself, with brightest glory crown'd,
His Seat has rear'd; while *Adam*'s Sons 55
The Earth (his Gift,) its tenants owns.

 Not Those whom death has snatch'd away
The debt of hallow'd praise shall pay,
Or wake his wonders to disclose,
But silent in the dust repose: 60
'Tis Ours, who still those wonders view,
The grateful labour to pursue;
Nor ever shall our lips decline
To crown with hymns the Name divine. *Hallelujah.*

PSALM CXVI.

How glows with grateful Love my breaſt!
  For God the voice of my requeſt
Accepts, and, while my hands I rear,
Bows to my plaint the willing ear.
For this, to Life's extremeſt hour   5
My lips to Him the pray'r ſhall pour.
While Death its ſnares around me threw,
The grave its horrors to my view
Preſenting, preſs'd with heavieſt grief,
From Thee, great God, I ſought relief.   10
" O ſave me, heav'nly Sire, I cried,
" And turn th' impending ſtroke aſide."
Juſt, good, and kind, is *Iſrael*'s Lord,
His breaſt with tend'reſt pity ſtor'd,
And prompt his Arm, when Ills invade,   15
The guileleſs and the meek to aid.
His Mercies, 'midſt thy deepeſt woe,
By bleſt experience taught to know,
Turn, turn thee to thy reſt, my Soul;
For He who ſits above the pole   20
(Tremendous Name,) has o'er thy head
The fulneſs of his bounty ſhed.
Thou, mightieſt Father, Thou wert nigh,
To ſave my ſoul from death, mine eye
From tears, to guard from lapſe my feet, 25
And bid me in this earthly Seat
(Life's wide dominion,) ſtill reſide,
To Thee in filial fear allied.

PSALM CXVI.

    To God my heart refign'd its care;
To Him my tongue addrefs'd its pray'r.   30
While, ftruck with terrors as I ftood,
A fea of forrows round me flow'd,
" No more, my Soul, no more, I cried,
" In Man's fallacious aid confide."
    O, what requital at my hand   35
Shall Mercies, Lord, like Thine demand?
By Thee from each diftrefs enlarg'd,
The Cup with benediction charg'd
I take, and, touch'd with holy flame,
Invoke my great Deliv'rer's name.   40
Ev'n now, before th' affembled Train,
Ev'n now, within thy facred Fane,
Behold me at thine altar bow,
And, pleas'd, abfolve my offer'd vow.
Who Thy Decrees, great God, obey,   45
Secure on Thee their hope fhall ftay;
Great is thy care on fuch beftow'd,
Nor worthlefs in thine eye their blood.
In Me thy Servant, Lord, in Me
The Offspring of thy Handmaid fee,   50
Who, late in heavieft fetters bound,
From Thee my full releafe have found.
For this, my Soul from day to day
The facrifice of praife fhall pay,
And, touch'd by Thee with holy flame,   55
Invoke my great Deliv'rer's Name.
Ev'n now, before th' affembled Train,
Ev'n now, within thy facred Fane,

(That Fane, whose walls, on firmest base
Uprear'd, fair *Salem*'s confines grace,) 60
Behold me at thine altar bow,
And, pleas'd, absolve my offer'd vow. *Hallelujah.*

PSALM CXVII.

1.

LET thy various Realms, O Earth,
 Praises yield to Heav'n's high Lord;
Praise him All of human birth,
And his wondrous Acts record.

2.

See his Mercy o'er our Land
Spread its ever-healing wing,
And his Truth through ages stand;
Praise, O praise, th' eternal King.

PSALM CXVIII.

LIFT your voice, and thankful sing
 Praises to your heav'nly King;
For his Mercies far extend,
And his Bounty knows no end.
Israel, thy Creator bless, 5
And with joyous tongue confess,
That his Mercies far extend,
And his Bounty knows no end.
Aaron, let thy chosen Line
Grateful in th' avowal join, 10
That his Mercies far extend,
And his Bounty knows no end.

Ye who make his Will your care,
With assenting voice declare,
That his Mercies far extend, 15
And his Bounty knows no end.
To my plaint propitious, He
Bade my captive Soul go free.
He shall in my Cause appear;
Let not Man excite my fear. 20
He amid my Helpers stands;
Struck by Him, th' opposing Bands
Instant from before mine eye
Back in wild retreat shall fly.
O, how safe the Man, whose mind 25
Rests on *Jacob*'s God reclin'd!
Safer far than They who trust
On the help of breathing dust,
Or, when threat'ning Ills invade,
Boast a Monarch's pow'r their aid. 30
Gather'd from each distant Coast
Round me press'd th' embattled Host;
But my Arm, by God upheld,
Strew'd with slaughter'd heaps the field.
Round me, thirsting for my blood, 35
Round me adverse myriads stood;
But my Arm, by God upheld,
Strew'd with slaughter'd heaps the field.
Round me, see! as Bees they dwell,
Bees, that, issuing from their cell, 40
Mix in swarms, and on the wing
Arm'd with fury onward spring:

Fierce awhile the Battle burn'd;
But, their legions backward turn'd,
Like the thorn-enkindled fire   45
See its flames at once expire,
While my Arm, by God upheld,
Strews with flaughter'd heaps the field.
Soon thy ftroke, relentlefs Foe,
Soon thy ftroke had laid me low,   50
Had not God's fupporting hand
Bid my fault'ring feet to ftand:
He my Strength, and He my Song,
Lo! my days I yet prolong,
And, each hoftile force o'erthrown,   55
Him my great Salvation own.
Shouts of health and hymns of praife
Wifdom's faithful followers raife,
While amid their peaceful Seat
Thus the ear their accents greet: 60
" O how ftrong the hand divine!
" O what wonders, Lord, are thine!"
See that hand, from Heav'n reveal'd,
Wonders yet on wonders yield.
Vaunt thy terrors, Death, no more: 65
He whom *Ifrael*'s Sons adore,
He, each danger chac'd away,
Bids me ftill, from day to day,
Speak his Acts, who, juft and kind,
Trials to my lot affign'd,   70
Yet amidft the doubtful ftrife
Refcued from the fword my life.

              Ope

Ope the gates of Righteousness;
Let my feet, with full access,
Walk its sacred Courts along;
Let me there with thankful tongue
Bless my great Deliv'rer's Name,
And his boundless Love proclaim.
   Here the hallow'd Gate behold;
See its valves at once unfold,
Pleas'd t' admit the chosen Train,
Pure from Sin's infectious stain.
   Thee, the God inthron'd above,
Thee my lips shall sing, whose Love
To my voice attention gave,
Prompt to hear, and strong to save.
   See the Stone, that, cast aside
By the Builders' erring pride,
In the Dome assumes its place,
Own'd the Angle's noblest grace.
'Thou the Work, great God, hast wrought;
In its scenes our wond'ring Thought
Joys thy clemency to trace,
Seal'd to *Jacob*'s favour'd Race.
Lit by thy auspicious ray
Downward streams the wish'd for Day,
Big with Acts that shall suggest
Endless mirth to *Israel*'s breast.
Save, O save, eternal Lord,
And thy prosp'ring aid afford.
Blest the Man, who, sent by God,
Visits *Salem*'s lov'd abode:

Come,

Come, ye Saints, and in his Train
Tread with licens'd step her Fane,
While from out her sacred Tow'r   105
Blessings on your head we pour.
Safe in *Israel*'s Lord confide;
He is God, and None beside:
See his fav'ring beams arise
To his People's longing eyes.   110
Fair, and innocent of spot,
Let the victim Lamb be brought,
And beside his Altar stand,
Fetter'd in the writhen band.
Thee my God, in lengthen'd lays,   115
Thee my raptur'd lips shall praise;
Thee my God (its ev'ry chord
By the skilful touch explor'd,)
Shall my harp aloud proclaim,
Zealous to exalt thy fame.   120
 Lift your voice, and thankful sing
Praises to your heav'nly King;
For his Mercies far extend,
And his Bounty knows no end.

PSALM CXIX.

ALEPH.

HOW blest, who Thee, great God, obey,
 And stedfast walk th' all-perfect way!
How blest, whose hearts with will intire
Thy presence seek, Almighty Sire;

Whose

Whose feet thy guidance own; whose mind
Has each nefarious act declin'd.
Thy voice has charg'd us to fulfill
The dictates of thy heav'nly Will:
Such, Lord, thy Charge; and O may I
Attentive to the task apply.
My steps conform'd to thy Decrees,
Nor shame nor dread my Soul shall seize;
Thy precepts on my mind impress'd
Shall swell with joy my faithful breast,
Thy Justice prompt my tongue to raise
The song of gratitude and praise.
Thy Law my love shall claim: Do Thou
Thy ear to my petition bow;
Nor leave me, helpless and forlorn,
The absence of thy grace to mourn.

BETH.

How, early wise, shall Youth, O say,
In innocence direct its way?
Thy Word its steps, to Thee resign'd,
The ever faithful Guide shall find.
Hail, best Instructor! Thee my Thought
With full desire, great God, has sought:
O let me not, by Error's sway
Impell'd, from thy direction stray.
Thy Precept, in my breast conceal'd,
From Sin's assault my heart shall shield.
Blest is thy Name, eternal Lord!
O write within my mind thy Word;

That

That Word, whose rules from day to day
My lips with grateful zeal display:
These, my best wealth, my treasur'd store,   35
I keep, and view them o'er and o'er:
Thy Dictates still, my constant Joy,
My soul's attention shall employ;
Nor aught shall from my sight withdraw
Thy path, or from my thought thy Law.   40

GIMEL.

Thy Mercy let thy Servant see,
Grant me to live conform'd to Thee,
And let my Soul, each mist away,
The wonders of thy Law survey.
Behold me, absent from my home,   45
Through Life's wild maze a Pilgrim roam,
Nor Thou to my desiring eye
Thy Word's directing beams deny.
With ardent zeal, with strong desire,
My thoughts to thy Decrees aspire.   50
O Thou, whose threat the proud subdues,
Whose wrath the sinner's steps pursues,
My soul, of each transgression pure,
From scorn and fierce reproach secure.
While Princes with malignant aim   55
Assembled wound my honest fame,
My Life, thy Will its fix'd pursuit,
Shall each opprobrious tongue refute.
Thy Laws my ev'ry thought controul,
While, fill'd with sacred joy, my Soul   60

It's

Its ever faithful Friends in Thefe
And Inmates of its counfel fees.
DALETH.
Low in the duft my Soul is laid;
O reach me, Lord, thy promis'd aid.
Thou, as my heart its guilt avow'd,   65
Thy pitying ear, great God, haft bow'd;
O let me, leffon'd in thy way,
The wonders of thy Grace furvey:
While on my Soul, that melts with woe,
That Grace its fuccours fhall beftow,   70
(Such hope thy Word has bid me form;)
Let me, with holy tranfport warm,
And privileg'd thy Law to learn,
From falfehood's path abhorrent turn.
Truth, Lord, my fteady thoughts purfue,   75
Thy Judgements fix'd before my view
In full difplay: Exempt from fhame
O give me Thou by Thefe to frame
My courfe; and mark with what delight,
(As onward Thefe my fteps invite,)   80
Its bands by Thee diffolv'd, my Soul
Anticipates the diftant goal.
HE.
Teach me, O teach me, Lord, thy Way;
So to my life's remoteft day,
By thy unerring Precepts led,   85
My willing feet its paths fhall tread.
Inform'd by Thee, with facred awe
My heart fhall meditate thy Law,

And

And with celestial Wisdom fill'd
To Thee its full obedience yield.   90
Give me to know thy Words aright,
(Thy Words, my soul's supreme delight,)
That, purg'd from thirst of gold, my mind
In Them its better wealth may find.
O turn from Vanity mine eye,   95
To Me thy quick'ning strength supply,
And with thy promis'd mercy chear
A heart devoted to thy fear.
My dreaded shame, great God, remove:
Thy Judgements, Lord, my thoughts approve; 100
Thy wise Commands my breast inflame;
O haste, and to my inmost frame
Permit thy Justice to dispense
Its all-reviving influence.

V A U.

O let me, Lord, thy Mercy know;   105
Thy promis'd health, great God, bestow;
So from my Soul, on Thee reclin'd,
Shall each reproach an answer find.
My trust thy Judgements, mightiest Lord,
Support; O let not then thy Word   110
(Thy Word, by Truth eternal seal'd,)
Be ever from my lips withheld:
That Word to Life's extremest stage
My just remembrance shall engage,
My Soul to thy Decrees incline,   115
And make the paths of freedom mine.

The

The Heav'n-taught Truths that warm my breast
My tongue to Monarchs shall suggest,
And, rapt with zeal, each check disclaim
Of servile dread, and infant shame. 120
Thy Law, *Jehovah*, still shall share
My ardent Love, my constant Care,
And, while from Thee with lifted hands
Pleas'd I receive its just commands,
My Life, submitted to its rein, 125
Shall speak them not receiv'd in vain.

Z A I N.

Thy promises, Almighty Sire,
Accomplish: These my hope inspire;
These, when oppress'd with ills I lie,
With vital strength my soul supply; 130
Nor loud reproach and hostile scorn
My heart from thy obedience turn.
Amid my woes, through ages past
In long memorial backward trac'd
Thy Judgements have my trust upheld, 135
And sorrow's heaviest cloud dispell'd.
How trembles, Lord, my heart to see
The souls that err from thy Decree!
Long as within this seat of clay,
My house of Pilgrimage, I stay, 140
Thy Statutes are my Song; thy Name
Wakes in my breast the holy flame,
That heav'n-ward lifts my thoughtful soul,
When night's dark shades invest the pole.

What hopes, great God, are mine, what joy, 145
While thy Commands my care employ!

CHETH.

My heart's best portion, Lord, art Thou;
To Thee my Thoughts obedience vow:
To Thee with ardent zeal I pray;
Thy promis'd mercy, Lord, display, 150
While back my yet unfinish'd race
With scrutiny severe I trace,
Thy Law with full acceptance greet,
And turn to Thee my willing feet.
With studious haste I ran, I flew, 155
Intent thy Dictates to pursue,
Nor These forget, though troops of foes
Amid their snare my steps inclose.
Thy just Decrees within my breast
Revolv'd, I quit my bed of rest, 160
And pleas'd, at midnight's awful hour,
In thanks to Thee my spirit pour.
I mark where'er the souls I find
To Thy Commands, great God, inclin'd;
I mark them, and with such reside 165
In friendship's strictest bands allied.
That Mercy, Lord, whose beams extend
Far as to Earth's remotest end,
That Mercy to my soul impart,
And grave thy precepts on my heart. 170

TETH.

My grateful heart thy Love has known,
O Thou, whose words and deeds are one:

O still

O still that Love impart, and store
My Soul with thy celestial Lore,
Whose thought its full assent resigns 175
To what thy sacred Will injoins.
In devious paths awhile I trod,
E'er yet corrected by thy rod,
But disciplin'd, great Sire, by Thee
Obsequious bow to thy Decree. 180
Thy Mercies, Lord, exhaustless flow;
O give my Soul thy Will to know:
While Crouds, whose hearts thy fear disclaim,
With studied falsehood blast my fame,
Thee, Lord, I seek; by thy Command 185
My Acts, my Thoughts, directed stand:
Amidst their rage, with joyful view
My heart thy Precepts can pursue,
While folly theirs from truth withholds,
And round them wraps its thickest folds. 190
Blest be thy hand, severely kind,
Whose stroke recall'd my erring Mind,
And urg'd me, as to Thee I turn,
Thy hallow'd Institutes to learn,
And, taught their worth, to prize them more 195
Than heaps of *Ophir*'s richest ore.

J o d.

Thy plastic art, throughout my frame,
Each limb, each nerve, great God, proclaim;
O give me Thou with mind sincere
To learn th' Instructions of thy Fear: 200

So shall the Souls, that Fear who know,
With social joy, my God, o'erflow,
And pleas'd my constant heart approve,
That waits, with Them, thy plighted Love.
Thy Judgements praise eternal claim,   205
Wise, just, and good; with friendliest aim
Thy faithful hand each woe I feel
Inflicts, and wounds me but to heal.
O let thy promis'd mercy shed
Its quick'ning effluence on my head,   210
And comfort to my Soul instill,
That loves the dictates of thy Will.
Let shame th' Aggressors proud repay,
Who seek my footsteps to betray:
Thine aid I ask, eternal Lord,   215
And treasure in my heart thy Word.
With Me in sacred friendship join
The souls that to thy fear incline,
And from the well-spring of thy Law
Exhaustless streams of knowledge draw.   220
O let my heart, to Thee subdu'd,
Guilt, and its offspring Shame, exclude.

CAPH.

Behold, while wearied with delay
My soul, my sight, consume away,
Thy Servant o'er th' ethereal plain   225
Send the long look, but send in vain.
O when to my expecting eyes,
When, shall thy wish'd Salvation rise,

Through

Through ſtruggling clouds its promis'd ray
Tranſmit, and o'er me pour the day? 230
Faſt as the wine-exhauſted hide
Amid the circling ſmoke is dried,
I waſte; yet never from my heart
Shall thy Commands, great God, depart.
How long ſhall I my days, O ſay, 235
In ſad ſucceſſion roll'd ſurvey,
How long to haughtieſt inſult yield,
Thy vengeance from my foes withheld?
Behold them with inſidious care
Their pits before my feet prepare, 240
And, taught thy Precepts to deſpiſe,
(Thy Precepts, Lord, how juſt, how wiſe!)
With cauſeleſs rage my ſoul invade:
Behold; and reach me, Lord, thine aid.
How nigh had Conqueſt crown'd their aim, 245
And rooted from the earth my name!
While ſtill thy paths, eternal God,
With undiverted ſtep I trod.
O let thy Mercy to my heart
Its life-ſuſtaining pow'r impart; 250
So ſhall my Soul with ſacred awe,
And juſt obſervance, hear thy Law.

LAMED.

Fix'd in the Heav'ns, eternal Lord,
On firmeſt baſis reſts thy Word;
Thy Truth, unconſcious of decay, 255
Sees waſting ages roll away:

Pois'd on its centre by thy hand
Earth long has stood, and yet shall stand:
For Earth, and Heav'n, and Seas, each hour
Subservient own thy sov'reign Pow'r: 260
Their course in Order's strictest line
Thy firm Decrees, great God, confine.
How had I perish'd, 'midst my woes,
But that within my bosom rose
The joys which thy Injunctions yield, 265
And each invading grief dispell'd!
O never, never, shall my heart,
Forgetful, from thy Law depart,
Which, instant, kindliest succour gave,
And wrought my rescue from the grave: 270
Behold me, Lord, behold me thine;
Thy ear to my request incline,
And save a Soul whose wakeful Thought
With fervent zeal thy Truths has sought,
And still shall seek them, though their snare 275
The Impious for my life prepare.
Mine eyes Perfection's limit see
Through Nature's Works; but thy Decree
No period, mightiest Monarch, knows,
Nor bounds of space its breadth inclose. 280

M E M.

With what desire, great God, I burn
Thy sacred Oracles to learn!
Each day, each hour, with stedfast mind
Thy Truths I meditate, and find

The

The knowledge to my foes denied
To Me in fulleſt weight ſupplied.
My Teachers, while from out thy Law
The leſſons of my life I draw,
My guidance aſk; the Aged Me
Their Elder in diſcretion ſee,
As, onward led, with ſteady pace
The Heav'n-appointed paths I trace.
How have I kept my feet from ill,
Intent thy Mandate to fulfill,
My ear to diſcipline reſign'd,
Nor ever from its rules declin'd!
In full ſatiety of joy
Abſorpt, thy Words my thought employ,
And ſweeter on my palate dwell
Than honey dropping from its cell.
My Soul, by thy Inſtruction wiſe,
From Error's path abhorrent flies.

N u n.

Thy Law, from *Sinai*'s mount reveal'd,
A lantern to my feet ſhall yield,
A light, whoſe beams ſhall o'er me dwell,
And night's incircling ſhades diſpell.
Thy Precepts (thus my tongue has ſworn,
Nor aught my purpoſe, Lord, ſhall turn;)
Thy Precepts, juſt, and wiſe, and true,
My ſteps, unwearied, ſhall purſue.
Beneath a weight of woes I bend;
Thy promis'd aid, my God, extend.

My lips their willing off'rings pay:
Accept them gracious; and display
Thy Judgements to my longing eyes: 315
While ceaseless dangers round me rise,
My soul just ready to resign,
To These my thoughts I still incline,
Nor impious force, or hostile snare,
Shall alienate from These my care. 320
These, while their worth my Soul inflames,
Its lasting heritage it claims,
And pleas'd the dictates of thy Will
To Life's last period shall fulfill.

SAMECH.

Far hence each Superstition vain, 325
Wild offspring of the human brain;
The Truths that fill thy hallow'd page
My happier choice, great God, engage.
Safe on thy Word my trust I build,
O Thou, my Refuge, and my Shield. 330
Ye impious, from my sight away;
My Soul shall God's behests obey.
O ever faithful to thy Word,
Do Thou thy vital strength afford;
Thy help impart, eternal Sire, 335
Nor let my hope in shame expire.
Sustain'd by thy almighty aid,
What danger shall my Soul invade?
In vain in all Sin its arts apply
To turn from thy Decrees mine eye. 340

Subverted

Subverted by their own deceit,
And fpurn'd beneath thy conqu'ring feet,
Thy wrath the rebel tribes deplore;
Spurn'd,— as the drofs, that from the ore
(Amid the glowing furnace caft,) 345
Is fever'd by the fiery blaft.
For this, with ardent Love thy Law
I feek; for this, while rev'rent Awe
And holy Horror fhake my frame,
Thy Juftice, mightieft Lord, proclaim. 350

A I N.

While Juftice o'er my life prefides,
Each act, each word, each purpofe guides,
Friend of the guiltlefs! nigh me ftand,
And fave me from th' Oppreffor's hand.
O ftill thy wonted grace difclofe; 355
Still in my quarrel interpofe
Thine arm, nor let my haughty foe
Exulting triumph in my woe.
My wafting eyes with earneft view
Thy promis'd health, my God, purfue: 360
Thy mercies to thy Servant fhow,
And give, O give me, Lord, to know
Each Heav'n-taught Rule: Behold me thine,
And let thy influence on me fhine,
Till, each illufion purg'd away, 365
My Soul thy myftic Truths furvey.
Thy wife Injunctions caft afide,
The fons of Infolence and Pride

With oft-repeated crimes demand
Th' unwilling vengeance from thy hand. 370
Thy Dictates on my thought impress'd
With sweet delight shall fill my breast;
Not Gold like These my love shall claim,
Gold sev'n times tortur'd in the flame.
These, Lord, I keep, and, fix'd, decree 375
To shun each path that leads from Thee.

P E.

O how the Wonders of thy Law
My heart to just obedience awe!
What streams of purest knowledge yield
Thy Words in full display reveal'd! 380
By These the Souls untaught before
To heights of heav'nly Science soar:
With sacred thirst my bosom burn'd;
To These my op'ning mouth I turn'd,
And from thy Precept wise and true 385
Its life-imparting spirit drew.
What grace thy Saints are blest to know,
That grace on Me, great God, bestow.
Thy Dictates to my soul convey,
And level to my steps thy way. 390
Redeem from Error's growth my mind,
Nor leave one baleful root behind.
O save me from Oppression's hand;
So shall my soul thy wise command
Observe: Indulgent on me shine, 395
And make the paths of knowledge mine.

My

My tears, great God, my zeal disclose,
And down the copious torrent flows,
As oft, with inward anguish torn,
Thy violated Laws I mourn. 400

   T s a d d i.
 Hail, Arbiter supreme! thy Will
Truth, Equity, and Justice seal:
Truth, Justice, Equity, thy Voice
Prescribes to favour'd *Israel*'s choice:
These while my foe presumptuous spurns, 405
With zeal consum'd my bosom burns.
O how thy Precepts, in the fire
Long prov'd, thy servant's Love inspire!
To indigence and scorn resign'd,
These still I seek with studious mind. 410
Eternal Rectitude is thine;
Truth to thy Laws adjusts its line;
Thy Laws, my Soul's best comfort found,
When pains and sorrows wrapt me round.
Thy just Decrees shall Time survive; 415
Them teach me, and my Soul shall live.

   K o p h.
 O Maker, Guide, and Judge of All!
With earnest voice to Thee I call:
To Thee I call: propitious hear;
So shall the Precepts of thy fear 420
My Soul inform, and, Thou my aid,
My ev'ry Act by These be sway'd.
E'er yet the dawn has streak'd the sky,
God of my Life, to Thee I cry;

         My

My hope (nor shall that hope be vain,) 425
Thy sacred promises sustain:
On thy Decrees, great God, intent,
My Thoughts the early watch prevent:
O let thy Mercy, while I pray,
My night illumine, guide my day, 430
Thy Word within my inmost frame
Awake the everliving flame.
Behold a Croud, from Thee estrang'd,
In dire alliance near me rang'd:
But Thou, my God, art nearer still: 435
My Soul the dictates of thy Will
Fix'd on eternal base has view'd,
And owns them wise, and just, and good.

RESH.

Behold my griefs; my Soul preserve;
For ne'er from thy direction swerve 440
My thoughts: Do Thou my cause defend;
O let thy Word its aid extend,
And, instant, to my breast dispense
It's All-reviving influence.
In vain thy grace the Souls would heal, 445
Whose crimes their just rejection seal;
Who, bold each impious deed to try,
Thy Laws oppose, thy Pow'r defy.
O let thy Mercy, Lord, (how great
That Mercy!) on thy Servant wait, 450
Its beams in full effusion give,
And teach my fainting heart to live.

While

While hostile Crouds around me stand,
My steps I guide by thy Command
Unvarying, and indignant see   455
The Souls whose Will has err'd from Thee.
Behold what love, what full delight,
Thy Precepts in my breast excite,
And let thy Favour o'er my head
Its vital pow'r incessant shed.   460
With truth thy Word, great God, was crown'd,
E'er time began its restless round:
Thy Laws through length of days extend,
First, midst, and last, and without end.

S C H I N.

 While princely Pow'r, without a cause, 465
The threat'ning sword against me draws,
My mind, to thy Commands applied,
Them fears, nor owns a fear beside.
My heart with secret transport swells,
While studious on thy Word it dwells;   470
Nor wealthiest spoils such joy bestow,
New wrested from the prostrate foe.
To Lies averse, thy Laws I love;
Thy just Decrees my Thoughts approve;
And sev'n times, each revolving day,   475
To Thee my grateful vows I pay.
Great is the peace prepar'd for All,
Whose willing feet obey thy Call;
Great is the peace for such prepar'd,
Nor aught their footsteps shall retard. 480
    B b   Thy

Thy health, my God, I wait, thy Will
With unremitted zeal fulfill,
And wrapt in love and filial fear
The Heav'n-defcended Truths revere.
Thy Truths my foul reveres: Each day,   485
Thy wife Inftructions I obey,
Affur'd that to thy fearching eyes
My life's whole path confpicuous lies.

T A U.

O let my cries thy heav'nly feat
Approach; my pray'r indulgent meet,   490
And give (for on thy Word relies
My hope;) O give me to be wife.
Behold, (for Mercy lives in Thee;)
Behold me fuppliant bend the knee,
And let thy promis'd aid difpell   495
The clouds of grief that o'er me dwell.
Thy facred Precepts taught to know,
How fhall my lips, great God, o'erflow
With praife, and, touch'd with holy flame,
The juftice of thy Laws proclaim!   500
While pleas'd I bow to thy Command,
Reach, in my refcue, reach thy hand:
O Thou, whofe Dictates warm my heart,
Thy long-expected health impart;
And let my Soul, to life reftor'd,   505
Thy Love in lafting hymns record,
While o'er my head its beams fhall fhine,
And make thy great Salvation mine.

Thine

Thine eyes in Me the Sheep behold,
Whose feet have wander'd from the fold; 510
That, guideless, helpless, strives in vain
To find its safe retreat again;
Now listens, if perchance its ear
The Shepherd's well-known voice may hear,
Now, as the tempests round it blow, 515
In plaintive accent vents its woe.
Great Ruler of this earthly Ball,
Do Thou my erring steps recall:
O seek thou Him who Thee has sought,
Nor turns from thy Decrees his thought. 520

PSALM CXX.

1.

TO God I cried, with anguish stung,
    Nor form'd a fruitless pray'r.
O save me from the lying tongue,
    And lips that would insnare.

2.

Thou Child of Guilt, to falsehood bred,
    Say, what shall be thine end?
See keenest arrows o'er thy head,
    And quenchless coals, impend.

3.

Ah! Woe is Me, to *Mesech*'s seat
    And *Kedar*'s tents confin'd;
Perpetual insult doom'd to meet
    From Men of restless mind.

4. When

4.

When offers mild of Peace I make,
 And friendlieſt terms prepare,
My words their ſlumb'ring rage awake,
 And arm them for the War.

PSALM CXXI.

1.

LO! from the Hills my help deſcends;
 To Them I lift mine eyes.
My ſtrength on Him alone depends,
 Who form'd the Earth and Skies.

2.

He, ever watchful, ever nigh,
 Forbids thy feet to ſlide;
Nor ſleep nor ſlumber ſeals the eye
 Of *Iſrael*'s Guard and Guide.

3.

He at thy hand, array'd in might,
 His ſhield ſhall o'er thee ſpread:
Nor Sun by day, nor Moon by night,
 Shall hurt thy favour'd head.

4.

Safe ſhalt thou go, and ſafe return,
 While He thy life defends,
Whoſe eyes thy ev'ry ſtep diſcern,
 Whoſe Mercy never ends.

PSALM CXXII.

1.

THE festal Morn, my God, is come,
That calls me to thy honour'd Dome,
    Thy presence to adore:
My feet the summons shall attend,
With willing step thy Courts ascend,
    And tread the hallow'd floor.

2.

Ev'n now to our transported eyes
Fair *Sion*'s tow'rs in prospect rise;
    Within her gates we stand,
And, lost in wonder and delight,
Behold her happy Sons unite
    In friendship's firmest band.

3.

Hither from *Judah*'s utmost end
The Heav'n-protected Tribes ascend;
    Their off'rings hither bring;
Here, eager to attest their joy,
In hymns of praise their tongues employ,
    And hail th' immortal King.

4.

By His Command impell'd, to Her
Contending Crouds their cause refer;
    While Princes from her Throne
With equal doom th' unerring Law
Dispense, who boast their birth to draw
    From *Jesse*'s favour'd Son.

PSALM CXXII.

5.

Be Peace by Each implor'd on Thee,
O *Salem*, while with bended knee
    To *Jacob*'s God we pray:
How bleſt, who calls himſelf thy Friend!
Succeſs his labour ſhall attend,
    And ſafety guard his way.

6.

O may'ſt thou, free from hoſtile fear,
Nor the loud voice of tumult hear,
    Nor war's wild waſtes deplore:
May Plenty nigh thee take her ſtand,
And in thy Courts with laviſh hand
    Diſtribute all her ſtore.

7.

Seat of my Friends and Brethren, hail!
How can my tongue, O *Salem*, fail
    To bleſs thy lov'd Abode?
How ceaſe the zeal that in me glows
Thy good to ſeek, whoſe walls incloſe
    The Manſion of my God?

PSALM CXXIII.

TO Thee, above the ſtarry ſpheres
    Inthron'd, his look thy ſuppliant rears:
As tow'rds their Lord the menial Band,
As Maidens tow'rds their Miſtreſs' hand
Obſervant caſt th' expecting eye,
So lift we ours, great God, on high,

Till Thou thy mercy shalt display,
And chase these clouds of grief away.
Enough thy People, Lord, have borne
Of insult keen, and hostile scorn: 10
O hear, in pity hear, the sighs
From our full hearts incessant rise,
While, round us rang'd, the Sons of pride
Our name revile, our woes deride.

PSALM CXXIV.

HAD God abandon'd from his care
Our cause, when adverse hosts to war
Uprose; had God, may *Israel* say,
Our cause abandon'd, in the day
When o'er the plain their troops were pour'd, 5
Alive by hostile rage devour'd
Down we had sunk; and o'er our head
The swelling floods their waves had spread:
Down we had sunk; but blest be God,
Whose arm the timely help bestow'd, 10
And, each invader chas'd away,
Snatch'd from their jaws th' expected prey.
See! as the Bird with sudden spring
Exulting mounts upon the wing,
Just rescu'd from the fowler's art, 15
So triumph We, with thankful heart,
And, sav'd by his preventing care,
Shake from our feet the broken snare.
When woes, when dangers round us rise,
On Him alone our strength relies, 20

Whose

Whose hand thy center fix'd, O Earth,
And gave th' enduring Heav'ns their birth.

PSALM CXXV.

WHO trust in God's protecting hand,
    Secure as *Sion*'s Mount shall stand,
That, proof to Ages, meets the skies,
And, fix'd, each adverse shock defies.
Behold fair *Salem*'s hallow'd ground,   5
By shadowing hills encompass'd round;
Thy presence thus, great God, we trace
Incircling *Jacob*'s chosen Race:
Nor distant times shall see thy Love
Its blessings from thy Saints remove.   10
Ne'er on the lot by These possess'd
Shall impious Pow'r its scepter rest,
Lest Sin, establish'd into Law,
Their hearts from thy obedience draw.
O still our Guardian, still our Friend,   15
Thy mercies to the Just extend;
While All, whose heart from Wisdom's way
Through paths perverse has lov'd to stray,
In suff'rings, as in guilt, allied,
Shall see the Peace to them denied   20
The fulness of its influence shed
On happier *Israel*'s favour'd head.

PSALM CXXVI.

IS this a Dream? amaz'd we cried,
  When, led by their celestial Guide,
Fair *Sion*'s captive Tribes again
Beheld her late deserted plain.
Then forth to laughter burst each tongue,   5
And songs of loudest triumph sung.
The Nations round, with secret awe,
The mighty work admiring saw:
And, " Great (they cried,) the Gift bestow'd
" On These, the favour'd of their God!"   10
" O, great the Gift!" Our hearts rejoin,
And joyful bless the hand divine.
  Let those, whose exile still we mourn,
Beneath thy conduct, Lord, return,
Fast as the copious torrents glide,   15
When, to its vacant bed their tide
Restoring, o'er the wastes they run,
That burn beneath the southern Sun.
Let scenes of Hope our thought employ:
Who sow in tears, shall reap in joy.   20
The weeping Hind, whose dubious hand
Now strews with grain the furrow'd land,
Shall homeward soon exulting bear
The Blessings of the loaded year.

PSALM CXXVII.

1.

A Race by God unbleſt who rear,
    A fruitleſs toil ſuſtain;
If God to ſhield the Town forbear,
    The Watchman wakes in vain.

2.

Why riſe Ye early, late take reſt,
    And eat the bread of care?
The balm of ſleep, his gift confeſt,
    His Children only ſhare.

3.

Know too thy Sons, that round thee ſtand,
    A gift by Him prepar'd;
Nor arrows in the Giant's hand
    Can yield ſo ſure a guard.

4.

Bleſt, who his quiver ſtores with Theſe:
    When hoſtile troops are near,
His gate the ſtorm approaching ſees,
    Yet ſees without a fear.

PSALM CXXVIII.

HOW bleſt the Souls, their God who fear,
    His Pow'r confeſs, his Law revere!
O happy Thou! ordain'd to ſhare
Thy Maker's ever conſtant care.
Thou privileg'd from want ſhalt ſtand,
And eat the labour of thy hand.

PSALM CXXVIII.

The Object of thy wedded Love
Prolific as the Vine shall prove,
Whose foliage o'er thy walls display'd
Spreads wide its amicable shade:	10
While, as the Olive-branches fair,
Around thy board thy infant Care
Shall croud, and bid thy heart o'erflow
With joys that only Parents know.

    Such Blessings, Lord, thy hands provide	15
For Each who makes thy fear his guide.

    Hail, favour'd Man! From *Sion*'s Tow'r
Thy God on Thee his gifts shall show'r:
Thou, thankful, to thy latest day
Shalt *Salem*'s prosp'ring state survey;	20
With lengthen'd joy, thine aged eyes
Shall see thy Children's Children rise,
And Peace her healing wings expand
O'er *Judah*'s Heav'n-distinguish'd Land.

PSALM CXXIX.

OFT from my youth, may *Israel* say,
    Oft from my youth, in close array
Against me rang'd, the hostile train
My ruin sought, but sought in vain.
My back with stripes the ploughers tore;	5
The lengthen'd furrows stream'd with gore;
But Thou, just God, hast burst their bands,
And sav'd me from their ruthless hands.

    Back let them fly in wild retreat,
Whose rage fair *Sion*'s hallow'd seat	10
                    Pursues:

PSALM CXXIX.

Pursues: Let shame their guilt repay;
And let them like the grass decay,
That, on the house-top seen to rise,
Stops in mid growth, and fades, and dies;
Nor fills the Mower's hand, nor gives   15
One grasp to him who binds the sheaves;
Nor prompts th' observing passenger
To greet them with the friendly pray'r:
" May Heav'n's high Lord your labours bless,
" And crown them with the wish'd success."   20

PSALM CXXX.

1.

TO Thee from out the Deeps I pray,
  With heaviest woes oppress'd:
Lord, let thine ears attentive weigh
  The voice of my request.

2.

If from the Sons of human birth
  Thy wrath its debt demand,
O who, throughout the peopled earth,
  Beneath that wrath shall stand?

3.

But Sin's worst wounds thy Mercy heals:
  As down its pow'rs descend,
The grateful Soul their influence feels,
  And trembles to offend.

4. Thee,

PSALM CXXX.

4.

Thee, Lord, I seek, the Wise, the Just;
   My soul, by Thee upheld,
Expectant waits (thy Word its trust,)
   Till Thou thy beams shalt yield.

5.

Not thus intent their longing sight
   The wearied Watchmen rear,
Not thus intent the growing light
   Observe, when morn is near.

6.

O trust in God; for Love in Him,
   And Grace abundant, reign:
He, *Jacob*, shall thy Sons redeem,
   And purge their ev'ry stain.

PSALM CXXXI.

THY eyes in Me nor lofty mind
   Nor haughty look, my God, shall find;
Nor Earth's vain pomp attracts my view,
Nor Honour's prize my thoughts pursue,
Or, touch'd by fell Ambition's fire,   5
To unpermitted heights aspire.
Behold me of affections mild,
Behold me humble as the Child,
That meek and silent sinks to rest,
Wean'd from the tender Parent's breast.   10
O, fonder than that Parent, see
Thy Maker, *Israel*, cherish Thee:

To latest times on him depend,
Thy Guide, thy Guardian, and thy Friend.

PSALM CXXXII.

GREAT Ruler of this earthly Ball,
Thy *David* to thy thought recall;
O think what pangs his bosom tore,
When to his God the Oath he swore,
And thus, with various pressures bow'd, 5
To *Jacob*'s Lord a Mansion vow'd.
Be Witness, if my floor I tread,
Be Witness, if my couch I spread,
If sleep these weary orbs shall seal,
Or slumber o'er mine eyelids steal, 10
Till to my search fair *Judah*'s Land
Some place present, whereon may stand,
Through future age, thy fix'd Abode,
The Seat of *Jacob*'s mighty God.
To Thee, O *Ephrata*, we came, 15
Inquisitive, and, led by fame,
The hallow'd Tabernacle found
Within the forest's ample bound.
Behold us, Lord, with willing feet
The mansion of thy presence greet, 20
(Each heart inflam'd with grateful zeal,)
And prostrate at thy footstool kneel.
Rise, *Israel*'s Father, God, and Friend;
Pleas'd to thy place of rest ascend,
Thou and thine Ark, tremendous shrine 25
Of Majesty and Pow'r divine.

While

PSALM CXXXII.

While Righteousness thy Priests arrays,
O let thy Saints their thankful lays
Prolong; and in thy *David*'s name
Let *Judah*'s King thy favour claim.   30
Thus to the Prince of *Jesse* born
God the reverseless Oath has sworn:
Thy throne, protected by my care,
The offspring of thy loyns shall heir;
Through distant times their hallow'd Line,   35
Long as to Me their hearts incline,
My Compact keep, my Laws obey,
Shall, uncontroul'd, extend their sway.
Thy Walls, O *Sion*, to thy Lord
His destin'd residence afford;   40
Here will I rest, nor e'er my Love
From thy distinguish'd seat remove.
Thy plenteous board my hand shall spread,
Distribute to thy Poor their bread,
Thy Priests with lasting health invest,   45
And wake to mirth each faithful breast.
Amid thy Race, O *David*, here
Salvation shall her standard rear,
While copious on th' anointed head
The heav'nly Lamp its beams shall shed: 50
Thy foes, with shame invelop'd o'er,
Their blasted counsels shall deplore,
And see the Crown that binds thy brow
With unextinguish'd splendors glow.

PSALM

PSALM CXXXIII.

1.

HOW blest the sight, the joy how sweet,
When Brothers join'd with Brothers meet
   In bands of mutual Love!
Less sweet the liquid fragrance, shed
On *Aaron*'s consecrated head,
   Ran trickling from above,

2.

And reach'd his beard, and reach'd his vest:
Less sweet the Dews on *Hermon*'s breast
   Or *Sion*'s Hill descend:
That Hill has God with Blessings crown'd,
There promis'd Grace that knows no bound,
   And Life that knows no end.

PSALM CXXXIV.

YE Servants of th' eternal King,
   Your grateful hymns triumphant sing:
To You I call, the chosen Band,
Who take amid his Courts your stand,
While, gliding round the dusky pole,   5
The starry Orbs in silence roll.
Within his Temple's vaulted frame
With lifted hands his praise proclaim.
And He, may He, whose pow'r has made
The Earth, and Heav'n's wide arch display'd,   10
From sacred *Sion* bid thee prove
The Blessings of his boundless Love.

PSALM CXXXV. *Hallelujah.*

YE Servants of your God, his fame
   In songs of highest praise proclaim:
Ye who, on his behests intent,
The Courts of *Israel*'s Lord frequent,
And pleas'd within his hallow'd gate   5
In regular succession wait:
Him praise, the everlasting King,
And Mercy's unexhausted spring:
Haste, to his Name your voices rear;
What Name like his the heart can chear?   10
Whose Love from out the num'rous Birth,
That crowns the wide-extended earth,
Selects the Race of *Isaac*'s Sons,
And *Jacob* his possession owns.
'Thy Greatness, Lord, my thoughts attest,   15
With awful gratitude impress'd,
Nor know, among the Seats divine,
A Pow'r that shall contend with Thine;
O Thou, whose All-disposing Sway
The Heav'ns, the Earth, and Seas obey;   20
Whose Might through all extent extends,
Sinks through all depth, all height transcends,
From Earth's low margin to the skies
Now bids the pregnant Vapours rise,
The Lightning's pallid sheet expands,   25
And glads with show'rs the furrow'd lands;
Now from thy Storehouse, built on high,
Permits th' imprison'd Winds to fly,

And, guided by thy Will, to sweep
The surface of the foaming Deep. 30
By thy resistless stroke assail'd,
Her Eldest-born proud *Egypt* wail'd:
Nor rag'd thy sword on Man alone;
Her flocks, her herds, its fury own,
While Nature's varied pow'rs conspire, 35
At thy Decree, Almighty Sire,
With scenes of dread to strike her eyes,
The haughty Tyrant to chastise,
And Each who lent th' assisting hand
To execute his stern command. 40
From *Egypt*'s desolated shore
Its course thy vengeance onward bore,
To distant realms by Justice led;
And mightiest Kings beneath it bled:
Their Monarch *Hesbon*'s Coasts deplor'd, 45
And *Basan* wept her Giant Lord,
While fell Destruction stalks around
Far as to *Canaan*'s utmost bound,
And vindicates her forfeit lands
To conqu'ring *Israel*'s chosen Bands. 50
Thy Name shall ever live; thy Praise,
Immortal God, through longest days
Extend: From Thee we wait our doom:
Thou, Lord, the balance wilt assume,
And, prompt thy People's woes to heal, 55
The sentence of thy wrath repeal.
Behold on each polluted shore
The heathen tribes their Gods adore,

Of

PSALM CXXXV.

Of silver form'd, or fusile gold,
That late within the guiding mould   60
To shapes prescrib'd obedient ran,
The Creatures of thy Creature Man;
Of sense-belying parts possess'd,
In useless imag'ry express'd,
Of Mouth, but not for speech design'd,   65
Of Ears and Eyes, yet deaf and blind:
Whose lips, by Nature's finger seal'd,
Ne'er knew the vital breath to yield:
Unvisited by Wisdom's ray
Their breast: Nor less insensate They,   70
Who made their mimic forms, or, made,
With fruitless pray'r invoke their aid.
Jehovah's praise with grateful tongue
Proclaim, ye Tribes from *Israel* sprung;
Him bless, ye Sons of *Aaron*'s race;   75
Ye who your birth from *Levi* trace,
And All whose heart his Laws delight,
In thanks to Him your songs unite.
Let *Sion* with enraptur'd ear
His fame throughout her precincts hear,   80
Who 'midst her walls, eternal Guest,
Has fix'd the Mansion of his rest.   *Hallelujah.*

PSALM CXXXVI.

I.

LIFT your voice, and thankful sing
Praises to your heav'nly King;
For his Blessings far extend,
And his Mercy knows no end.

2.
Be the Lord your only theme,
Who of Gods is God supreme;
 For his Blessings far extend,
 And his Mercy knows no end.

3.
He to whom All Lords beside
Bow the knee, and vail their pride;
 For his Blessings &c.

4.
Who asserts his just Command
By the Wonders of his hand;
 For his &c.

5.
He, whose Wisdom, thron'd on high,
Built the Mansions of the sky;
 For his &c.

6.
He, who bade the watry Deep
Under Earth's foundation sleep,
 For his &c.

7.
And the Orbs that gild the pole
Through the boundless Æther roll;
 For his &c.

8.
Thee, O Sun, whose pow'rful ray
Rules the Empire of the Day;
 For his &c.

9.
You, O Moon and Stars, whose light
Breaks the horrors of the Night.
  For his &c.

10.
When his vengeful wrath he shed,
Egypt mourn'd her Firstborn dead;
  For his &c.

11.
Thence by Him from bondage freed
March'd all *Israel*'s chosen seed,
  For his &c.

12.
While his mighty hand he rear'd,
And his outstretch'd arm appear'd.
  For his &c.

13.
Aw'd by Him, from side to side
Lo, th' obedient Deeps divide;
  For his &c.

14.
At his word the billows stay,
Part, and give his People way;
  For his &c.

15.
At his word again they close
O'er the head of *Jacob*'s foes.
  For his &c.

PSALM CXXXVI.

16.
Safe in his Almighty aid
Israel o'er the Desert stray'd;
    For his &c.

17.
Kings, unable to withstand,
Felt the vengeance of his hand:
    For his &c.

18.
Chiefs for hardiest deeds renown'd
Prostrate fell, and bit the ground:
    For his &c.

19.
Sihon fierce, who forth to fight
Led the harness'd *Amorite*;
    For his &c.

20.
Mightiest *Og*, beneath whose sway
Basan's fertile region lay.
    For his &c.

21.
These he slew, and from their hands
Took the forfeit of their Lands;
    For his &c.

22.
Lands, which erst by promise due,
Sons of *Jacob*, fell to You.
    For his &c.

PSALM CXXXVI.

23.

On our forrows from on high
He with pity caft an eye;
   For his &c.

24.

In our battles o'er each head
He the fhield of fafety fpread.
   For his &c.

25.

He with food fuftains, O Earth,
All who claim from Thee their birth.
   For his &c.

26.

Lift your voice, and thankful fing
Praife to Heav'n's eternal King;
   For his Bleffings far extend,
   And his Mercy knows no end.

PSALM CXXXVII.

WHERE *Babylon*'s proud water flows,
   We fate and wept, while in us rofe
The dear remembrance of thy name,
O fair, O loft, *Jerufalem!*
Our filent harps the willows bore,   5
Whofe boughs along th' extended fhore
Their fhades outfpread: when thus the Foe
Infulting aggravates our woe:
  " Come, tune to mirth your fullen tongue;
  " Rife, *Hebrew* flaves, and give the fong;   10
                      " Such

PSALM CXXXVII.

"Such strains as wont your fane to fill,
"On captive *Sion*'s boasted Hill."
How shall we yield to the demand?
How, exiles in a heathen Land,
Presume the Heav'n-taught song to raise,   15
And desecrate the hallow'd lays?
If *Sion* from my breast depart,
Forget my hand its tuneful art:
Fast to my palate cleave my tongue,
If, when I form my sprightliest song,   20
Aught to my mirth supply a theme,
But Thou, O lov'd *Jerusalem*.
Think, Lord, O think, when *Sion* lay
Abandon'd to the dreadful day,
How, as thy heaviest wrath she tried,   25
"Down, down, exulting *Edom* cried,
"Down let the hated City fall,
"And level to the dust her wall."
Daughter of *Babylon*, that woe,
Depress'd, consum'd, thyself shalt know,   30
Which We, dire Murth'ress, found from Thee:
And Blest, who shall by God's Decree
Warn from thy fate each distant Land
To dread the Justice of his hand;
Commission'd lead the slaughter on,   35
And dash thine Infants on the stone.

PSALM CXXXVIII.

THEE, Lord, my harp's awaken'd strings
   Shall praise, and to the ear of Kings,
Whose pow'rs thy sacred impress bear,
The ardor of my zeal declare.
In low prostration, tow'rd thy shrine,   5
His knees thy Servant shall incline,
And thankful teach the rapt'rous lay
Thy Faith and Mercy to display,
Whose Sanctity all height transcends;
Whose word eternal Truth attends;   10
Whose Pow'r, while Thee my pray'r address'd,
Has fill'd with Heav'n-born strength my breast.
Earth's Lords, by thy instructions led,
With *Israel*'s sons thy path shall tread,
And, joyous, as they march along,   15
Thy Glory chaunt in grateful song,
Thee Nature's only Lord attest,
Of boundless excellence possess'd,
Inthron'd above the loftiest sky,
Yet wont the Humble to descry,   20
And, from thy distant seat, deride
The frantic boasts of human pride.
When hostile troops excite my fear,
Thy quick'ning Grace my heart shall chear,
Thy hand compose their furious strife,   25
And rescue from the sword my life.
What bliss thy promise bids me share,
Haste, Lord, to yield; nor from thy care

(O ever faithful, wife and good,)
The creature of thy hands exclude.   30

PSALM CXXXIX.

THOU, Lord, haft fearch'd me out; thine eyes
    Mark when I fit, and when I rife;
By Thee my future thoughts are read;
Thou round my path, and round my bed,
Attendeft vigilant; each word,   5
E'er yet I fpeak, by Thee is heard.
Life's maze, before my view outfpread,
Within thy prefence wrapt I tread,
And touch'd with confcious horror ftand
Beneath the fhadow of thy hand.   10
How deep thy Knowledge, Lord, how wide!
Long to the fruitlefs tafk applied,
That mighty Sea my thoughts explore,
Nor reach its depth, nor find its fhore.
Where fhall I fhun thy wakeful eye,   15
Or whither from thy Spirit fly?
Aloft to Heav'n my courfe I bear;
In vain; for Thou, my God, art there:
If prone to Hell my feet defcend,
Thou ftill my footfteps fhalt attend: 20
If now, on fwifteft wings upborne,
I feek the regions of the Morn,
Or hafte me to the weftern Steep,
Where Eve fits brooding o'er the Deep,
Thy hand the fugitive fhall ftay,   25
And dictate to my fteps their way.

                    Perchance

PSALM CXXXIX.

Perchance within its thickeſt veil
The Darkneſs ſhall my head conceal:
But, inſtant, Thou haſt chas'd away
The gloom, and round me pour'd the day. 30
Darkneſs, great God, to Thee there's none;
Darkneſs and Light to Thee are one;
Nor brighter ſhines to Thee diſplay'd
The Noon than Night's obſcureſt ſhade.
My reins, my fabrick's ev'ry part, 35
The wonders of thy plaſtic art
Proclaim, and prompt my willing tongue
To meditate the grateful ſong:
With deepeſt awe my Thought their frame
Surveys:—" I tremble that I am." 40
While yet a ſtranger to the day
Within the burthen'd womb I lay,
My bones, familiar to thy view,
By juſt degrees to firmneſs grew:
Day to ſucceeding day conſign'd 45
Th' unfiniſh'd Birth; thy mighty Mind
Each limb, each nerve, e'er yet they were,
Contemplated diſtinct and clear;
Thoſe nerves thy curious finger ſpun,
Thoſe limbs it faſhion'd one by one; 50
And, as thy pen in fair deſign
Trac'd on thy book each ſhadowy line,
Thy Handmaid Nature read them there,
And made the growing work her care,
Conform'd it to th' unerring plan, 55
And gradual wrought me into Man.

PSALM CXXXIX.

With what delight, great God, I trace
The Acts of thy stupendous Grace!
To count them, were to count the sand
That lies upon the sea-beat strand.   60
When from my temples sleep retires,
To Thee my thankful heart aspires,
And with thy sacred presence blest
Joys to receive the awful Guest.
Shall impious Men thy will withstand,   65
Nor feel the vengeance of thy hand?
Hence, Murth'rers, hence, nor near me stay;
Ye Sons of Violence, away.
When lawless Crouds with insult vain
Thy Works revile, thy Name profane,   70
Can I unmov'd those insults see,
Nor hate the Wretch that hateth Thee?
Indignant, in thy Cause I join,
And all thy foes, my God, are mine.
Searcher of hearts, my thoughts review;   75
With kind severity pursue
Through each disguise thy Servant's mind,
Nor leave one stain of guilt behind.
Guide through th' eternal path my feet,
And bring me to thy blissful Seat.   80

PSALM CXL.

MY impious foes, great God, repell;
Their rage by pow'r superior quell;
Who toil, on fierce contention bent,
New arts of mischief to invent;

Whet,

Whet, as the Asp, their tongues, and dip
In Death's worst gall their venom'd lip.
O save me from the hand of Wrong,
And backward turn the frantic Throng,
That, pleas'd, in dire alliance meet,
And tempt to fatal lapse my feet.
The murth'rous trap, th' intwining snare,
The Sons of Violence prepare,
And guileful, onward as I tread,
Beside my path their net outspread.
Thou art my God; thine ear apply:
(Thus prostrate at thy throne I cry:)
Strength of my health, indulgent Lord,
Thy Arm unseen each adverse sword,
As o'er the field the battle burn'd,
Preventive from my head has turn'd.
O let not the remorseless Band
(Each counsel by thy prosp'ring hand
Accomplish'd, and each wish supplied,)
Their conquests, with augmented pride,
Exulting boast; but on their heads
(While round the hostile circle spreads,
Intent my guiltless Soul to slay,)
The mischief of their lips repay.
Let rushing flames their sin chastise;
Prone tow'rd the pit (no more to rise,)
Let each with fault'ring footsteps bend,
And headlong to its depths descend.
The tongue to Wisdom unsubdu'd
From bliss its Owner shall exclude:

The feet to violence inclin'd 35
Deſtruction, following faſt behind,
Shall hunt, and with unwearied pace
Through ſin's dark maze their path ſhall trace.
My heart has known thee, Lord, prepar'd
The helpleſs and the poor to guard, 40
To ſave them from Oppreſſion's jaws,
And vindicate their injur'd cauſe.
The Souls ſubjected to thy fear
To Thee the thankful voice ſhall rear,
And, ſtudious of thy juſt Command, 45
Within thy ſight accepted ſtand.

PSALM CXLI.

TO Thee I call; O haſte thee near;
My voice, great God, indulgent hear;
With grateful odour to the ſkies
As incenſe let my pray'r ariſe,
And let my hands, uplifted high, 5
With full acceptance meet thine eye,
As Victims on thy altar laid,
When eve extends its deep'ning ſhade.
O let my mouth to guilt be barr'd,
And o'er its portal plant a guard. 10
Turn, turn from ſin's purſuit my will,
Nor let th' artificers of ill
In Me the wiſh'd aſſociate greet,
Or ſee me to their path my feet
Incline, and, caught in Error's ſnare, 15.
Their feaſtful board luxurious ſhare:

Let

Let Virtue's Friends, severely kind,
With welcome chastisement my mind
Correct; but give not These to shed
The balm of flatt'ry o'er my head,   20
Lest sudden from thy wrath I feel
The stroke, that none shall know to heal.
The pray'r, that from my lips proceeds,
My just abhorrence of their deeds
Shall speak; nor Thou that pray'r despise,   25
But, while before their startled eyes
From rocky heights their Chiefs are thrown,
Incline their stubborn hearts to own
How sweet my words, and, taught thy fear,
The lessons of thy truth to hear.   30
Behold the grave's wide mouth display'd,
Our bones in heaps before it laid,
As when beneath the Woodman's stroke
From the tall Ash or spreading Oak
The branches fall, and scatter'd round   35
In wild disorder strew the ground.
Father of All! to Thee mine eyes
I lift: on Thee my hope relies:
Do Thou, as 'mid the toils I tread
By Men of impious heart outspread,   40
My danger (nor regardless,) see,
And let me, while by thy decree
Wrapt in the snare themselves I view,
With step secure my path pursue.

PSALM

PSALM CXLII.

TO God I cry; to Him my pray'r
   Address; to Him my heart its care
Shall pour, and to his ear disclose
In sad recital all its woes.
Thine eyes, great God, with steady view   5
Through sorrow's gloom my steps pursue,
And see my foes athwart my way
The cover'd snare insiduous lay.
I turn'd me, anxious, on the right,
I turn'd, and round me cast my sight   10
With fruitless search; no friend was nigh,
Th' expected succour to supply,
With lenient tongue my griefs to chear,
Or pitying drop the social tear.
Forlorn of help, Thee, mightiest Lord,   15
My Soul with humble trust implor'd:
In Thee, All-bounteous God, I cried,
In Thee alone my hopes reside;
While life along my veins shall stream,
Its portion Thee and bliss supreme   20
My heart shall own: O gracious hear,
While worn with griefs my voice I rear,
And let my foe's superior might
Thy pity to my aid excite.
Do Thou my prison doors unbar;   25
So shall my tongue thy Love declare
In hymns of praise, while, joy'd in Me
Th' event of pious Hope to see,

The Souls that own thy juſt Command
With thankful wonder round me ſtand.   30

PSALM CXLIII.

THINE ear, my God, propitious lend;
   O ever juſt and true, extend
Thy pity, while to Thee I pray,
Nor ſcrutinize with ſtrict ſurvey
Thy ſervant's Acts; for who, O who,   5
Shall pure of guilt approach thy view?
Thou ſeeſt the Foe with furious ſtrife
My ſoul purſue; to earth my life
He treads, and in the horrid gloom,
(As thoſe who 'mid the ſilent tomb   10
Through ages ſleep,) from human eye
Secluded far, has bid me lie.
I feel my vital ſtrength depart,
And wild amazement fills my heart.
But, backward borne to periods paſt,   15
Thy Mercies, Lord, my thoughts have trac'd;
And in my breaſt recorded ſtand
The wonders of thy mighty hand.
Aloft my ſuppliant palms I ſpread;
Nor more the glebe, its moiſture fled,   20
Longs the deſcending ſhow'r to ſee,
Than thirſts my wearied ſoul for Thee.
O haſte to hear me, haſte to ſave;
Nor let me (leſt the yawning grave
Enwrap me in its dreary reign,)   25
Thy chearing preſence ſeek in vain.

O

PSALM CXLIII.

O let the hour that wakes the day
Thy Mercy to my ear convey.
While (for on Thee my hope depends;)
In fervent thought my mind ascends,   30
Expectant, tow'rd thy heav'nly Seat,
Train to the paths of Truth my feet.
To Thee, my refuge, Lord, I fly;
Do Thou the deaths that wait me nigh
Repell. My will to thine (for Thou,   35
Thou, art my God;) corrective bow,
And give me, by thy Spirit led,
Auspicious Guide, the Land to tread
Where Righteousness has fix'd her Throne;
Thy Mercy, long to *Israel* known,   40
True to thy Name, to Me impart,
And quicken with thy grace my heart.
O let thy Justice interpose,
My sorrows to relieve, my foes
To crush, and from their rage remove   45
A Soul devoted to thy Love.

PSALM CXLIV.

BLEST be the Lord my strength, whose aids,
   When lawless force my peace invades,
My fingers for their task prepare,
And discipline my hands to War:
My hope, my shield, my strongest tow'r,   5
The Friend that in the dang'rous hour
My life protects, my trust sustains,
Gives to my steady grasp the reins.

PSALM CXLIV.

Of Pow'r, and bids each hoſtile Land
Subjected own my juſt command.   10
Lord, what is Man, that in thy care
His humble lot ſhould find a ſhare?
Or what the Son of Man, that THOU
Thus to his wants thine ear ſhouldſt bow?
(Himſelf, when in the balance weigh'd, 15
A Nothing, and his Life a ſhade.)
Deſcend, from Heav'n's vaſt height deſcend:
Its wide-ſpread arch beneath thee bend:
Touch the proud hills, eternal Sire;
And ſee them quick in ſmoke aſpire!   20
Let fierceſt lightnings through the air
Now ruſhing now reverting tear
Thy ſtubborn foes; and, edg'd with flame,
Swift at their heads thy arrows aim.
Stretch to my aid thine arm, and ſave   25
My life from the devouring wave:
Back let the vengeful foe retire,
Whoſe lips, whoſe hands, in fraud conſpire.
So ſhall my finger's artful ſtroke
The harp and tenſtring'd lute provoke   30
New ſtrains t' attempt, and with my tongue
In ſweet diviſion form the ſong.
Guardian of Kings! whoſe fav'ring might
Thy *David* through the thickeſt fight
With watchful care vouchſaf'd to guide, 35
And turn'd each threat'ning ſword aſide,
Back let the vengeful foe retire,
Whoſe lips, whoſe hands, in fraud conſpire.

So,

So, nurs'd beneath indulgent skies,
Our Sons with full increase shall rise, 40
Like youngling plants in order rang'd,
Of healthful stem, and leaf unchang'd,
Our Daughters as the column fair,
That, fashion'd by the Artist's care,
Claims in the regal Dome a place, 45
The polish'd angle's noblest grace.
While the rich harvest's gather'd store
Loads with its heap th' extended floor,
Our Oxen strong for toil behold!
The teeming Mothers of the fold 50
See, scatter'd o'er the rural scene,
Their thousands and their myriads yean.
No more our Streets the cries of fear
Or shouts of violence shall hear:
Thou, Lord, the tumults shalt assuage 55
Of hostile force, and civil rage.
O happy We, while thus our Race
The signals of thy Love shall grace!
O blest the People, that in Thee
Their God and faithful Guardian see! 60

PSALM CXLV.

THEE will I bless, my God and King,
   Nor cease thy wondrous Acts to sing.
From earliest morn to latest eve
Thy praises on my tongue shall live;
To Thee my harp shall wake each string, 5
Nor cease thy wondrous Acts to sing.

Great

PSALM CXLV.

 Great is our God : In vain our praise
His Excellence in equal lays
Would celebrate; in vain the Mind
Its height, its depth, essays to find.   10
Age to succeeding age thy Might
Shall speak, thy Works, blest Lord, recite.
My tongue thy glory shall proclaim,
The faithful witness of thy fame,
Bid Contemplation's inmost thought   15
Survey the wonders thou hast wrought,
And with assenting myriads join
To bless the Majesty divine.
Thy dreaded Pow'r shall each rehearse,
Thy Greatness shall my thankful verse   20
Inspire, thy Righteousness and Love
Our hearts inflame, our songs improve.
Thee good and kind shall Mortals own,
To anger slow, to pity prone.
Thy Mercies on the sons of Earth,   25
On All whom Thou hast call'd to birth,
Far as Creation's bounds extend,
Thy Mercies, heav'nly Lord, descend.
One chorus of perpetual praise
To Thee thy various works shall raise,   30
Thy Saints to Thee in hymns impart
The transports of a grateful heart,
The splendors of thy Kingdom tell,
Delighted on thy Wonders dwell,
And bid the World's wide realms admire   35
The glories of th' Almighty Sire,

Whose Throne shall Nature's wreck survive,
Whose Pow'r through endless Ages live.
His Promise Truth eternal guides,
And Mercy o'er his Act presides.   40
The feet whose steps to lapse incline
With faithful care the Arm divine
Shall prop; the Spirit bow'd with woe
His All-supporting aid shall know.
From Thee, great God, while ev'ry eye   45
Expectant waits the wish'd supply,
Their bread proportion'd to the day
Thy op'ning hands to each convey.
Thy Ways eternal Justice guides,
And Mercy o'er thine Act presides: 50
Who ask thine aid with heart sincere,
Thee ever gracious, ever near,
Shall own; their pray'r, in each distress,
To Thee thy Servants, Lord, address,
And find thee (verging on the grave,)   55
Nor slow to hear, nor weak to save.
 Ye Souls among his Saints inroll'd,
In God your sure defence behold,
While fierce Destruction at his word
Shall bathe in impious blood its sword.   60
 Long as I breathe, my grateful tongue
To Him shall meditate the song;
From Man's whole Race his hallow'd Name
Shall thanks and endless honour claim.

PSALM

PSALM CXLVI. *Hallelujah.*

PRAISE, praise thy God, my Soul; his Name
   To Life's last date my thanks shall claim,
And, long as I exist, my lyre
Shall wake to sing th' eternal Sire.
O seek not, with presumption vain,   5
Your hope on Princes to sustain,
Nor trust, when threat'ning ills invade,
The strengthless prop of human aid.
His breath resign'd, on earth's low bed
Behold the Mortal rest his head;   10
Nor farther shall his thoughts extend,
But with him to the grave descend.
Blest, who their help in Thee alone,
The God to *Jacob*'s Offspring known,
Have found, and to the hand divine   15
In each distress their care resign:
That hand, that form'd the Heav'ns and Earth,
And call'd the watry Deep to birth,
With All that in the ample round
Of Nature's utmost Reign is found.   20
'Tis God's, whose Truth, through ages past
Confirm'd, shall time's extent outlast,
'Tis His, the injur'd cause to right,
And crush the arm of lawless Might;
With bread the hungry to sustain,   25
And loose the wretched Captive's chain,
The blind restore, the weak uprear,
And to the souls that own his fear

His Mercies, each revolving day,
In endless series to display: 30
Through distant regions doom'd to roam,
In Him the stranger finds a home;
'Tis His, the Orphan's breast to chear,
And wipe the heart-swoln Widow's tear.
From His Decrees who dare to stray, 35
Shall reap the error of their way.
O *Sion*, in thy God confide,
And know how fix'd his Reign, how wide:
O'er subject Worlds his just Command
To endless age confirm'd shall stand. *Halleiujah.* 40

PSALM CXLVII.

O Bless *Jehovah:* Sweet the joy,
When tasks like these the voice employ;
To Him our highest thanks belong,
And Praise sits comely on our tongue.
'Tis He, who builds fair *Salem*'s walls, 5
And *Israel*'s exil'd sons recalls;
Yields to the contrite heart relief,
And binds its wounds, and sooths its grief;
Assigns the starry flock their names,
(As, scatter'd wide, their vivid flames 10
Adorn the bright ethereal plain,)
And numbers with his eye their train.
Great is our God: beyond all bound
His Pow'r, beyond all search is found
His Knowledge; in his Arm the Meek 15
With sure success their Aid shall seek;—

That

PSALM CXLVII.

That Arm, whose unresisted stroke
On Each who dares his Wrath provoke
With swift descent its aim shall guide,
And level to the dust their pride. 20
Let ev'ry tongue, let ev'ry chord,
Exalt the name of *Jacob*'s Lord,
Whose hand with clouds the Heav'n obscures;
On Earth the genial moisture pours;
Bids the green herb its mantle spread, 25
Luxuriant, o'er the Mountain's head:
With lib'ral care th' unconscious Beast
Sustains, and stills the Raven's nest,
When urg'd by want her clam'rous Brood
Request from Him their wonted food. 30

 If o'er the field the battle bleed,
Regardless of the strengthful Steed,
Regardless of the Chiefs, whose feet
Unmov'd the shock of legions meet,
On You, in whom his Fear resides, 35
On You, whose heart in Him confides,
His Grace its signals shall bestow,
His Arm with conquest bind your brow.

 O *Solyma*, his lov'd Abode,
Him praise, unceasing! Bless thy God, 40
O *Sion*, who thy gates has barr'd;
Whose various gifts thy Sons have shar'd;
Who crowns with peace thy happy plain;
Calls from thy glebe the purest grain;
Whose Word, from heav'n in swift career 45
Convey'd, suggests to Nature's ear

The Laws that regulate her frame,
And gives her ev'ry act its aim.
Flak'd by his Art, the woolly snow
Falls silent on the ground below;   50
By Him the frost, as ashes hoar,
Lies sprinkled earth's wide surface o'er:
In harden'd fragments through the air,
While Man its rigours shuns to bear,
His hail descends; in icy chains   55
His hand the gliding stream detains,
Till, at his word, th' instructed wind
With friendly breath the wave unbind,
And bid it, onward borne, again
With liquid lapse its course maintain.   60
   Such is the God, and such his Might,
Whose Precepts *Israel*'s Love invite,
And to his Tribes in full display
His Life-directing truths convey.
What Realm, through earth's extended Coasts, 65
His Care, like thine, O *Judah*, boasts,
Or, taught, as Thou, his fear to own,
The dictates of his Will has known?
O come, your thankful voices join,
And bless the Majesty divine.   70

PSALM CXLVIII. *Hallelujah.*

YE Blest Inhabitants of Heav'n,
  To God be all your praises giv'n;
O praise him from the realms that lie
Above the reach of mortal eye.

Him.

PSALM CXLVIII.

Him praise, ye Angels of his Train,
Him All whom Heav'n's vast Hosts contain;
Praise Him, Thou Sun, that round the pole
With restless course art seen to roll,
And Thou, O Moon, whose sharpen'd horns
A lustre not their own adorns;
Praise Him, ye Stars: His praise repeat,
Thou Heav'n of Heav'ns, his awful Seat,
And You, ye Floods, that, heap'd on high,
Press with your weight th' extended sky.
Let These to God their voices rear,
Who bade them be; and strait they were:
Who bids them stand; and stand they shall;
Nor aught the Mandate shall recall,
That, fix'd by his Almighty Mind,
To endless age their date assign'd.

   Nor let the Heav'n his praise confine;
O All of Earth the chorus join:
Ye Whales, ye Deeps, in praise conspire,
Snow, Vapour, Hail, and bick'ring Fire,
And ev'ry Wind, and ev'ry Storm,
That duteous his behests perform;
Ye lesser Hills, ye Mountains high,
Ye Trees, whose fruits Man's food supply,
Ye Cedars, whose expanded Shade
Nor Storms nor Ages teach to fade,
Ye Beasts, that range th' uncultur'd soil,
Or patient lend to Man your toil:
Praise Him, each Bird that wings the air,
Each Reptile, nurtur'd by his care;

Ye

Ye Kings and Nations of the Earth; 35
O praife him All of princely birth,
And Ye, whofe Doom, as Juftice guides,
The long-contefted caufe decides.
Ye Youthful Bands and Virgin Choir,
Each lifping Babe, and hoary Sire, 40
Wake to his Name your grateful fongs;
To Him alone all Praife belongs;
His glory Earth's wide bounds o'erflows,
Nor higheft Heav'n its limit knows.
Ye Tribes, exalted by his Arm, 45
You, chief, the heav'nly Theme fhall warm,
Bleft Sons of *Ifrael*'s hallow'd Land,
Who neighb'ring to his prefence ftand.
 O come, your thankful voices raife,
And confecrate to Him your praife. 50

PSALM CXLIX. *Hallelujah.*

SING to our God the new-form'd lay;
 Ye Souls who his commands obey,
Affembling join your thankful tongues,
And hallow with his praife your Songs.
O *Ifrael*, let thy Maker's Name 5
With joyous zeal thy breaft inflame,
And *Sion*'s fons exulting fing
The Mercies of their heav'nly King.
Range in the dance the facred Band,
And urge the Minftrel's well-taught hand 10
(Its touch with varying force applied,)
The reins of harmony to guide,

       While

While with the loud-resounding lyre
The timbrels in his praise conspire.
With what delight, great God, behold   15
Thine eyes the People of thy fold!
Thy Strength the Souls of humble frame
Their ever present Aid proclaim.
With conquest crown'd, and rapt in joy,
Let All whom thy Decrees employ   20
Thy Name exalt with thankful mind,
Nor cease, when on their beds reclin'd,
The silent midnight's list'ning ear
With songs of loudest mirth to chear.
Thy Mercy let their lips record;   25
Give to their grasp the two-edg'd sword;
And let them, guided by thy hand,
Thy vengeance through each Heathen Land
Distribute, and the Tribes chastise
Whose impious Arm thy pow'r defies,   30
Triumphant in the iron chain
Their Nobles and their Kings detain,
And while, inspir'd with active zeal,
Thy prescript thus their hands fulfill,
The glories wear for All prepar'd,   35
Whose hearts thy just behests regard.   *Hallelujah.*

PSALM CL. *Hallelujah.*

PRAISE, O praise, the Name divine;
   Praise it at the hallow'd Shrine;
Let the Firmament on high
To its Maker's praise reply:

                               Let

Let his Acts, and Pow'r supreme, 5
To your Songs suggest a theme:
Be the harp no longer mute;
Sound the trumpet, touch the lute;
Wake to life each tuneful string;
Bring the pipe, the timbrel bring; 10
Let the organ in his praise
Learn its loudest note to raise,
And the cymbal's varying sound
From the vaulted roof rebound.
All who vital breath enjoy, 15
In his praise that breath employ,
And in one great Chorus join;
Praise, O praise, the Name divine.

GLORIA PATRI.

1. IN Thee, O Heav'n, O Earth, in Thee
    Be Glory to th' Eternal Three;
   That Glory, which through ages past
   Was; is; and shall for ever last.

OR THIS.

2. To Father, Son, and Spirit blest,
    Be praise in Heav'n and Earth address'd,
   As was, and is, and yet shall be,
   When Time its latest hour shall see.

OR THIS.

3. To Father, Son, and Spirit blest,
    Be praise in loudest notes address'd,

Such

Such as the Stars of Morning sung,
When Earth was on its balance hung,
Such praise as from th' Angelic Choirs,
And Saints whom zeal like theirs inspires,
In Heav'n above and Earth below
Still flows, and shall for ever flow.

ANOTHER.

4. All Glory to th' Eternal Three;
Thee, Father; Thee, O Son; and Thee,
 The Spirit ever blest:
That Glory, which through ages past
Unchang'd has stood, and yet shall last,
 When Time has sunk to rest.

ANOTHER.

5. All Glory to th' Eternal Three,
 As was, e'er Time began to roll,
As is, nor yet shall cease to be,
 When Time has reach'd its destin'd goal.

ANOTHER.

6. Be Glory to th' Eternal Three
 Ascrib'd, and highest Praise,
As was, and is, and still shall be
 Beyond the end of days.

ANOTHER.

7. To th' Eternal Three be giv'n
Praise on Earth, and Praise in Heav'n;
Such as was through ages past,
Is, and shall for ever last.

☞ *The Translations of the* Gloria Patri, *here given, exhibit a Specimen of five different Sorts of Metre used in the Version or Paraphrase of the Psalms.*

A TABLE of REFERENCES

TO THE

English BIBLE Translation of the PSALMS;

SHEWING

To what Parts of the above VERSION or PARAPHRASE the several Verses of each PSALM correspond.

Bible Transl.	*Paraphrase.*	*Bible Transl.*	*Paraphr.*
PSALM I.		**Pſ. IV.**	
Verſe 1, 2.	Line 1—10.	v. 1.	Line 1—6.
v. 3.	11—22.	v. 2.	7—10.
v. 4.	23—26.	v. 3.	11—14.
v. 5, 6.	27—34.	v. 4, 5.	15—22.
		v. 6.	23—28.
		v. 7.	29—34.
Pſ. II.		v. 8.	35—38.
v. 1, 2, 3.	1—8.		
v. 4, 5.	9—12.		
v. 6.	13—16.	**Pſ. V.**	
v. 7.	17—22.	v. 1, 2, 3.	1—8.
v. 8.	23—26.	v. 4, 5, 6.	9—16.
v. 9.	27—32.	v. 7.	17—20.
v. 10, 11, 12.	33—44.	v. 8, 9.	21—30.
		v. 10, 11, 12.	31—44.
Pſ. III.		**Pſ. VI.**	
v. 1, 2.	1—6.	v. 1, 2, 3, 4.	1—10.
v. 3, 4.	7—12.	v. 5.	11—14.
v. 5, 6.	13—18.	v. 6, 7.	15—26.
v. 7.	19—24.	v. 8, 9, 10.	27—32.
v. 8.	25—28.		**Pſ. VII.**

A TABLE of REFERENCES.

Bible Transl.	Paraphr.	Bible Transl.	Paraphr.
Pſ. VII.		**Pſ. XIII.**	
v. 1, 2.	1—8.	v. 1, 2.	1—8.
v. 3, 4, 5.	9—18.	v. 3, 4.	9—18.
v. 6, 7, 8, 9.	19—32.	v. 5, 6.	19—26.
v. 10, 11.	33—38.		
v. 12, 13.	39—44.	**Pſ. XIV.**	
v. 14, 15, 16.	45—52.	v. 1.	1—8.
v. 17.	53—56.	v. 2, 3.	9—18.
		v. 4, 5, 6.	19—30.
Pſ. VIII.		v. 7.	31—40.
v. 1.	1—4.		
v. 2.	5—10.	**Pſ. XV.**	
v. 3, 4.	11—22.	v. 1, 2.	1—8.
v. 5, 6, 7, 8, 9.	23—38.	v. 3.	9—14.
		v. 4, 5.	15—28.
Pſ. IX.			
v. 1, 2.	1—7.	**Pſ. XVI.**	
v. 3, 4.	8—14.	v. 1, 2, 3.	1—12.
v. 5, 6.	15—24.	v. 4.	13—18.
v. 7, 8.	25—30.	v. 5, 6.	19—24.
v. 9, 10.	31—38.	v. 7, 8.	25—32.
v. 11, 12.	39—46.	v. 9, 10, 11.	33—48.
v. 13, 14.	47—54.		
v. 15, 16, 17, 18.	55—68.	**Pſ. XVII.**	
v. 19, 20.	69—76.	v. 1, 2.	1—6.
		v. 3, 4, 5.	7—16.
Pſ. X.		v 6, 7.	17—24.
v. 1, 2, 3.	1—12.	v. 8, 9, 10, 11, 12.	25—36.
v. 4, 5.	13—20.	v. 13, 14.	37—44.
v. 6.	21—26.	v. 15.	45—50.
v. 7, 8, 9, 10.	27—46.		
v. 11.	47—50.	**Pſ. XVIII.**	
v. 12, 13.	51—56.	v. 1, 2, 3.	1—10.
v. 14.	57—64.	v. 4, 5, 6.	11—20.
v. 15.	65—68.	v. 7, 8.	21—28.
v. 16, 17, 18.	69—80.	v. 9, 10.	29—36.
		v. 11, 12, 13, 14, 15.	37—56.
Pſ. XI.		v. 16, 17, 18, 19, 20.	57—74.
v. 1, 2.	1—8.	v. 21, 22, 23, 24.	75—84.
v. 3, 4, 5.	9—20.	v. 25, 26.	85—90.
v. 6, 7.	21—30.	v. 27, 28, 29.	91—104.
		v. 30, 31, 32, 33, 34, 35, 36.	105—130.
Pſ. XII.		v. 37, 38, 39, 40.	131—142.
v. 1, 2.	1—6.	v. 41, 42.	143—150.
v. 3, 4.	7—14.	v. 43, 44, 45.	151—160.
v. 5.	15—20.	v. 46, 47, 48, 49.	161—170.
v. 6.	21—24.	v. 50.	171—176.
v. 7, 8.	25—30.		

A TABLE of REFERENCES.

Bible Transl.	Paraphr.	Bible Transl.	Paraphr.
Pf. XIX.		v. 4, 5, 6, 7. –	3, 4.
v. 1, 2, 3. – –	1 — 10.	v. 8, 9, 10, 11, 12.	5, 6, 7, 8.
v. 4, 5, 6. – –	11 — 24.	**Pf. XXVII.**	
v. 7, 8. – – –	25 — 38.	v. 1, 2, 3. – –	1 — 12.
v. 9, 10, 11. –	39 — 52.	v. 4, 5, 6. – –	13 — 28.
v. 12, 13. – –	53 — 62.	v. 7, 8, 9. – –	29 — 42.
v. 14. – – –	63 — 70.	v. 10, 11, 12. –	43 — 56.
Pf. XX.		v. 13, 14. – –	57 — 66.
v. 1, 2, 3. – –	1 — 12.	**Pf. XXVIII.**	
v. 4, 5, 6. – –	13 — 24.	v. 1, 2, 3. – –	1 — 16.
v. 7, 8, 9. – –	25 — 36.	v. 4, 5. – – –	17 — 32.
Pf. XXI.		v. 6, 7. – – –	33 — 42.
v. 1, 2, 3. – –	1 — 12.	v. 8, 9. – – –	43 — 52.
v. 4, 5, 6, 7, 8. –	13 — 22.	**Pf. XXIX.**	
v. 9, 10, 11, 12, 13.	23 — 40.	v. 1, 2. – – –	1 — 6.
Pf. XXII.		v. 3, 4, 5, 6, 7, 8. –	7 — 28.
v. 1, 2, 3. – –	1 — 12.	v. 9, 10, 11. –	29 — 42.
v. 4, 5, 6, 7, 8.	13 — 26.	**Pf. XXX.**	
v. 9, 10, 11, 12, 13.	27 — 42.	v. 1, 2, 3. – –	1 — 10.
v. 14, 15. – –	43 — 52.	v. 4, 5. – – –	11 — 24.
v. 16, 17, 18. –	53 — 66.	v. 6, 7, 8, 9, 10.	25 — 42.
v. 19, 20, 21. –	67 — 76.	v. 11, 12. – –	43 — 50.
v. 22, 23, 24. –	77 — 90.	**Pf. XXXI.**	
v. 25, 26. – –	91 — 102.	v. 1, 2, 3, 4, 5. –	1 — 20.
v. 27, 28. – –	103 — 108.	v. 6, 7, 8. – –	21 — 34.
v. 29, 30, 31. –	109 — 122.	v. 9, 10, 11, 12.	35 — 54.
Pf. XXIII.		v. 13, 14, 15, 16, 17, 18.	55 — 76.
v. 1, 2, 3, 4. –	1 — 20.	v. 19, 20. – –	77 — 88.
v. 5, 6. – – –	21 — 30.	v. 21, 22. – –	89 — 98.
Pf. XXIV.		v. 23, 24. – –	99 — 106.
v. 1, 2. – – –	1 — 8.	**Pf. XXXII.**	
v. 3, 4, 5, 6. –	9 — 22.	v. 1, 2. – – –	1 — 8.
v. 7, 8, 9, 10. –	23 — 38.	v. 3, 4, 5. – –	9 — 30.
Pf. XXV.		v. 6, 7. – – –	31 — 42.
v. 1, 2, 3. – –	1 — 10.	v. 8, 9, 10, 11. –	43 — 58.
v. 4, 5, 6, 7. –	11 — 22.	**Pf. XXXIII.**	
v. 8, 9, 10, 11. –	23 — 36.	v. 1, 2, 3. – –	1 — 10.
v. 12, 13, 14. –	37 — 52.	v. 4, 5, 6, 7. –	11 — 22.
v. 15, 16, 17, 18.	53 — 62.	v. 8, 9. – – –	23 — 28.
v. 19, 20, 21, 22.	63 — 74.	v. 10, 11, 12. –	29 — 40.
Pf. XXVI.		v. 13, 14, 15. –	41 — 46.
v. 1, 2, 3. –	Stanza 1, 2.		

A TABLE of REFERENCES.

Bible Transl.	Paraphr.	Bible Transl.	Paraphr.
v. 16, 17, 18, 19.	47—60.	v. 19, 20, 21, 22.	53—64.
v. 20, 21, 22.	61—63.		

Pf. XXXIX.

		v. 1, 2, 3.	1—16.

Pf. XXXIV.

v. 1, 2, 3.	1—8.	v. 4, 5, 6.	17—32.
v. 4, 5, 6.	9—20.	v. 7, 8, 9, 10.	33—44.
v. 7, 8.	21—30.	v. 11.	45—54.
v. 9, 10.	31—36.	v. 12, 13.	55—66.
v. 11, 12, 13, 14, 15, 16.	37—52.		

Pf. XL.

v. 17, 18, 19, 20.	53—66.	v. 1, 2.	Stanza 1.
v. 21, 22.	67—74.	v. 3, 4, 5.	2, 3.
		v. 6, 7, 8.	4, 5, 6.

Pf. XXXV.

v. 1, 2, 3.	1—8.	v. 9, 10, 11.	7, 8.
v. 4, 5, 6.	9—18.	v. 12,13,14,15,16,17.	9, 10, 11, 12.
v. 7, 8, 9, 10.	19—40.		

Pf. XLI.

v. 11, 12, 13, 14.	41—64.	v. 1, 2, 3.	1—14.
v. 15, 16.	65—74.	v. 4, 5, 6.	15—28.
v. 17, 18.	75—82.	v. 7, 8, 9.	29—40.
v. 19, 20, 21.	83—92.	v. 10, 11, 12, 13.	41—58.
v. 22, 23, 24, 25.	93—104.		

Pf. XLII.

v. 26, 27, 28.	105—118.	v. 1, 2.	1—6.
		v. 3, 4.	7—20.

Pf. XXXVI.

		v. 5.	21—26.
v. 1, 2, 3, 4.	1—12.	v. 6, 7.	27—36.
v. 5, 6, 7, 8, 9.	13—36.	v. 8, 9, 10, 11.	37—56.
v. 10, 11, 12.	37—46.		

Pf. XLIII.

		v. 1, 2.	1—8.

Pf. XXXVII.

v. 1, 2, 3.	1—10.	v. 3, 4, 5.	9—24.
v. 4, 5, 6.	11—18.		

Pf. XLIV.

v. 7, 8, 9, 10.	19—32.		
v. 11.	33—38.	v. 1, 2, 3.	1—18.
v. 12, 13, 14, 15.	39—54.	v. 4, 5, 6, 7, 8.	19—34.
v. 16, 17, 18, 19, 20.	55—72.	v. 9, 10, 11, 12, 13, 14, 15, 16.	35—56.
v. 21, 22, 23, 24.	73—84.	v. 17, 18, 19, 20, 21.	57—68.
v. 25, 26.	85—92.	v. 22, 23, 24, 25, 26.	69—86.
v. 27, 28, 29, 30, 31.	93—108.		

Pf. XLV.

v. 32, 33, 34.	109—120.		
v. 35, 36.	121—126.	v. 1, 2.	1—10.
v. 37, 38, 39, 40.	127—136.	v. 3, 4, 5.	11—22.
		v. 6, 7, 8, 9.	23—40.

Pf. XXXVIII.

		v. 10, 11.	41—48.
v. 1, 2, 3, 4, 5.	1—12.	v. 12, 13, 14, 15.	49—64.
v. 6, 7, 8, 9, 10.	13—24.	v. 16, 17.	65—74.
v. 11, 12, 13, 14.	25—38.		
v. 15, 16, 17, 18.	39—52.		

A TABLE of REFERENCES.

Bible Transl.	Paraphr.	Bible Transl.	Paraphr.
Pſ. XLVI.		v. 6.	29 — 38.
v. 1, 2, 3.	1 — 12.		
v. 4, 5, 6.	13 — 26.	**Pſ. LIV.**	
v. 7, 8, 9.	27 — 36.	v. 1, 2.	Stanza 1.
v. 10, 11.	37 — 44.	v. 3, 4, 5, 6, 7.	2, 3.
Pſ. XLVII.		**Pſ. LV.**	
v. 1, 2, 3, 4.	Stanza 1, 2, 3.	v. 1, 2, 3, 4, 5.	1 — 10.
v. 5, 6, 7, 8.	4, 5, 6, 7.	v. 6, 7, 8.	11 — 20.
v. 9.	8, 9.	v. 9, 10, 11.	21 — 28.
		v. 12, 13, 14.	29 — 42.
Pſ. XLVIII.		v. 15, 16, 17.	43 — 54.
v. 1, 2, 3.	Stanza 1, 2, 3.	v. 18, 19, 20, 21.	55 — 72.
v. 4, 5, 6, 7.	4, 5.	v. 22, 23.	73 — 84.
v. 8, 9, 10.	6, 7, 8, 9.		
v. 11, 12, 13, 14.	10, 11, 12, 13.	**Pſ. LVI.**	
		v. 1, 2, 3, 4.	1 — 10.
Pſ. XLIX.		v. 5, 6, 7.	11 — 18.
v. 1, 2, 3, 4.	1 — 12.	v. 8, 9, 10, 11.	19 — 32.
v. 5, 6, 7, 8, 9.	13 — 28.	v. 12, 13.	33 — 38.
v. 10, 11, 12, 13.	29 — 46.		
v. 14, 15.	47 — 62.	**Pſ. LVII.**	
v. 16, 17.	63 — 70.	v. 1, 2, 3.	1 — 14.
v. 18, 19, 20.	71 — 82.	v. 4, 5, 6.	15 — 28.
		v. 7, 8, 9, 10, 11.	29 — 48.
Pſ. L.			
v. 1, 2, 3.	1 — 10.	**Pſ. LVIII.**	
v. 4, 5, 6.	11 — 22.	v. 1, 2.	1 — 10.
v. 7, 8, 9.	23 — 32.	v. 3, 4, 5.	11 — 22.
v. 10, 11, 12, 13, 14, 15.	33 — 52.	v. 6, 7, 8.	23 — 34.
v. 16, 17, 18, 19, 20.	53 — 70.	v. 9, 10, 11.	35 — 50.
v. 21, 22, 23.	71 — 84.		
		Pſ. LIX.	
Pſ. LI.		v. 1, 2, 3, 4, 5.	1 — 16.
v. 1, 2, 3, 4.	1 — 12.	v. 6, 7, 8, 9, 10.	17 — 30.
v. 5, 6, 7.	13 — 26.	v. 11, 12, 13.	31 — 46.
v. 8, 9, 10, 11, 12, 13.	27 — 48.	v. 14, 15, 16, 17.	47 — 58.
v. 14, 15, 16, 17.	49 — 64.		
v. 18, 19.	65 — 72.	**Pſ. LX.**	
		v. 1, 2, 3, 4, 5.	1 — 20.
Pſ. LII.		v. 6, 7, 8.	21 — 34.
v. 1, 2, 3, 4.	Stanza 1, 2, 3.	v. 9, 10, 11, 12.	35 — 48.
v. 5, 6, 7.	4, 5, 6.		
v. 8, 9.	7, 8.	**Pſ. LXI.**	
		v. 1, 2, 3, 4, 5.	1 — 18.
Pſ. LIII.		v. 6, 7, 8.	19 — 28.
v. 1, 2, 3.	1 — 18.		
v. 4, 5.	19 — 28.	**Pſ. LXII.**	

A TABLE of REFERENCES.

Bible Transl.	Paraphr.
Pf. LXII.	
v. 1, 2, 3, 4.	1—20.
v. 5, 6, 7, 8.	21—32.
v. 9.	33—38.
v. 10, 11, 12.	39—52.
Pf. LXIII.	
v. 1, 2, 3, 4.	1—18.
v. 5, 6, 7, 8.	19—34.
v. 9, 10, 11.	35—46.
Pf. LXIV.	
v. 1, 2, 3, 4.	1—14.
v. 5, 6, 7.	15—28.
v. 8, 9, 10.	29—38.
Pf. LXV.	
v. 1, 2, 3.	1—10.
v. 4, 5, 6, 7.	11—30.
v. 8, 9, 10, 11.	31—44.
v. 12, 13.	45—54.
Pf. LXVI.	
v. 1, 2, 3, 4.	1—14.
v. 5, 6, 7.	15—30.
v. 8, 9, 10, 11, 12.	31—50.
v. 13, 14, 15.	51—58.
v. 16, 17, 18, 19, 20.	59—70.
Pf. LXVII.	
v. 1, 2.	1—6.
v. 3, 4, 5.	7—18.
v. 6, 7.	19—24.
Pf. LXVIII.	
v. 1, 2, 3.	1—12.
v. 4, 5, 6.	13—30.
v. 7, 8, 9, 10.	31—48.
v. 11, 12.	49—56.
v. 13, 14.	57—70.
v. 15, 16.	71—78.
v. 17.	79—86.
v. 18.	87—96.
v. 19, 20, 21, 22, 23.	97—116.
v. 24, 25, 26, 27.	117—134.
v. 28, 29.	135—140.
v. 30, 31.	141—154.

Bible Transl.	Paraphr.
v. 32, 33, 34, 35.	155—170.
Pf. LXIX.	
v. 1, 2, 3.	1—10.
v. 4, 5, 6, 7, 8.	11—30.
v. 9, 10, 11, 12.	31—44.
v. 13, 14, 15, 16, 17, 18, 19.	45—66.
v. 20, 21.	67—76.
v. 22, 23, 24.	77—86.
v. 25, 26, 27, 28.	87—100.
v. 29, 30, 31.	101—110.
v. 32, 33, 34, 35, 36.	111—124.
Pf. LXX.	
v. 1, 2.	Stanza 1.
v. 3, 4, 5.	2, 3.
Pf. LXXI.	
v. 1, 2, 3, 4.	1—14.
v. 5, 6.	15—22.
v. 7, 8, 9.	23—34.
v. 10, 11.	35—40.
v. 12, 13, 14, 15, 16, 17.	41—58.
v. 18, 19, 20, 21.	59—80.
v. 22, 23, 24.	81—90.
Pf. LXXII.	
v. 1, 2, 3, 4.	1—14.
v. 5, 6, 7.	15—26.
v. 8, 9, 10, 11.	27—42.
v. 12, 13, 14, 15.	43—56.
v. 16, 17.	57—68.
v. 18, 19.	69—78.
Pf. LXXIII.	
v. 1, 2, 3.	1—10.
v. 4, 5, 6.	11—20.
v. 7, 8, 9.	21—30.
v. 10, 11.	31—38.
v. 12, 13, 14, 15, 16, 17.	39—62.
v. 18, 19, 20.	63—72.
v. 21, 22, 23, 24, 25, 26.	73—90.
v. 27, 28.	91—98.
Pf. LXXIV.	

A TABLE of REFERENCES.

Bible Tranſl.	Paraphr.	Bible Tranſl.	Paraphr.
Pſ. LXXIV.		v. 67, 68, 69, 70, 71, 72.	201—220.
v. 1, 2.	1—12.		
v. 3, 4.	13—20.	**Pſ. LXXIX.**	
v. 5, 6, 7, 8.	21—40.	v. 1, 2, 3.	1—14.
v. 9, 10, 11.	41—54.	v. 4, 5, 6, 7.	15—26.
v. 12, 13, 14.	55—68.	v. 8, 9, 10.	27—44.
v. 15, 16, 17.	69—82.	v. 11, 12, 13.	45—54.
v. 18, 19, 20, 21.	83—98.		
v. 22, 23.	99—104.	**Pſ. LXXX.**	
		v. 1, 2, 3.	1—14.
Pſ. LXXV.		v. 4, 5, 6, 7.	15—26.
v. 1, 2, 3.	1—12.	v. 8, 9, 10, 11, 12, 13.	27—48.
v. 4, 5, 6, 7.	13—26.	v. 14, 15, 16, 17, 18, 19.	49—72.
v. 8, 9, 10.	27—38.		
		Pſ. LXXXI.	
Pſ. LXXVI.		v. 1, 2, 3.	1—10.
v. 1, 2, 3, 4.	1—14.	v. 4, 5, 6, 7.	11—24.
v. 5, 6, 7.	15—30.	v. 8, 9, 10.	25—34.
v. 8, 9, 10, 11, 12.	31—46.	v. 11, 12.	35—42.
		v. 13, 14, 15, 16.	43—54.
Pſ. LXXVII.			
v. 1, 2, 3.	1—14.	**Pſ. LXXXII.**	
v. 4, 5, 6, 7, 8, 9.	15—30.	v. 1, 2, 3, 4.	1—10.
v. 10, 11, 12.	31—38.	v. 5, 6, 7, 8.	11—24.
v. 13, 14, 15.	39—50.		
v. 16, 17, 18.	51—62.	**Pſ. LXXXIII.**	
v. 19, 20.	63—70.	v. 1, 2, 3, 4, 5.	1—18.
		v. 6, 7, 8.	19—28.
Pſ. LXXVIII.		v. 9, 10, 11, 12.	29—44.
v. 1, 2, 3, 4.	1—10.	v. 13, 14, 15, 16, 17, 18.	45—62.
v. 5, 6, 7, 8.	11—22.		
v. 9, 10, 11, 12.	23—30.	**Pſ. LXXXIV.**	
v. 13, 14, 15, 16.	31—44.	v. 1, 2.	1—6.
v. 17, 18, 19, 20.	45—58.	v. 3, 4.	7—16.
v. 21, 22, 23, 24, 25.	59—68.	v. 5, 6, 7.	17—30.
v. 26, 27, 28, 29, 30, 31.	69—82.	v. 8, 9, 10, 11, 12.	31—50.
v. 32, 33, 34, 35, 36, 37.	83—96.	**Pſ. LXXXV.**	
v. 38, 39.	97—106.		
v. 40, 41, 42, 43.	107—118.	v. 1, 2, 3, 4.	1—12.
v. 44, 45, 46, 47, 48.	119—136.	v. 5, 6, 7.	13—22.
v. 49, 50, 51.	137—148.	v. 8, 9, 10.	23—38.
v. 52, 53, 54, 55, 56, 57.	149—170.	v. 11, 12, 13.	39—48.
v. 58, 59, 60, 61, 62.	171—186.		
v. 63, 64.	187—194.	**Pſ. LXXXVI.**	
v. 65, 66.	195—200.	v. 1, 2, 3, 4, 5.	1—12

A TABLE of REFERENCES.

Bible Tranſl.	Paraphr.
v. 6, 7, 8.	13—18.
v. 9, 10.	19—26.
v. 11, 12, 13.	27—36.
v. 14, 15, 16, 17.	37—54.

Pſ. LXXXVII.

Bible Tranſl.	Paraphr.
v. 1, 2, 3.	1—10.
v. 4, 5, 6.	11—34.
v. 7.	35—42.

Pſ. LXXXVIII.

Bible Tranſl.	Paraphr.
v. 1, 2, 3, 4.	1—8.
v. 5, 6, 7, 8, 9.	9—22.
v. 10, 11, 12.	23—34.
v. 13, 14, 15, 16, 17, 18.	35—50.

Pſ. LXXXIX.

Bible Tranſl.	Paraphr.
v. 1, 2, 3, 4.	1—14.
v. 5, 6, 7, 8, 9.	15—34.
v. 10, 11.	35—44.
v. 12, 13, 14.	45—56.
v. 15, 16, 17, 18.	57—70.
v. 19, 20, 21, 22, 23, 24, 25.	71—96.
v. 26, 27, 28, 29, 30, 31, 32.	97—112.
v. 33, 34, 35, 36, 37.	113—124.
v. 38, 39, 40, 41.	125—136.
v. 42, 43, 44, 45.	137—146.
v. 46, 47, 48.	147—162.
v. 49, 50, 51, 52.	163—176.

Pſ. XC.

Bible Tranſl.	Paraphr.
v. 1, 2.	1—6.
v. 3, 4.	7—16.
v. 5, 6, 7, 8, 9.	17—34.
v. 10.	35—42.
v. 11, 12.	43—48.
v. 13, 14, 15, 16, 17.	49—70.

Pſ. XCI.

Bible Tranſl.	Paraphr.
v. 1, 2, 3, 4, 5, 6.	1—20.
v. 7, 8, 9, 10.	21—32.
v. 11, 12, 13.	33—44.
v. 14, 15, 16.	45—52.

Pſ. XCII.

Bible Tranſl.	Paraphr.
v. 1, 2, 3.	1—12.
v. 4, 5, 6, 7.	13—28.
v. 8, 9, 10, 11.	29—42.
v. 12, 13, 14, 15.	43—56.

Pſ. XCIII.

Bible Tranſl.	Paraphr.
v. 1, 2.	Stanza 1, 2.
v. 3, 4, 5.	3, 4.

Pſ. XCIV.

Bible Tranſl.	Paraphr.
v. 1, 2, 3, 4.	1—10.
v. 5, 6, 7, 8.	11—22.
v. 9, 10, 11.	23—32.
v. 12, 13, 14, 15.	33—48.
v. 16, 17, 18, 19.	49—60.
v. 20, 21, 22, 23.	61—74.

Pſ. XCV.

Bible Tranſl.	Paraphr.
v. 1, 2, 3, 4, 5.	1—20.
v. 6, 7, 8, 9.	21—36.
v. 10, 11.	37—48.

Pſ. XCVI.

Bible Tranſl.	Paraphr.
v. 1, 2, 3.	1—6.
v. 4, 5, 6.	7—14.
v. 7, 8, 9.	15—24.
v. 10, 11, 12, 13.	25—42.

Pſ. XCVII.

Bible Tranſl.	Paraphr.
v. 1, 2, 3, 4, 5.	1—16.
v. 6, 7, 8, 9.	17—34.
v. 10, 11, 12.	35—48.

Pſ. XCVIII.

Bible Tranſl.	Paraphr.
v. 1, 2, 3.	1—14.
v. 4, 5, 6, 7, 8, 9.	15—32.

Pſ. XCIX.

Bible Tranſl.	Paraphr.
v. 1, 2, 3.	Stanza 1, 2.
v. 4, 5.	3, 4.
v. 6, 7.	5, 6, 7.
v. 8, 9.	8, 9.

Pſ. C.

Bible Tranſl.	Paraphr.
v. 1, 2, 3.	1—10.
v. 4, 5.	11—18.

Pſ. CI.

Bible Tranſl.	Paraphr.
v. 1, 2, 3, 4, 5.	1—26.

A TABLE of REFERENCES.

Bible Transl.	Paraphr.	Bible Transl.	Paraphr.
v. 6, 7, 8.	27—42.	v. 6, 7, 8, 9.	15—30.
		v. 10, 11, 12, 13.	31—44.
Pſ. CII.		v. 14, 15, 16.	45—54.
v. 1, 2.	1—6.	v. 17, 18, 19, 20, 21, 22.	55—70.
v. 3, 4, 5.	7—16.	v. 23, 24, 25.	71—86.
v. 6, 7, 8.	17—30.	v. 26, 27, 28.	87—96.
v. 9, 10, 11.	31—42.	v. 29, 30, 31.	97—104.
v. 12, 13, 14.	43—56.	v. 32, 33.	105—114.
v. 15, 16, 17, 18.	57—70.	v. 34, 35, 36, 37, 38.	115—128.
v. 19, 20, 21, 22.	71—86.	v. 39, 40, 41, 42.	129—138.
v. 23, 24, 25, 26, 27, 28.	87—118.	v. 43, 44, 45, 46.	139—148.
		v. 47, 48.	149—164.
Pſ. CIII.		**Pſ. CVII.**	
v. 1, 2, 3, 4, 5.	1—16.	v. 1, 2, 3.	Stanza 1, 2, 3.
v. 6, 7, 8, 9, 10, 11, 12.	17—34.	v. 4, 5, 6, 7, 8.	4, 5, 6, 7.
v. 13, 14, 15, 16.	35—52.	v. 9, 10, 11, 12.	8, 9, 10, 11.
v. 17, 18.	53—58.	v. 13, 14, 15.	12, 13.
v. 19, 20, 21, 22.	59—72.	v. 16, 17, 18.	14, 15, 16.
		v. 19, 20, 21, 22.	17, 18, 19.
Pſ. CIV.		v. 23, 24, 25, 26, 27.	20, 21, 22, 23.
v. 1, 2, 3.	1—14.	v. 28, 29, 30, 31, 32.	24, 25, 26, 27.
v. 4, 5.	15—20.	v. 33, 34, 35, 36, 37, 38.	28, 29, 30, 31, 32, 33.
v. 6, 7, 8, 9, 10, 11.	21—42.	v. 39, 40, 41, 42, 43.	34, 35, 36, 37, 38.
v. 12, 13, 14, 15.	43—54.		
v. 16, 17, 18.	55—68.	**Pſ. CVIII.**	
v. 19, 20, 21, 22.	69—84.	v. 1, 2, 3.	1—14.
v. 23, 24, 25, 26.	85—102.	v. 4, 5, 6.	15—24.
v. 27, 28, 29, 30.	103—118.	v. 7, 8, 9.	25—38.
v. 31, 32.	119—126.	v. 10, 11, 12, 13.	39—52.
v. 33, 34, 35.	127—140.	**Pſ. CIX.**	
Pſ. CV.		v. 1, 2, 3, 4, 5.	1—14.
v. 1, 2, 3, 4.	1—12.	v. 6, 7, 8.	15—28.
v. 5, 6, 7, 8, 9, 10, 11.	13—30.	v. 9, 10, 11, 12, 13.	29—44.
v. 12, 13, 14, 15.	31—44.	v. 14, 15, 16.	45—54.
v. 16, 17, 18, 19, 20, 21, 22.	45—68.	v. 17, 18, 19.	55—68.
v. 23, 24, 25.	69—82.	v. 20, 21, 22.	69—76.
v. 26, 27, 28.	83—96.	v. 23, 24, 25.	77—86.
v. 29, 30, 31.	97—108.	v. 26, 27, 28, 29, 30, 31.	87—100.
v. 32, 33, 34, 35.	109—124.		
v. 36, 37, 38.	125—138.		
v. 39, 40, 41, 42.	139—152.		
v. 43, 44, 45.	153—164.		
Pſ. CVI.		**Pſ. CX.**	
v. 1, 2, 3, 4, 5.	1—14.	v. 1, 2.	1—10.

A TABLE of REFERENCES.

Bible Transl.	Paraphr.	Bible Transl.	Paraphr.
v. 3.	11—20.	v. 19, 20, 21.	73—86.
v. 4.	21—24.	v. 22, 23, 24.	87—98.
v. 5, 6.	25—32.	v. 25, 26.	99—106.
v. 7.	33—38.	v. 27, 28, 29.	107—124.

Pſ. CXI.

v. 1, 2, 3.	Stanza 1, 2.	v. 1, 2, 3.	1—6.
v. 4, 5.	3, 4.	v. 4, 5, 6, 7, 8.	7—20.
v. 6, 7, 8, 9, 10.	5, 6, 7.	v. 9, 10, 11.	21—30.
		v. 12, 13, 14, 15, 16.	31—40.

Pſ. CXII.

v. 1, 2, 3.	Stanza 1, 2.	v. 17, 18, 19, 20.	41—50.
v. 4, 5, 6, 7, 8.	3, 4, 5.	v. 21, 22, 23, 24.	51—62.
v. 9, 10.	6, 7.	v. 25, 26, 27, 28, 29.	63—74.
		v. 30, 31, 32.	75—82.
		v. 33, 34, 35, 36.	83—94.

Pſ. CXIII.

v. 1, 2, 3, 4.	1—8.	v. 37, 38, 39, 40.	95—104.
v. 5, 6, 7, 8, 9.	9—22.	v. 41, 42, 43, 44, 45.	105—116.
		v. 46, 47, 48.	117—126.
		v. 49, 50, 51, 52.	127—136.

Pſ. CXIV.

v. 1, 2, 3, 4.	Stanza 1, 2, 3.	v. 53, 54, 55, 56.	137—146.
v. 5, 6, 7, 8.	4, 5, 6, 7.	v. 57, 58, 59, 60.	147—156.
		v. 61, 62, 63, 64.	157—170.
		v. 65, 66, 67, 68.	171—182.

Pſ. CXV.

v. 1, 2, 3.	1—10.	v. 69, 70, 71, 72.	183—196.
v. 4, 5, 6, 7, 8.	11—28.	v. 73, 74, 75.	197—208.
v. 9, 10, 11, 12, 13.	29—48.	v. 76, 77, 78, 79, 80.	209—222.
v. 14, 15, 16.	49—56.	v. 81, 82, 83.	223—234.
v. 17, 18.	57—64.	v. 84, 85, 86, 87, 88.	235—252.
		v. 89, 90, 91, 92.	253—266.
		v. 93, 94, 95, 96.	267—280.

Pſ. CXVI.

		v. 97, 98, 99, 100.	281—292.
v. 1, 2.	1—6.	v. 101, 102, 103, 104.	293—302.
v. 3, 4, 5, 6, 7.	7—22.	v. 105, 106, 107, 108.	303—315.
v. 8, 9.	23—28.	v. 109, 110, 111, 112.	316—324.
v. 10, 11.	29—34.	v. 113, 114, 115, 116.	325—336.
v. 12, 13, 14, 15.	35—48.	v. 117, 118, 119, 120.	337—350.
v. 16, 17, 18, 19.	49—62.	v. 121, 122, 123, 124, 125.	351—366.

Pſ. CXVII.

		v. 126, 127, 128.	367—376.
v. 1.	Stanza 1.	v. 129, 130, 131.	377—386.
v. 2.	2.	v. 132, 133, 134, 135, 136.	387—400.

Pſ. CXVIII.

		v. 137, 138, 139, 140.	401—408.
v. 1, 2, 3, 4.	1—16.	v. 141, 142, 143, 144.	409—416.
v. 5, 6, 7, 8, 9.	17—30.	v. 145, 146, 147, 148, 149.	417—432.
v. 10, 11, 12.	31—48.	v. 150, 151, 152.	433—438.
v. 13, 14, 15, 16, 17, 18.	49—72.		v. 153,

A TABLE of REFERENCES.

Bible Tranſl.	Paraphr.
v. 153, 154, 155, 156.	439—452.
v. 157, 158, 159, 160.	453—464.
v. 161, 162, 163, 164.	465—476.
v. 165, 166, 167, 168.	477—488.
v. 169, 170, 171, 172.	489—500.
v. 173, 174, 175, 176.	501—520.

Pſ. CXX.
v. 1, 2, 3, 4.	Stanza 1, 2.
v. 5, 6, 7.	3, 4.

Pſ. CXXI.
v. 1, 2, 3, 4.	Stanza 1, 2.
v. 5, 6, 7, 8.	3, 4.

Pſ. CXXII.
v. 1, 2, 3.	Stanza 1, 2.
v. 4, 5.	3, 4.
v. 6, 7, 8, 9.	5, 6, 7.

Pſ. CXXIII.
v. 1, 2.	1—8.
v. 3, 4.	9—14.

Pſ. CXXIV.
v. 1, 2, 3, 4, 5, 6.	1—12.
v. 7, 8.	13—22.

Pſ. CXXV.
v. 1, 2.	1—10.
v. 3, 4, 5.	11—22.

Pſ. CXXVI.
v. 1, 2, 3.	1—12.
v. 4, 5, 6.	13—24.

Pſ. CXXVII.
v. 1, 2.	Stanza 1, 2.
v. 3, 4, 5.	3, 4.

Pſ. CXXVIII.
v. 1, 2, 3, 4.	1—16.
v. 5, 6.	17—24.

Pſ. CXXIX.
v. 1, 2, 3, 4.	1—8.
v. 5, 6, 7, 8.	9—20.

Bible Tranſl.	Paraphr.

Pſ. CXXX.
v. 1, 2, 3.	Stanza 1, 2.
v. 4, 5, 6, 7, 8.	3, 4, 5, 6.

Pſ. CXXXI.
v. 1.	1—6.
v. 2, 3.	7—14.

Pſ. CXXXII.
v. 1, 2, 3, 4, 5.	1—14.
v. 6, 7, 8, 9, 10.	15—30.
v. 11, 12, 13, 14.	31—42.
v. 15, 16, 17, 18.	43—54.

Pſ. CXXXIII.
v. 1, 2, 3.	Stanza 1, 2.

Pſ. CXXXIV.
v. 1.	1—6.
v. 2, 3.	7—12.

Pſ. CXXXV.
v. 1, 2, 3.	1—10.
v. 4, 5, 6, 7.	11—30.
v. 8, 9, 10, 11, 12.	31—50.
v. 13, 14, 15, 16, 17, 18.	51—72.
v. 19, 20, 21.	73—82.

Pſ. CXXXVI.
The Number of each Stanza, in the Paraphraſe of this Pſalm, anſwers reſpectively to that of each Verſe.

Pſ. CXXXVII.
v. 1, 2, 3.	1—12.
v. 4, 5, 6.	13—22.
v. 7.	23—28.
v. 8, 9.	29—36.

Pſ. CXXXVIII.
v. 1, 2, 3.	1—12.
v. 4, 5, 6.	13—22.
v. 7, 8.	23—30.

Pſ. CXXXIX.

A TABLE of REFERENCES.

Bible Transl.	Paraphr.	Bible Transl.	Paraphr.
Pf. CXXXIX.		**Pf. CXLV.**	
v. 1, 2, 3, 4, 5, 6.	1—14.	v. 1, 2.	1—6.
v. 7, 8, 9, 10, 11, 12.	15—34.	v. 3, 4, 5, 6, 7, 8, 9.	7—28.
v. 13, 14, 15, 16.	35—56.	v. 10, 11, 12, 13.	29—40.
v. 17, 18.	57—64.	(See the *Septuagint*, at Ver. 13.)	
v. 19, 20, 21, 22.	65—74.	v. 14, 15, 16, 17.	41—50.
v. 23, 24.	75—80.	v. 18, 19, 20, 21.	51—64.
Pf. CXL.		**Pf. CXLVI.**	
v. 1, 2, 3.	1—6.	v. 1, 2, 3, 4.	1—12.
v. 4, 5, 6, 7.	7—20.	v. 5, 6, 7, 8.	13—30.
v. 8, 9, 10, 11.	21—38.	v. 9, 10.	31—40.
v. 12, 13.	39—46.	**Pf. CXLVII.**	
Pf. CXLI.		v. 1, 2, 3, 4.	1—12.
v. 1, 2.	1—8.	v. 5, 6, 7, 8, 9.	13—30.
v. 3, 4.	9—16.	v. 10, 11.	31—38.
v. 5, 6.	17—30.	v. 12, 13, 14, 15.	39—48.
v. 7, 8, 9, 10.	31—44.	v. 16, 17, 18.	49—60.
		v. 19, 20.	61—70.
Pf. CXLII.		**Pf. CXLVIII.**	
v. 1, 2, 3.	1—8.	v. 1, 2, 3, 4.	1—14.
v. 4, 5, 6, 7.	9—30.	v. 5, 6.	15—20.
Pf. CXLIII.		v. 7, 8, 9.	21—30.
v. 1, 2, 3.	1—12.	v. 10, 11, 12, 13.	31—44.
v. 4, 5, 6, 7.	13—26.	v. 14.	45—50.
v. 8, 9, 10, 11, 12.	27—46.	**Pf. CXLIX.**	
Pf. CXLIV.		v. 1, 2, 3.	1—14.
v. 1, 2.	1—10.	v. 4, 5.	15—24.
v. 3, 4.	11—16.	v. 6, 7, 8, 9.	25—36.
v. 5, 6, 7, 8.	17—28.	**Pf. CL.**	
v. 9, 10, 11.	29—38.	v. 1, 2, 3, 4.	1—12.
v. 12, 13, 14, 15.	39—60.	v. 5, 6.	13—18.

ERRATA.

Pfalm VII. Line 21. read *Nor let my*.
Pf. XXII. l. 17. read *wifh'd for*.
Pf. XXX. l. 21. read *obtrufive*.
Pf. LXIX. l. 27. read *Domeftic*.
Pf. LXXVIII. l. 203. read *Dwellings*.
Pf. LXXXIX. l. 51. read *thine Arm*.
Pf. XCIX. Stanza 5. dele the Comma after *Aaron*.
Pf. CVIII. l. 30. infert a Comma after *and*.
Pf. CXLII. l. 8. read *infidious*.

Published by the same Author,

1. THE Destruction of Troy, translated from the *Greek* of Tryphiodorus into *English Verse*, with Notes. To which is added the *Greek* Original corrected and enlarged from a Manuscript: With *Frischlinus*'s Translation in Latin Verse, and Notes, partly selected from other Comments, and partly composed by the Editor. 8vo. 1742.

2. A Dissertation on Proverbs, Chap. IX. 1, 2, 3, 4, 5, 6. Containing occasional Remarks on other Passages in Sacred and Profane Writers. 4to. 1744. Price 1s.

3. Poems on Sacred Subjects. 4to. Price 1s.

4. A Letter to the Rev. Mr. Joseph Warton, chiefly relating to the Composition of *Greek* Indexes, and the Advantage to be received from it in learning the *Greek* Language. Price 3d.

5. Annotations, Critical and Grammatical, on St. John, Chap. I. Ver. 1—14. Being Part of a Work, particularly designed for the Use of Young Persons, as an Introduction to the Study of the *Greek Testament*. To which is prefixed A Preliminary Discourse, exhibiting an easy Method of studying the *Greek* Language. Price 6d.

6. Prayers for a Time of Earthquakes and violent Floods: Suited to the various Occasions and Circumstances of Persons who are apprehensive of such Calamities, or have already felt the Effects of them. Price 1d. or 7s. a Hundred.

7. An Encouragement to a Good Life: Particularly addressed to some Soldiers quartered in Reading, Berks, 1759. Price 3d. a Dozen, or 2s. a Hundred.

8. A Morning Prayer and an Evening Prayer. Price Eight for 1d. or 1s. a Hundred.

www.ingramcontent.com/pod-product-compliance
Lightning Source LLC
Chambersburg PA
CBHW030321240426
43673CB00040B/1237